Paul and the Popular Philosophers

Other Books by
Abraham J. Malherbe

Gregory of Nyssa: The Life of Moses
The Cynic Epistles: A Study Edition
Social Aspects of Early Christianity
Moral Exhortation: A Greco-Roman Sourcebook
Paul and the Thessalonians
Ancient Epistolary Theorists

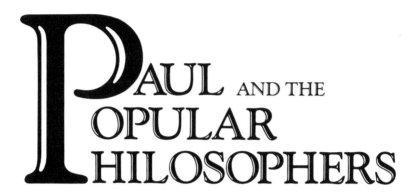

Paul AND THE Popular Philosophers

Abraham J. Malherbe

Fortress Press   Minneapolis

Library of Congress Cataloging-in-Publication Data

Malherbe, Abraham J.
    Paul and the popular philosophers / Abraham J. Malherbe.
        p. cm.
    Essays originally published 19861986.
    Includes bibliographies and indexes.
    ISBN 0-8006-2410-6
    1. Bible. N.T. Epistles of Paul—Philosophy. 2. Philosophy,
Ancient—Influence. 3. Paul, the Apostle, Saint. I. Title.
BS2650.2.M35 1989
227'.067—dc20   89-36042
                                                                      CIP

The paper used in this publication meets the minimum requirements of American National Standard for Information Sciences—Permanence of Paper for Printed Library Materials, ANSI Z329.48-1984.   ∞™

Manufactured in the U.S.A.   AF 1-2410
93   92   91   90   89   1   2   3   4   5   6   7   8   9   10

For
Leander E. Keck
and
Wayne A. Meeks
Friends and Colleagues

Contents

Preface

The studies presented in this volume represent some of the technical investigations that underlie my recent book, *Paul and the Thessalonians: The Philosophic Tradition of Pastoral Care* (Fortress Press, 1987). Readers of that book have expressed an interest in having the essays more readily available, and I am thankful to John A. Hollar, Senior Editor of Fortress Press, for his initiative and constant encouragement in seeing this book through the press. Since nine of the eleven chapters were published as articles during the last decade, I have decided to confine my alterations to occasional matters of style and corrections of typographical errors and references. Ken Cukrowski, Chris Hutson and my wife, Phyllis, have contributed to the production of the book by checking and correcting references, compiling indexes and typing the manuscript. I am grateful to them, as I am to the Council of Fellows of Yale University for an A. Whitney Griswold Faculty Award, and to the Yale Divinity School for assistance from its Faculty Research Fund. Without their support, publication of this volume would not have been undertaken.

Acknowledgments

I am thankful to the original publishers for permission to republish the following essays in this book:

"Self-Definition among the Cynics," in *Jewish and Christian Self-Definition. Vol. 3: Self-Definition in the Greco-Roman World,* ed. B. F. Meyer and E. P. Sanders (Philadelphia: Fortress Press, 1982), 3.48–59, 193–97.

"*Mē Genoito* in the Diatribe and Paul," *HTR* 73 (1980): 231–40.

" 'Gentle as a Nurse': The Cynic Background to 1 Thessalonians 2," *NovT* 12 (1970): 203–17.

"Exhortation in First Thessalonians," *NovT* 25 (1983): 238–56.

"Paul: Hellenistic Philosopher or Christian Pastor?" *ATR* 68 (1986): 3–13.

"The Beasts at Ephesus," *JBL* 87 (1968): 71–80.

"Antisthenes and Odysseus, and Paul at War," *HTR* 76 (1983): 143–73.

"Medical Imagery in the Pastoral Epistles," in *Texts and Testaments: Critical Essays on the Bible and Early Christian Fathers,* ed. W. E. March (San Antonio, Texas: Trinity Univ. Press, 1980), 19–35.

" 'In Season and Out of Season': 2 Timothy 4:2," *JBL* 103 (1984): 235–43.

" 'Not in a Corner': Early Christian Apologetic in Acts 26:26," *The Second Century* 5 (1985/86): 193–210.

"A Physical Description of Paul," HTR 79 (1986): 170–75.

Abbreviations

Ancient Sources

For most ancient authors the texts, translations and titles of the Loeb Classical Library have been used. The letters attributed to Crates, Diogenes, Heraclitus and Socrates and the Socratics are cited according to *The Cynic Epistles,* ed. A. J. Malherbe, SBLSBS 12 (Missoula, Mont.: Scholars Press, 1977). In addition, the following have been used:

P. Aelii Aristidi opera quae exstant omnia, ed. C. A. Behr (Leiden: E. J. Brill, 1976)

Anonyme Latin, Traité de physiognomie, ed. Jacques André, Budé (Paris: Belles Lettres, 1981)

Antisthenis fragmenta, ed. F. Decleva Caizzi (Milan: Cisalpino, 1966)

Cleomedes de motu circulari corporum caelestium libri duo, ed. H. Ziegler (Leipzig: B. G. Teubner, 1891)

Epicteti dissertationes ab Arriano digestae, ed. H. Schenkl (Leipzig: B. G. Teubner, 1916)

Epicurea, ed. H. Usener (Leipzig: B. G. Teubner, 1887)

Ancient Epistolary Theorists, ed. A. J. Malherbe, SBLSBS 19 (Atlanta: Scholars Press, 1988)

Epistolographi Graeci, ed. R. Hercher (Paris: Didot, 1873)

Erotiani vocum Hippocraticarum collectio cum fragmentis, ed. E. Nachmannson (Goteborg: Eranos, 1918)

Euripidis tragoediae, ed. A. Nauck, 3 vols. (Leipzig: B. G. Teubner, 1854)

Fragmenta philosophorum graecorum, ed. F. W. A. Mullach, 3 vols. (Paris: Didot, 1860–81)

Claudii Galeni opera omnia, ed. C. G. Kuhn (reprint, Hildesheim: Olms, 1965)

Gnomologium Vaticanum, ed. L. Sternbach (reprint, Berlin: Walter de Gruyter, 1963)

Héraclite: Allégories d'Homère, ed. F. Buffière, Budé (Paris: Belles Lettres, 1962)

Oeuvres complètes d'Hippocrate, ed. É. Littré, 10 vols. (Paris: Baillière, 1839)

Lucilius: Satiren, ed. W. Krenkel, Schriften und Quellen der Alten Welt 23 (Leiden: E. J. Brill, 1970)

Maximi Tyrii philosophumena, ed. H. Hobein (Leipzig: B. G. Teubner, 1910)

Menandri sententiae, ed. S. Jaekel (Leipzig: B. G. Teubner, 1964)

Menander Rhetor, ed. and trans. D. A. Russell and N. G. Wilson (Oxford: Clarendon Press, 1981)

C. Musonii Rufi reliquiae, ed. O. Hense (Leipzig: B. G. Teubner, 1905)

Oeuvres d'Oribase, ed. and trans. C. Daremberg and U. C. Bussemaker, 6 vols. (Paris: Imprimerie nationale, 1851–76)

Flavii Philostrati Heroicus, ed. L. de Lannou (Leipzig: B. G. Teubner, 1977)

Flavii Philostrati opera, ed. C. L. Kayser, vol. 1 (Leipzig: B. G. Teubner, 1870)

Scriptores Physiognomici graeci et latini, ed. R. Foerster (Leipzig: B. G. Teubner, 1893)

Rhetores Graeci, ed. L. Spengel, 3 vols. (Leipzig: B. G. Teubner, 1854–56)

Socraticorum reliquiae, ed. G. Giannantoni, 4 vols. (Rome: Edizioni dell'Ateneo, 1983–85)

Sorani Gynaeciorum vetus translatio latina, ed. V. Rose (Leipzig: B. G. Teubner, 1882)

Ioannis Stobaei anthologium, ed. C. Wachsmuth and O. Hense, 5 vols. (Berlin: Weidmann, 1884–1912)

Synesios von Kyrene: Dion Chrysostomos, oder Vom Leben nach seinem Vorbild, ed. and trans. K. Treu (Darmstadt: Wissenschaftliche Buchgesellschaft, 1959)

Scholia in Theocritum vetera, ed. C. Wendel (Stuttgart: B. G. Teubner, 1966)

Vettii Valentis anthologium libri, ed. W. Kroll (Berlin: Weidmann, 1908)

Introduction

The dimension of Paul's life and practice represented by these studies has in recent decades enjoyed renewed attention.[1] That is not to say that ancient philosophy is generally regarded as having had an influence on the writers of the New Testament. Three giants, on whose shoulders all students of ancient Christianity wittingly or unwittingly stand, may be taken to represent one perception. Arthur Darby Nock, while recognizing the importance of philosophy for Christians from the second century on, was skeptical about its significance for the New Testament.[2] So, also, Henry Chadwick discerned in Acts 17 and the Prologue to the Fourth Gospel only anticipations of the engagement with philosophy which would enter a new stage with such figures as Clement of Alexandria and Origen.[3] And Werner Jaeger claimed that no direct impact of Greek philosophy on the New Testament had been confirmed by modern historical research; doctrinal influence on Christian thought belonged to later generations.[4]

One could have begun a recitation of denials of philosophic influence with Tertullian's question, which calls for the reply that Athens has nothing whatever to do with Jerusalem.[5] Tertullian, of course, was interested in preserving what was distinctive about the Christian faith.[6] So are some apologists to this day, who are convinced that the authority of the New Testament would be weakened if it could be demonstrated that its "essential beliefs" were derived from its pagan milieu.[7] What is evidently at stake in this question-begging assertion is the normativity ascribed to the canon. But why the same

---

[1] For an account, see A. J. Malherbe, "Hellenistic Moralists and the New Testament," *ANRW* 2.26/1 (forthcoming).

[2] See A. D. Nock, *Early Gentile Christianity and Its Hellenistic Background* (New York: Harper & Row, Torchbook, 1964), 94–97. Nock's interests lay in religion rather than philosophy. It is noteworthy that in his introduction to this volume, in which his 1928 essay is reprinted, the only passage to which philosophy is related is Acts 17.

[3] H. Chadwick, *Early Christian Thought and the Classical Tradition: Studies in Justin, Clement, and Origen* (Oxford: Oxford Univ. Press, 1966), 3–4.

[4] W. Jaeger, *Early Christianity and Greek Paideia* (Cambridge, Mass.: Harvard Univ. Press, 1961), 105-106 n. 2.

[5] Tertullian *On Prescription Against Heresies* 7: "What has Athens to do with Jerusalem?"; cf. *Apology* 47.

[6] See Chadwick, *Early Christian Thought and the Classical Tradition,* 1–2.

[7] See, e.g., R. H. Nash, *Christianity and the Hellenistic World* (Grand Rapids: Zondervan, 1984), 13.

1

strictures would not on canonical grounds apply to influence from contemporary Judaism is not clear. After all, as a prominent specialist in hellenistic philosophy has recently reminded us, "early Christianity developed out of a culture which, so far as most of the older theologians were concerned, was more Greek and Roman than Jewish."[8] Why the New Testament, on *a priori* theological grounds, should have been kept safe from the taint of Hellenism requires a more cogent explanation than has been offered since early Christianity has become the object of modern historical research.

Chadwick claims that the New Testament writers did not philosophize. He thinks that is "of providential importance since in consequence the gospel is not inextricably associated with a first-century metaphysical structure."[9] What is of interest here is not the nature of the theological claims Chadwick makes, but the nature of the influence which he and the other historians cited above have in mind. He is concerned with metaphysical structure. That is also the sort of influence of which Nock and Jaeger see only glimmers in Acts 17 and the Johannine Prologue. This is not the philosophical dimension which has recently attracted the attention of New Testament scholars or with which this book deals.[10] Jaeger, as had many others before him, identified Christian mission preaching as the decisive moment in the encounter between Greeks and Christians: in their mission preaching Christians borrowed their arguments and forms of address from Greek philosophers who for centuries in their protreptic discourses had sought to lead their hearers to a better life. Christians, Jaeger believes, first adopted and adapted these resources when they preached to hellenized Jews, and then further developed what they had borrowed when they preached to Greeks.[11]

---

[8]A. A. Long, "Epicureans and Stoics," in *Classical Mediterranean Spirituality: Egyptian, Greek, Roman,* ed. A. H. Armstrong (New York: Crossroad, 1986), 135. Long has in mind such writers as Tertullian, Origen, and Clement of Alexandria, who are important sources for Stoicism despite their frequent disagreements with the Stoics. Pagans as well as Christians found striking similarities between philosophic and Christian teachings. See E. Hatch, *The Influence of Greek Ideas and Usages Upon the Christian Church* (London: Williams & Norgate, 1897), 126–28; *The Octavius of Marcus Minucius Felix,* trans. and ed. G. W. Clarke, ACW 39 (New York: Newman Press, 1974), 351 n. 570, on Minucius Felix *Octavius* 34.5.

[9]*Early Christian Thought and the Classical Tradition,* 4–5.

[10]For the kind of interest not treated here, see R. G. Tanner, "St. Paul and Panaetius," in *Studia Biblica 1978: III. Papers on Paul and Other New Testament Authors,* ed. E. A. Livingstone, Sixth International Congress on Biblical Studies, JSNTSup 3 (Sheffield: Journal for the Study of the Old Testament, 1980), 361–74; J. W. Thompson, *The Beginnings of Christian Philosophy: The Epistle to the Hebrews,* CBQMS 13 (Washington, D. C.: Catholic Biblical Association of America, 1982). Neither do the essays in the book deal with the broader subject of Paul's relationship to hellenistic culture, as does N. Hugede, *Saint Paul et la culture grecque* (Geneva: Editions Labor et Fides, 1966).

[11]Jaeger, *Early Christianity and Greek Paideia,* 9–11. For the continuing awareness of Greek philosophy in early Christian protreptic, see J. Daniélou, *Gospel Message and Hellenistic Culture,* trans. and ed. J. A. Baker (Philadelphia: Westminster Press, 1973).

It is with this protreptic endeavor, broadly understood, that this book is concerned. My studies belong to a tradition of scholarship that flourished around the turn of the century. A number of factors contributed to the vigor with which early Christianity was then situated in its Greco-Roman context. The history-of-religions approach to the study of early Christianity made it natural to examine Christianity in its cultural context, particularly since those young scholars who would shape their discipline for the twentieth century received their early training under some of the leading classicists of their day. Thus Hans Lietzmann was for seven semesters a member of Hermann Usener's seminar in classical philology while the latter was preparing his edition of *The Art of Rhetoric,* falsely attributed to Dionysius of Halicarnassus.[12] In this context Johannes Weiss analyzed some aspects of Paul's style and issued an invitation to specialists in ancient rhetoric to relate his analysis to rhetorical practice. The invitation was unfortunately not accepted, and the interest in rhetoric soon fell into desuetude.[13]

A not inconsiderable factor in determining scholarly interest is the publication of new texts. Witness the excitement caused by the discoveries at Qumran and Nag Hammadi! Something similar happened ninety years ago as critical editions were published of long-known but equally long-neglected works of hellenistic authors. Around the turn of the century it was hellenistic philosophers who attracted attention as excellent editions of their works were issued, especially in the series initiated in 1849 by the publishing house of Benedict Gotthelf Teubner. So impressed was Johannes Weiss by the affinity between these authors and much of the New Testament that he insisted that students of the New Testament should know Seneca, Epictetus, Plutarch, Lucian, Musonius, Marcus Aurelius, and Cicero intimately, and pursue the study of the New Testament with Hans von Arnim's collection of Stoic texts at their elbows.[14] Weiss's great commentary on 1 Corinthians shows that he had followed his own advice, and the commentary on 2 Corinthians by his student, Hans Windisch, shows that his influence continued after his death in 1914 at the age of fifty-one.[15]

---

[12]*Dionysii Halicarnasei quae fertur Ars rhetorica,* ed. H. Usener (Leipzig: B. G. Teubner, 1895). See Lietzmann's account of his education in *Die Religionswissenschaft der Gegenwart in Selbstdarstellungen,* ed. E. Stange (Leipzig: F. Meiner, 1926), 2.12–13.

[13]J. Weiss, "Beiträge zur paulinischen Rhetorik," in *Theologische Studien, Bernhard Weiss zu seinem 70. Geburtstag dargebracht* (Göttingen: Vandenhoeck & Ruprecht, 1897), 165–247. See the excellent discussion by H. D. Betz, "The Problem of Rhetoric and Theology according to the Apostle Paul," in *L'Apôtre Paul: Personalité, style et conception du ministère,* ed. A. Vanhoye, BETL 73 (Louvain: Louvain Univ. Press, 1986) 1, 16–48.

[14]J. Weiss, *Die Aufgaben der neutestamentlichen Wissenschaft in der Gegenwart* (Göttingen: Vandenhoeck & Ruprecht, 1908), 4, 11, 55.

[15]J. Weiss, *Der erste Korintherbrief,* KEK (Göttingen: Vandenhoeck & Ruprecht, 1910), still the best commentary on the letter; H. Windisch, *Der zweite Korintherbrief,* KEK (Göttingen: Vandenhoeck & Ruprecht, 1924), a monument to erudition, which unfortunately does not allow the detailed information to illuminate Paul's letter.

Another of Weiss's students, Rudolf Bultmann, heavily dependent on Heinrich Schenkl's Teubner text of Epictetus, had written his dissertation on the diatribe, which he understood to represent the oral style of popular philosophical propaganda, and which he thought had influenced Paul's oral style.[16] Bultmann shared his teacher's interest in the art of persuasion. But Bultmann focused on the style he thought preachers to the masses had developed as they attempted to turn their listeners to the rational life, rather than on the formal rhetoric taught in the classrooms of teachers of rhetoric. To this interest in style was added an interest in the minor literary and rhetorical conventions used by the moral philosophers in their instruction.[17] So, for example, Ernst von Dobschutz and Hans Lietzmann drew attention to the Greek elements in the virtue and vice lists which appear in the New Testament, and Martin Dibelius suggested that Colossians 3:18—4:1, a so-called household code *(Haustafel)*, was borrowed, with some slight adaptation, from the Stoics.[18]

It is fair to say that, with few exceptions, both the philosophic material introduced into the discussion as well as the insights offered by these pioneers continued to be accepted for decades almost without question by the majority of critical scholars. Despite a few efforts to extend the investigation of form and style along the lines already laid out,[19] and some attempts to understand Paul in comparison with the philosophers,[20] original work had virtually come to a standstill. Only during the last two decades has dissatisfaction with this state of affairs led to new original work on the relationship between the moral philosophers and the New Testament.[21] These newer studies, like those of

---

[16]R. Bultmann, *Der Stil der paulinischen Predigt und die kynisch-stoische Diatribe,* FRLANT 13 (Göttingen: Vandenhoeck & Ruprecht, 1910).

[17]For representative texts illustrating various aspects of moral instruction, see A. J. Malherbe, *Moral Exhortation: A Greco-Roman Sourcebook,* Library of Early Christianity 4 (Philadelphia: Westminster Press, 1986).

[18]E. von Dobschütz, *Die urchristlichen Gemeinden: Sittengeschichtliche Bilder* (Leipzig: J. C. Hinrichs, 1902), 277–84; H. Lietzmann, *An die Römer,* HNT 9 (Tübingen: J. C. B. Mohr [Paul Siebeck], 1906), excursus on Rom. 1:28-31; M. Dibelius, *An die Kolosser, an die Epheser, an Philemon,* HNT 12 (Tübingen: J. C. B. Mohr [Paul Siebeck], 1913), excursus after comment on Col. 4:1.

[19]For example, K. Weidinger, Dibelius's student, wrote *Die Haustafeln: Ein Stück urchristlicher Paränese,* UNT 14 (Leipzig: J. C. Hinrichs, 1928); Bultmann's student, H. Thyen, applied his teacher's analysis of the diatribe to what he considered examples of synagogue preaching in *Der Stil der jüdisch-hellenistischen Homilie,* FRLANT 47 (Göttingen: Vandenhoeck & Ruprecht, 1955); and A. Vögtle, *Die Tugend-und Lasterkataloge im Neuen Testament,* NA 16.4/5 (Münster: Aschendorff, 1936), pushed further on the catalogues of virtues and vices.

[20]See, for example, K. Deissner, *Das Idealbild des stoischen Weisen,* Greifswalder Universitätsreden 24 (Greifswald: L. Bamberg, 1930); idem, "Das Sendungsbewusstsein der Urchristenheit," *ZsysTh* 7 (1930): 772–90; and, to some degree, but less clear in method, H. Windisch, *Paulus und Christus: Ein biblisch-religionsgeschichtlicher Vergleich,* UNT 24 (Leipzig: J. C. Hinrichs, 1934).

[21]See Malherbe, "Hellenistic Moralists and the New Testament," (n. 1 above) for an extended *Forschungsbericht,* and, further, D. L. Balch, "Household Codes," in *Greco-Roman Literature and the New Testament: Selected Forms and Genres,* ed. D. E. Aune, SBLSBS 21 (Atlanta: Scholars Press, 1988), 25-50; S. K. Stowers, "The Diatribe," ibid., 71–83.

the first two decades of this century, are characterized by their direct engagement with the ancient philosophical sources, only now with a range wider than the Stoicism favored by Weiss, Bultmann, and Dibelius.

It is now recognized that Platonists, Peripatetics, Cynics, Stoics, Epicureans, and Pythagoreans must all come under consideration. They are all of interest to the topics pursued in this book, not for their different metaphysical systems, although these systems are not completely irrelevant, but because they all aimed at moral reformation. They shared not only this goal, but much of the substance of their moral instruction and many of the devices and methods they used to attain it. This has contributed to a view of a syncretistic philosophical *Koine* in which Stoicism was of greatest importance. Such an understanding of the matter is increasingly seen to be inadequate. The nature of syncretism itself is coming under close scrutiny. For instance, syncretism is no longer regarded as a process of homogenization in which contributing elements lose their individuality.[22] On the contrary, engagement may very well lead to an accentuation of uniqueness. This was clearly so as philosophical schools disputed with each other and members of the same school debated their school's doctrines. My studies in this book share in this attempt to gain greater precision in our understanding of contemporary philosophy and of Paul's relationship to it.

The first chapter attempts to shed more light on the Cynics (its original form included a short discussion of Epicureans). There is a growing appreciation of the importance of these philosophers who were constantly in the public eye. It had become customary to deny them an independence by joining them by means of a hyphen to Stoics. "Stoic-Cynic," however, obscures some major differences between the two and does not suggest that there were considerable differences among the Cynics themselves.[23] To my knowledge, this is the first effort to concentrate on Cynic sources, letters attributed to ancient worthies but reflecting a Cynic viewpoint, as the basis for interpreting Cynicism. While the discussion is not related to the New Testament, the matters taken up systematically here are important for the other studies which do.

Although Bultmann focused his analysis of the diatribe on Epictetus, who taught in a schoolroom, he made generalizations about the social setting

---

[22]See A. J. Malherbe, "Graeco-Roman Religion and Philosophy and the New Testament," in *The New Testament and Its Modern Interpreters,* ed. E. J. Epp and G. W. McRae (Philadelphia: Fortress Press; Atlanta: Scholars Press, 1989), 3–26.

[23]For a brief description of Cynicism, see A. J. Malherbe, "Cynics," *IDBS* (1976): 201–3, and for Cynics and Stoics, see idem, "Pseudo Heraclitus, Epistle 4: The Divinization of the Wise Man," *JAC* 21 (1978): 42–64. For the renewed vigor of Cynicism in the early Empire, see M. Billerbeck, "La réception du cynicisme à Rome," *AC* 51 (1982): 151–73; J. L. Moles, " 'Honestius quam ambitiosus?' An Explanation of the Cynic's Attitude to Moral Corruption in His Fellow Men," *JHS* 103 (1983): 103–23.

where the style was usually adopted. Bultmann thought that the diatribe was the form in which philosophers addressed the masses on street corners and in the marketplace. Bultmann's study of Paul's style assumed that the diatribal elements in it were clues to Paul's public preaching. Furthermore, he thought that Paul's adaptation of that style reflected a mind more indebted to experience than the rationality of an Epictetus. By concentrating on a key element of diatribal style, I seek to show that Bultmann's generalizations do not hold. Paul and Epictetus use that element, a peculiar way in which a false inference is rejected, but other representatives of the diatribe do not. Paul is also more deliberate in using the diatribal rejection in finely constructed argumentation than Epictetus. The way in which Paul uses the rejection does not portray someone depending on experience; indeed, Paul's use of the style would have been more at home in the classroom than the street corner, and there is no reason to assume that he had appropriated the style from other hellenistic Jews.

Then follow three studies on 1 Thessalonians, which to an exceptional degree reveals Paul's appropriation of the style and commonplaces of his philosophic contemporaries. The "frankness" *(parrēsia)* with which philosophers pointed out the shortcomings of their listeners easily became harsh railing, which led to long reflection on the proper nature of philosophic frankness. Chapter 3, "Gentle as a Nurse," claims for Paul an awareness of these discussions. It demonstrates that Paul's description of himself as a nurse to the Thessalonians (1 Thess. 2:7) is especially intelligible in light of such discussions among philosophers, and it details some of the similarities between Paul's account of his ministry in Thessalonica and contemporary descriptions of the ideal Cynic.

The more general study on exhortation in 1 Thessalonians (chapter 4) focuses on the letter itself rather than Paul's demeanor when he was in Thessalonica. It places the letter more securely in the ancient hortatory tradition, but is careful to point out Paul's adaptation of that tradition and how Paul differs from it. In discussing the epistolary character of the letter, attention is given to its paraenetic features and an attempt is made to set the letter in the context of ancient epistolary theory.[24] As to rhetorical classification, 1 Thessalonians is shown to be a paraenetic letter.

The chapter on Paul as pastor (chapter 5) is based on other studies in this volume and is an abstract of a longer study on Paul as a founder, shaper, and nurturer of a church.[25] It attempts to sketch a social history of a young

---

[24]*Ancient Epistolary Theorists,* ed. A. J. Malherbe, SBLSBS 19 (Atlanta: Scholars Press, 1988).
[25]A. J. Malherbe, *Paul and the Thessalonians: The Philosophic Tradition of Pastoral Care* (Philadelphia: Fortress Press, 1987).

church during the first months after its founding by describing Paul's activity in light of the philosophers' "pastoral" practice. This is one aspect of the philosophic tradition that has not, so far as I am aware, been accorded by New Testament scholars the importance it deserves. The material introduced, from Platonists, Epicureans, and Stoics, draws attention to the psychological condition and social circumstances of recent converts in order to clarify Paul's method of dealing with the church. When this is done, the paraenetic features of Paul's letter are seen to have a pastoral function.

Two studies on Paul's correspondence with the Corinthians deal with Paul's self-understanding. His statement that he had fought with beasts at Ephesus (1 Cor. 15:32) is to be taken metaphorically (chapter 6). This is the way Cynics, especially, described their opposition to hedonists, who were frequently described as Epicureans. Paul uses the language to describe his opposition to hedonists in Ephesus. The study on Paul's use of martial imagery (chapter 7) again demonstrates that he had a sophisticated knowledge of the way Stoics and Cynics used the image to describe their own understanding of themselves and their work. Indeed, Paul was aware of the differences among Cynics, and deftly situated himself in the philosophical landscape. As in the other chapters, equal attention is given to the ways in which Paul differs from his contemporaries. What emerges is a Paul who directly, without depending on Jewish predecessors, used the philosophic tradition to describe himself as a warrior for God as he engaged his opponents in Corinth.

The last four studies deal with followers and interpreters of Paul. Two on the Pastoral Epistles present a Paul quite different from the other letters that have come under consideration. The Paul who is represented as writing these letters is thoroughly at home in the traditions with which this book is concerned. But the way in which the traditions are used differ from Paul's use. The medical imagery in the letters is derived from the philosophers and is used to describe opponents who are antisocial, harsh, and beyond hope (chapter 8). As such, they are to be avoided, for they are incapable of benefiting from the type of pastoral therapy employed by Paul. One such difference is examined in chapter 9: on being ready to act "in season and out of season" (2 Tim. 4:2). This advice flies in the face of good pastoral practice as envisaged by responsible philosophers and practiced by Paul. True physicians of the soul were at pains to find the right occasion on which to be stern or gentle. The Pastoral Epistles allow no such modulation when confronting heretics who are out to destroy the church.

The Book of Acts has an interest in presenting Christianity as a public, world religion. Paul claims this public character in his last defense, before Festus (Acts 26:26), and he does so in language derived from the philosophers.

The study which explores Paul's claim (chapter 10) sketches Luke's presentation of Paul as a philosopher and shows that Luke in a number of respects anticipates the concerns as well as the responses, albeit inchoately, of the apologists of the second century.

The final study (chapter 11) moves in the curious world of ancient physiognomy. A well-known description of Paul usually not regarded as flattering is discovered to belong, in fact, to a tradition which describes heroes in the same terms. Among these heroes was Heracles, a patron saint of the Cynics.

The Paul that emerges from these essays is one who was thoroughly familiar with the traditions used by his philosophic contemporaries. As his use of them to conduct his argument or to describe his own self-understanding as a Christian apostle shows, he knew these traditions first-hand and not through the mediation of other Jews who before him had to come to terms with the Greek experience. Paul's followers and interpreters took his familiarity with moral philosophy for granted and therefore did not think it incongruous to represent him as *Paulus hellenisticus*. Paul himself used the philosophic traditions with at least as much originality as his contemporaries did. A major difference between them is that Paul is neither as schoolbookish nor self-conscious in using the traditions as they were. His letters, after all, are not tractates on psychagogic practice but are themselves examples of that practice. In his letters Paul does not discuss those traditions overtly. He does not engage in disputes about the proper practice, as the philosophers did; indeed, he does not even focus on the traditions in an attempt to discover what was to be appropriated or rejected. Paul has another agenda, and if the question of influence is to be addressed, it is to be done in more subtle and nuanced ways than has often been the case.

The traditions Paul uses were given a hard edge by the Cynics through their very, often dramatic, presence as well as their sharp formulation of issues. The Cynics figure prominently in these studies, partly because they had been slighted in earlier discussions and the balance had to be redressed, and partly because they had been lumped uncritically with the Stoics. But they are also treated at great length because Paul's practice and teaching are seen in sharper profile against a background to which they belong. Paul, however, was no Cynic. He addressed some of the issues they raised, and he used their language, but he shrank, for example, from the Cynics' preoccupation with the individual, either themselves or others. Paul, on the other hand, was a founder of communities, of which the Cynics had none.

In his communal concern, Paul was more like the Epicureans, although we know little about contemporary Epicurean communities. In his concern for proper care of people he approximated responsible people like Plutarch, and the substance of his teaching at times reminds us of someone like Musonius Rufus. Paul could use the same devices in his argumentation as Epictetus did, and he could put a paraenetic style to his own, pastoral purpose.

Yet for all this he remains *Paulus christianus,* but without that making him any the less *Paulus hellenisticus.* After all, like Tennyson's Ulysses, and like the eclectic Plutarch or Musonius, we are part of all we have met. So was Paul.

1

Self-Definition
among the Cynics

The Cynics and the Cynicism of the first century A.D. are known to us for the most part through Stoic interpreters, and the temptation is great, on the basis of Seneca's account of Demetrius, Musonius Rufus, Epictetus, and Dio Chrysostom, to draw a picture of Cynicism which obscures the differences between Stoicism and Cynicism and among the Cynics themselves. In the second century, the diversity among the Cynics emerges more clearly as such personalities as Oenomaus of Gadara, Demonax, and Peregrinus Proteus appear on the scene. Unfortunately, only fragments of Oenomaus's writings have been preserved, and only a few comments, mostly negative, are made about him by Julian, and we are largely but not wholly dependent on Lucian's interpretations of Demonax and Peregrinus for information about them. It is therefore fortunate that in the Cynic epistles we do have primary sources for the sect in the Empire. These neglected writings are more than the school exercises they have been thought to be, and enable us to determine the points at issue among the Cynics themselves.[1]

The Definition of Cynicism

Diogenes Laertius already experienced difficulty in describing common Cynic doctrine, and records that some considered it, not a philosophical school (*hairesis*), but a way of life (*Lives of Eminent Philosophers* 6.103).[2] He seems

---

[1]The texts are readily available in *Epistolographi Graeci,* ed. R. Hercher (reprint, Amsterdam: Hakkert, 1965). For introduction, text and translation of the most important letters, see *The Cynic Epistles: A Study Edition,* ed. A. J. Malherbe, SBLSBS 12 (Missoula, Mont.: Scholars Press, 1977).
[2]Cf. Diogenes Laertius *Lives of Eminent Philosophers* 1.19–20, for Hippobotus's refusal to list the Cynics as a philosophical school. For *hairesis* as a school of thought, see J. Glucker, *Antiochus and the Late Academy* (Göttingen: Vandenhoeck & Ruprecht, 1978), 166–92. On Diogenes's passion for classification, see J. Mejer, *Diogenes Laertius and His Hellenistic Background,* Hermes Einzelschrift 40 (Wiesbaden: Franz Steiner, 1978), 52. Julian, who also describes it as a way of life (*Oration* 6.181D, 201A), nevertheless insists that it is a form of philosophy, a gift of the gods, but that it should be studied from the Cynics' deeds rather than their writings (*Oration* 6.132C–189B).

to incline to the view that it is a philosophical school, but notes that Cynics dispensed with logic and physics, and confined themselves to ethics. Cynics have generally been perceived as having an aversion to encyclopaedic learning and placing no premium on education in the pursuit of virtue. As a distinctively anti-social sect, they attached greatest importance to a way of life that gave chief emphasis to personal decision.[3] Yet this generalization holds only partly. While it is true that in the hellenistic period Cynicism did not require adherence to an organized system of doctrine, the major figures known to us, in contrast to the charlatans Lucian describes, were by no means anti-intellectual. Oenomaus reflects a knowledge of philosophical arguments about free will and providence,[4] Demonax is said to have been eclectic although in dress he was a Cynic,[5] Peregrinus is thought to have been influenced by Neopythagoreanism,[6] and the Socratic epistles betray at least an openness to philosophy and its possible contribution to one's progress toward virtue.[7]

Cynics differed among themselves in their philosophical eclecticism as they did in other matters, but a personal preference for or use in debate of one system does not appear to have been a major issue in determining who was a Cynic. What made a Cynic was his dress and conduct, self-sufficiency, harsh behavior toward what appeared as excesses, and a practical ethical idealism, but not a detailed arrangement of a system resting on Socratic-Antisthenic principles. The result was that Cynicism was compatible with views that shared its ethical demands even if they were at cross purposes with its fundamentally different teaching in other matters.[8] The resulting diversity makes an attempt at a detailed definition of Cynicism difficult, especially if it is based on the idealized presentations of Epictetus, Lucian, Maximus of Tyre, and Julian.[9] Epictetus's description has often been taken to represent the true

---

[3]See, for example, R. Höistad, *Cynic Hero and Cynic King* (Uppsala: C. W. K. Gleerup, 1948), 34 and *passim*.

[4]See D. R. Dudley, *A History of Cynicism from Diogenes to the Fifth Century A.D.* (London: Methuen, 1937), 169; D. Amand, *Fatalisme et liberté dans l'antiquité grecque* (Louvain: Bibliothèque de l'Université, 1945), 127–34.

[5]Lucian *Demonax* 5, 62, but see 14.

[6]Cf. K. Praechter, *Die Philosophie des Altertums* (Berlin: S. Mittler, 1926), 512; Dudley, *A History of Cynicism,* 180. H. M. Hornsby, "The Cynicism of Peregrinus Proteus," *Hermathema* 48 (1933): 65-84, discusses the evidence and is skeptical of Neopythagorean influence on Peregrinus.

[7]Pseudo-Socrates *Epistle* 25. In *Epistle* 18.2 and *Epistle* 20 there is a positive evaluation of Socrates's *logoi,* in contrast to Lucian *Philosophies for Sale* 11, where education and doctrine are regarded as superfluous. Cf. Julian *Oration* 6.189A: "For Diogenes deeds sufficed."

[8]Praechter, *Die Philosophie des Altertums,* 659.

[9]Epictetus *Discourse* 3.22; cf. M. Billerbeck, *Epiktet: Vom Kynismus,* Philosophia Antiqua 34 (Leiden: E. J. Brill, 1978); Lucian *Demonax;* cf. K. Funk, "Untersuchungen über die Lucianische Vita Demonactis," *Philologus,* Suppl. 10 (1907): 561–674; Maximus of Tyre *Discourse* 36; Julian *Oration* 6, esp. 200C–202C.

Cynic without due allowance being made for his Stoicizing or for the fact that he is presenting an ideal.[10]

Although these accounts do contain genuine Cynic material and viewpoints, it is preferable to identify features that Cynics themselves consider central and to proceed from there. Among other sources, the Cynic epistles represent such information and must be introduced into the discussion. In view of the interest of the symposium, some major features of Cynic diversity in the second century A.D. will be touched on, and an attempt will be made to determine whether one form of Cynicism came to predominate in the third. Here, special attention will be given to the Cynic letters attributed to Socrates and his disciples.

The letters under consideration come from two authors, the former writing in the name of Socrates, probably in the first century A.D. (*Epistles* 1–7), the latter writing in the names of members of the Socratic circle in the third century (*Epistles* 8–27; 29–34). The letters may have originated in a school, but their value for the history of Cynicism is considerable. In addition to their propagandistic aim, they represent divergent Cynic views projected onto the Socratics to create an impression of Socrates and his disciples discussing issues important to Cynics.[11] The author of the Socratic letters, with

---

[10]This has been the case particularly with New Testament scholars who, impressed by Epictetus's view of the ideal Cynic as a messenger of God, have used his interpretation of Cynicism to illustrate the Christian apostolate and other Christian and pagan emissaries. See, e.g., K. Rengstorff, *"apostolos," TDNT* 1 (1964): 409–13, who qualifies the usefulness of Epictetus's description by saying, "in so far as Epictetus decribes for us the reality and not merely the ideal of the true Cynic" (409). W. Schmithals (*The Office of Apostle in the Early Church*, trans. J. E. Steely [Nashville: Abingdon Press, 1969], 111) impatiently dismisses any other possible descriptions of religious emissaries in Hellenism and confines himself to Epictetus's description of the "Cynic-Stoic" sage as the pre-eminent source for a figure close to the Christian apostle. D. Georgi (*The Opponents of Paul in Second Corinthians* [Philadelphia: Fortress Press, 1986], e.g., 28–29, 156–57) is similarly dependent on Epictetus and combines Epictetus's picture of Cynicism with that of other types of religious propagandists to construct a *theios anēr* figure on which Paul's Corinthians opponents are claimed to have modelled themselves. These scholars have not done justice to the Stoic elements in Epictetus's description, nor have they sufficiently recognized that he is describing an ideal Cynic. As to Epictetus's Stoicism in *Discourse* 3.22, the debate among specialists has not been whether it dominates that diatribe, but whether it reveals Epictetus as a follower of early Stoicism, as A. Bonhoeffer, *Die Ethik des Stoikers Epiktet* (Stuttgart: F. Enke, 1894), had argued, or whether the influence of Musonius and the evidence of Seneca for contemporary Stoicism should not be taken into consideration, as Billerbeck, *Epiktet,* does. Billerbeck, however, is more successful in distinguishing between Stoicism and Cynicism in Epictetus than between the varieties of Cynicism in the early Empire. Furthermore, Epictetus describes an ideal Cynic—from a Stoic point of view. Stoics were not at all sanguine about attaining the ideal. Epictetus himself claimed not to have done so, and his description is given to correct the popular misconception of Cynics for young men who may be considering entering that way of life. On the attainment of the ideal, see A. J. Malherbe, "Pseudo-Heraclitus, Epistle 4: The Divinization of the Wise Man," *JAC* 21 (1978): 54–56.

[11]On the composition and dating of the corpus I follow J. Sykutris, "Sokratikerbriefe," PW, Suppl. 5 (1931): 981–87; idem, *Die Briefe des Sokrates und der Sokratiker,* Studien zur Geschichte und Kultur des Altertums 18/2 (Paderborn: Ferdinand Schöningh, 1933). See also L. Köhler, "Die

the earlier collection before him, is embarrassed by the public fussing of Cynics among themselves,[12] and it is characteristic of his corpus that attempts are made to modify a radical Cynic individualism and attempt a *rapprochement* between the protagonists.

Lucian (*Demonax* 21) records an illustrative encounter between Demonax and Peregrinus. Peregrinus rebukes Demonax for his levity and jesting with people, and accuses him of not acting in the Cynic manner. Demonax replies that Peregrinus is not behaving in a human manner.[13] Lucian's biased interpretation of the lives of the two does not obscure the fact that both were Cynics, and that the argument between them involves the manner of life that can justifiably be called Cynic. Reflected here is a divergence into two types of Cynicism: an austere, rigorous one, and a milder, so-called hedonistic strain.[14] Despite Lucian's caricature of him, Peregrinus emerges as a Cynic of the austere type who modelled himself on Heracles. In his austerity he was not unlike Oenomaus.[15] Demonax, in contrast, was everybody's friend (*Demonax* 10; cf. 8 and 63) and, while he adopted Diogenes' dress and way of life, did not alter the details of his life for the effect it might have on the crowds.[16] He revered Socrates, except for his irony, and admired Diogenes,

---

Briefe des Sokrates und der Sokratiker," *Philologus,* Suppl. 20.2 (1928). On the appeal to Socrates by the Stoics and Cynics in the early Empire, see K. Döring, *Exemplum Socratis: Studien zur Sokratesnachwirkung in der kynisch-stoischen Popularphilosophie der frühen Kaiserzeit und in frühen Christentum,* Hermes Einzelschriften 42 (Wiesbaden: Franz Steiner, 1979), esp. 114–26 on the Socratic epistles. For the school setting of the letters, see Köhler, "Die Briefe des Sokrates und der Sokratiker," 4–5, and W. Obens, "Qua aetate Socratis et Socraticorum epistulae quae dicuntur scriptae sunt" (Diss., Muenster 1912), 6. For their propagandistic aim, see E. Norden, "Beiträge zur Geschichte der griechischen Philosophie," *Jahrbücher fur classische Philologie,* Suppl. 19 (1893): 393, and O. Schering, "Symbola ad Socratis et Socraticorum epistulas explicandas" (Diss., Greifswald, 1917), 32. I am indebted to B. Fiore, S. J., *The Function of Personal Example in the Socratic and Pastoral Epistles,* AnBib 105 (Rome: Biblical Institute Press, 1986), 101–26, for much of what follows.

[12]Pseudo-Socrates *Epistle* 23.3. Cf. Lucian *The Fisherman* 44, and for his awareness of the diversity among the Cynics, see R. Helm, "Lucian und die Philosophenschulen," *Neue Jahrbuch für das klassisches Altertum* 9 (1902): 264 n. 2; M. Caster, *Lucien et la pensée religieuse de son temps* (Paris: Les Belles Lettres, 1937), 71;

[13]For the Cynic as bestial and inhumane, see Lucian *Philosophies for Sale* 10–11; Julian *Oration* 7.209A.

[14]For the types, see G. A. Gerhard, *Phoinix von Kolophon* (Leipzig/Berlin: B. G. Teubner, 1909), 64–72, 165–68; idem, "Zur Legende vom Kyniker Diogenes," *ARW* 15 (1912): 388–408, and for a different interpretation, R. Höistad, "Cynicism," *Dictionary of the History of Ideas* (1968): 1.631–32; J. F. Kindstrand, *Bion of Borysthenes: A Collection of the Fragments with Introduction and Commentary,* Studia Graeca Upsaliensis 11 (Uppsala: Almqvist & Wiksell, 1976), 64-67.

[15]Despite their eclectic tendencies, Peregrinus's disciples also considered themselves Cynics (cf. Lucian *The Passing of Peregrinus* 2–4, 24, 26, 29, 36, 37, 43); he was remembered by others as an austere Cynic (Aulus Gellius *Attic Nights* 8.3; 12.11; Philostratus *Lives of the Sophists* 2.563). For Oenomaus's severity, see Eusebius *Preparation for the Gospel* 5.21 213C; 5.23 215D; 5.29 224C–225A; 5.33 228D; 6.6 254D; 6.7 261B, and Julian's criticism of his inhuman, bestial life (*Oration* 7.209AB).

[16]Lucian *Demonax* 5-6. Lucian's *ou paracharattōn ta eis tēn diaitan* ("not altering the details of his life") may be an allusion to the Cynic's *paracharattein to nomisma* ("to alter the coinage"); cf. Diogenes Laertius *Lives of Eminent Philosophers* 6.20, 71.

but loved Aristippus (6, 62). Lucian's stress on Demonax's culture and mildness does not hide the fact that he was not loved by the masses (11), and that his "witty remarks" in 12–62 are reminiscent of Diogenes's apophthegms preserved in Diogenes Laertius *Lives of Eminent Philosophers* 6.24–69. Demonax defended Cynic *parrēsia* (50), and even praised Thersites as a Cynic mob-orator (61). While retaining Cynicism's simplicity of life and dress and its indifference to presumed virtues and vices, Demonax rejected its hostility to education and culture, excessive asceticism, and shamelessness.[17]

What can be detected in Lucian finds elaboration in the Cynic epistles, where attempts at self-definition utilize as models early Cynics and heroes from Greek myth, appropriately interpreted to reflect a particular writer's proclivities. Certain letters attributed to Crates and Diogenes represent austere Cynicism. In obvious polemic against hedonistic Cynicism, pseudo-Crates affirms that Cynic philosophy is Diogenean and the Cynic someone who toils according to it, taking a short cut in doing philosophy by avoiding the circuitous route of doctrine. He wears the Cynic garb which is viewed as the weapons of the gods (*Epistle* 6).[18] The Cynic takes up this armament as a deliberate act to demonstrate that the simplicity of the soul finds expression in his deeds, in which he wars against appearances.[19] In contrast to Odysseus, who is made to represent the hedonistic Cynic, Diogenes is portrayed as consistent in his commitment to the Cynic life, austere, self-sufficient, self-confident, trusting in reason, and brave in his practice of virtue.[20] This brand of Cynicism does not simply consist in indifference to all things, but in the robust endurance of what others out of softness or opinion cannot endure.[21] The Cynic shamelessness is part of this rejection of opinions and conventions, and is the mark of the doggish philosopher.[22] The situation in which men find themselves requires, not philosophers like Plato and Aristippus, who in the doxographic tradition represent hedonistic Cynicism, but a harsh taskmaster who can bring the masses to reality.[23]

---

[17]Praechter, *Die Philosophie des Altertums,* 511.
[18]See V. Emeljanow, "The Cynic Short Cut to Virtue," *Mnemosyne,* n. s. 18/2 (1965): 182–84.
[19]Cf. pseudo-Diogenes *Epistles* 7; 15; 27; 34; 46. For extended discussion, see A. J. Malherbe, "Antisthenes and Odysseus, and Paul at War," *HTR* 76 (1983): 143–73 (= 91–119 in this volume).
[20]Pseudo-Crates *Epistle* 19. For Cynic interpretations of Odysseus, see Malherbe, "Pseudo-Heraclitus, Epistle 4" (n. 10 above), 50–51.
[21]Pseudo-Crates *Epistle* 29; pseudo-Diogenes *Epistle* 27; Lucian *Peregrinus* 27.
[22]Pseudo-Diogenes *Epistles* 42; 44. On Cynic *anaideia,* see Gerhard, *Phoinix von Kolophon,* 144–45. H. Schulz-Falkenthal, "Kyniker-Zur inhaltlichen Deutung des Namens," *WZHalle* 26.2 (1977): 41–49, and I. Nachov, "Der Mensch in der Philosophie der Kyniker," in *Der Mensch als Mass der Dinge,* ed. R. Müller (Berlin: Akademie-Verlag, 1976): 361–98, overstress the social and political motivations for Cynic conduct.
[23]Pseudo-Diogenes *Epistles* 29; 32. For Plato in the Cynic tradition, see A. Swift Reginos, *Platonica* (Leiden: E. J. Brill, 1976), 111–18, who does not, however, discuss the way in which the Plato anecdotes function in the debate under review. For Aristippus as representing the hedonistic Cynic, see R. F. Hock, "Simon the Shoemaker as an Ideal Cynic," *GRBS* 17 (1976): 48–52.

The issues between the two types are sharpened in six of the Socratic letters in which Simon the shoemaker (and Antisthenes) and Aristippus speak for them (*Epistles* 9–13). The topic discussed is whether the Cynic could associate with a tyrant. Antisthenes asserts that the Cynic should strive for self-sufficiency *(autarkeia),* and that he cannot associate with tyrants or the masses, for they are ignorant of it (*Epistle* 8). With biting irony the hedonist Aristippus replies that he was a steward of the teaching of Socrates in Dionysius's court (*Epistle* 9), and that his position there had resulted in his saving certain Locrian youths (*Epistles* 10; 11). Simon denies that a life of luxury is Socratic; his cobbling is done to make possible his admonition of foolish men, and his austerity is of value in the pursuit of *sōphrosynē.* He takes umbrage at Aristippus's jesting about his way of life (*Epistle* 12). Aristippus responds in conciliatory fashion. He is not ridiculing the humble life, for there is wisdom in it. But Simon would also have opportunity to practise his craft, and on a larger scale, in Syracuse. Aristippus assures Simon that he is his friend, in contrast to the harsh, bestial Cynics (*Epistle* 13).

The mild Cynic, therefore, defends his behavior by arguing that it benefits others and is more human. What is to be found in Lucian's description of Demonax thus also appears here. It is the rigorous Cynics who explicitly discuss "Cynicism" in their self-definition, and they do so in terms of their manner of life. The mild Cynic is more conciliatory, although this should not be overstated, and defends his behavior by pointing to its usefulness in influencing a larger audience.[24]

The Human Condition

Something more, however, than a difference in method used to attain an end seems to have been at the basis of Cynics' self-conceptions. They shared the view that man has to be reformed by being taught to unlearn his vices (Diogenes Laertius *Lives of Eminent Philosophers* 6.7–8). Unlike vice, which enters the soul spontaneously, they held that virtue was acquired by practice (pseudo-Crates *Epistle* 12), and happiness consisted in living according to nature (Diogenes Laertius *Lives of Eminent Philosophers* 6.71; Julian *Oration* 6.193D). Virtue could be taught, and, once acquired, could not be lost (Diogenes Laertius *Lives of Eminent Philosophers* 6.10, 105). What Cynics called for was a decision to improve oneself, to make a deliberate choice to change from one's previous condition (Diogenes Laertius *Lives of Eminent Philosophers* 6.56). Yet they differed in their assessments of the degree to which the

---

[24]Cf. Pseudo-Diogenes *Epistle* 46, for the rigorist's insistence that his way of life, too, is beneficial as a demonstration of self-sufficiency.

human condition had been corrupted and, consequently, on the methods that were to be applied to effect the desired change.

The rigoristic Cynics had an extremely pessimistic view of mankind, which earned them the charge of misanthropy.[25] This view is especially, but not exclusively, represented by most of the letters attributed to Crates, Diogenes, Heraclitus, and Hippocrates.[26] Most people, they held, are totally deluded, puffed up in their evil, and completely bereft of reason and self-control. Having sunk to the level of beasts in their ignorance and conduct, nature itself hates them, and takes vengeance on them by punishing them.[27] In contrast, the true Cynic, the epitome of virtue, knows nature and imitates it.[28] Whereas nature punishes them in deed, the Cynic does so in his speech (pseudo-Diogenes *Epistle* 28.5). It is by virtue alone that their souls can be purified of its diseases, and it is the Cynic who is the physician able to bring about their cure.[29] Their putrid condition requires no gentle treatment, but rather the cautery and surgery of scathing Cynic *parrēsia*.[30] It is not that the Cynic wishes to be morbid; their wickedness made him sullen and excised his gentleness (pseudo-Heraclitus *Epistles* 5.3; 7.2–3).

The worse the human condition, the greater is the virtue of the Cynic perceived to be. Not everyone is capable of Cynic virtue, and most people, complaining about Cynic indifference, flee the Cynic regimen when they see how hard it is.[31] The Cynic alone has brought moral practice to perfection,[32] and, when people prove to be beyond cure, he withdraws from them.[33] He separates from the bestial crowd who know neither nature, reason or truth, and associates only with those who understand the word of a Cynic (pseudo-Diogenes *Epistle* 28.8). He may explain, in self-defence, that it is men's vice, and not themselves, that he hates (pseudo-Heraclitus *Epistle* 7.2), but his

---

[25]See Gerhard, *Phoinix von Kolophon,* 64–72, 166–67, 170–76.

[26]The charlatans Lucian criticizes frequently affected the style of these Cynics, but for different reasons. They made up for the lack of content in their speeches by railing at the crowds (*Philosophies for Sale* 10-11) who, being simple people, admired them for their abusiveness (*Peregrinus* 18), delighted in their "therapy," and thought them to be superior persons by virtue of their belligerence (*The Runaways* 12; *The Carousal* 12–19).

[27]Pseudo-Diogenes *Epistles* 28; 29. Cf. pseudo-Heraclitus *Epistles* 2; 4; 5; 7; 9; pseudo-Hippocrates *Epistle* 17.

[28]Pseudo-Heraclitus *Epistles* 5.1; 9.3, 6.

[29]Pseudo-Diogenes *Epistles* 27; 49; pseudo-Hippocrates *Epistle* 11.7.

[30]E.g., pseudo-Diogenes *Epistles* 27; 28; 29. On the medical imagery, see A. J. Malherbe, "Medical Imagery in the Pastoral Epistles," in *Texts and Testaments: Critical Essays on the Bible and Early Church Fathers,* ed. W. E. March (San Antonio, Tex.: Trinity Univ. Press, 1980), 19–35 (= 121–36 in this volume).

[31]Pseudo-Crates *Epistle* 21; pseudo-Diogenes *Epistles* 21; 41.

[32]Cf. Pseudo-Diogenes *Epistle* 27; pseudo-Heraclitus *Epistle* 4.3; cf. Diogenes Laertius *Lives of Eminent Philosophers* 6.71.

[33]Pseudo-Heraclitus *Epistles* 2; 4; 7; 9; pseudo-Socrates *Epistle* 24. He would prefer, however, to live with men in order to provide for them an example to follow. Cf., pseudo-Crates *Epistles* 20; 35.2.

hatred for them and for association with them is nevertheless at times stated explicitly.[34]

This contempt for the masses raises the question of the harsh Cynic's motivation for speaking to them at all. It has been claimed that, despite the Cynic's consciousness of his superior virtue and his contempt for the masses, in reality he "was influenced by altruistic motives in a far higher degree than his ethics required him to be."[35] The Cynic, filled with philanthropy, according to this view, recognized his goal to be to benefit people.[36] His concern for others did not originate in a sense of duty, but stemmed from a real sympathy with human suffering and the unnatural bondage in which men find themselves. Having freed himself from evils, he was conscious of having a mission to free others.[37]

This is not, however, the self-portrait of the harsh Cynic who hardly stresses his philanthropy, and whose altruism, such as it is, is not a major characteristic. As its proponents acknowledge, this view of Cynic philanthropy seems at odds with Cynic individualism. Julian, whose understanding of Cynicism appears to be correct in this respect, provides us with some clarity on the matter. The Cynics' reproof of others, he says, was not their chief end and aim; rather,

> their main concern was how they might themselves attain to happiness and . . . they occupied themselves with other men and only in so far as they comprehended that man is by nature a social and political animal; and so they aided their fellow-citizens, not only by practicing but by preaching as well (*Oration* 6.201C).

The Cynic must therefore begin with himself, expelling all desires and passions and undertaking to live by intelligence and reason alone.[38] Julian is aware that many Cynics failed in this, and allowed themselves to be influenced by the masses (*Oration* 6.197B-D). The Cynic must free himself from popular opinion, but that does not mean

> that we ought to be shameless before all men and to do what we ought not; but all that we refrain from and all that we do let us not do or refrain from, merely

---

[34]Pseudo-Diogenes *Epistle* 28.2. Pseudo-Socrates *Epistle* 24 is more ambiguous: "Plato" is convinced that Timon was not a misanthrope. On Timon remembered as a misanthrope, see F. Bertram, "Die Timonlegende. Eine Entwicklungsgeschichte des Misanthropentypus in der Antiken Literatur," (Diss., Ruprecht-Karls-Universität zu Heidelberg, 1906), 33 n. 1, 38, 44–54.
[35]T. Gomperz, *Greek Thinkers* (New York: Charles Scribner's Sons, 1908), 2.163. See J. L. Moles, " 'Honestius quam ambitiosus?' An Exploration of the Cynic's Attitude toward Moral Corruption in His Fellow Men," *JHS* 103 (1983): 103–23, who still stresses the *philanthrōpia* of the Cynics.
[36]Gerhard, *Phoinix von Kolophon,* 32–33; Gomperz, *Greek Thinkers,* 2.166. For a more nuanced treatment, see Höistad, *Cynic Hero and Cynic King.*
[37]J. Kaerst, *Geschichte der hellenistischen Zeitalters* (Leipzig/Berlin: B. G. Teubner, 1909), 2.1.118–19, 120.
[38]Julian *Oration* 6.201D. Cf. 188B, 189AB, 192A, 198D; *Oration* 7.214BC.

because it seems to the multitude somehow honourable or base, but because it is forbidden by reason and the god within us, that is, the mind (*Oration* 6.196D).

Julian wishes to retain the Cynic's individualism, and warns against his simply defining himself over against the multitude.

The Superiority of the Austere Cynic

The harsh, austere Cynics stress their radical individualism, but cannot withstand the temptation to do so by defining themselves in opposition to the multitudes whom they hold in such contempt. At the risk of overstating the matter, it is important to note that their comments on themselves are made when they lambaste the multitude who are beyond the hope of cure, or when they compare themselves with the Cynics of milder mien who hold out some hope for society, whom they accuse of pandering to the crowd. What we meet here is not philanthropy or altruism; rather, the concern with the multitudes serves to highlight the superiority of the Cynic who has committed himself without reservation to the life of Diogenes. That sense of superiority emerges from everything that this type of Cynic does or says.

To begin with, all men are evil, and hate the Cynic (pseudo-Heraclitus *Epistles* 2; 7.10). Although their folly causes him hardships, and they maltreat him, and he cannot avoid them, still his virtue remains untouched (pseudo-Crates *Epistle* 35). He is superior to them because he has chosen the difficult, Diogenean, way to happiness.[39] It is hard to find a real Cynic (pseudo-Diogenes *Epistle* 29.4). One must be born to that life, otherwise one fears it and despairs of it (pseudo-Crates *Epistle* 21; pseudo-Diogenes *Epistles* 12; 41). But the Cynic is superior in his moral exercise, is more simple in his life, and more patient in hardship (pseudo-Diogenes *Epistle* 27). It is, in the first instance, what he is, as exemplified in his deeds rather than his words, that is important. Thus, the Cynic dress, which he invests with great importance, sets him off from other people by freeing him from popular opinion (pseudo-Diogenes *Epistles* 7; 34) and effectively separating him from undesirable people (pseudo-Crates *Epistle* 23).

The Cynic's superiority is also demonstrated in his begging. He begs to sustain himself, but he does so for the right reasons and in the right manner, which set him further apart. Begging is not disgraceful, for it is to satisfy a need arising from voluntary poverty (pseudo-Crates *Epistle* 17). By surrendering his private property and thus being freed from evil (pseudo-Crates *Epistle* 7), he shows himself superior to the values of popular opinion (pseudo-Diogenes *Epistle* 9). Furthermore, he is not really begging, but only demanding

---

[39]Pseudo-Crates *Epistles* 6; 13; 15; 16; pseudo-Diogenes *Epistles* 30; 37.

what belongs to him, for, since all things belong to God, friends have all things in common, and he is a friend of God, all things belong to him (pseudo-Crates *Epistles* 26, 27; pseudo-Diogenes *Epistle* 10.2). Nor is he indiscriminate in his begging, for vice must support virtue. Thus, he begs only from people who are worthy of him and his teaching (pseudo-Crates *Epistles* 2; 19; 22; 36; pseudo-Diogenes *Epistle* 38.3–4).

The Cynic's offensive public acts are demonstrations of his deliberateness in choice, and, rather than being blamed for them, he should be recognized as the more worthy of trust because of them (pseudo-Diogenes *Epistles* 42; 44). His goal is to live quietly and not to participate fully in society (pseudo-Crates *Epistle* 5). He may be ridiculed, yet he does not care what people think of him. The benefit that people will receive from him will not come to them because he had sought them out or tried to please them, but because they had observed the example he presented them in his life (pseudo-Crates *Epistle* 20).[40]

The Mild Cynic

In comparison with misanthropic Cynics, those of a milder disposition showed less pride. Their comparative tolerance did not place them on the same level with people they exhorted; nevertheless, they were decidedly more modest in the claims they made for themselves.[41] The Cynics of the Socratic epistles are not as preoccupied with nature or as pessimistic in their view of the human condition, yet they are certain that they know human nature, what people's shortcomings are, what is best for them, and that the greatest emphasis is to be placed on virtue (pseudo-Socrates *Epistles* 5; 6.3,5). These Cynics do not describe themselves, as Lucian does Demonax (*Demonax* 10), as everybody's friend, but their behavior does reflect a more positive attitude. While their self-sufficiency and rejection of popular values makes them different from the majority (pseudo-Socrates *Epistle* 6.2-4), on the ground that the "hedonistic" life does not affect their *phronēsis* (*Epistle* 9.3) they reject the misanthropists' claim that the only appropriate life for the sage is the austere one, and that he cannot associate with the ignorant masses (*Epistle* 8).

In their various social roles these Cynics differ radically from the antisocial Cynics. Unlike Peregrinus, for example, they have no desire to upset

---

[40]On the pride of the misanthropic Cynic, see Gerhard, *Phoinix von Kolophon,* 67–72.

[41]Gerhard, *Phoinix von Kolophon,* 65–66, is unconvincing in his assertion that the use of the first person plural in Teles points to such an identification. Pseudo-Socrates *Epistle* 23.2, "we do not have such great wisdom, but only enough not to harm people in our association with them," is a *captatio benevolentiae.*

the social order. A Cynic of this sort will accept no political office or military appointment, for it is beyond his powers to rule men. But he does remain in the city in the capacity that he does have, that of a counsellor who constantly points out what is profitable for the city (*Epistle* 1.1,10-12).[42] He seeks only that fame which comes from being prudent and just (*Epistle* 6.2), and remains constant in his endurance and contempt for riches (*Epistle* 5). He is fully aware of the injustice in the state (*Epistle* 7) and meets with opposition (*Epistle* 5), but Socrates is his exemplar, not only of the treatment that the sage may receive at the hands of unjust men (*Epistles* 14; 16), but also of the benefits that can accrue from his life and death (*Epistle* 17). This Cynic therefore does not despair of improving society, and consequently justifies his involvement by the potential benefit he might render. Like Demonax, he is mild in the exercise of his *parrēsia,* accommodating himself to his audience, and distancing himself from the antisocial Cynics.[43]

Living as a resident Cynic rather than an independent, wandering preacher required special justification, which "Socrates" provides in *Epistles* 1 and 6.[44] It is clear that these letters are responding to charges of harsh Cynics that it is out of mercenary motives that the resident Cynic confines himself to esoteric teaching in lecture halls. In response, "Socrates" denies that he is unapproachable or mercenary, and offers a number of reasons for his decision to remain in the city. First, he has done so because God had commanded him to remain (*Epistle* 1.2, 7). He knows that this argument may be unacceptable to many Cynics, and therefore uses the Socratic tradition to bolster it (*Epistle* 1.8–9).[45] Furthermore, he claims to meet the needs of his country in the capacity in which he can render some benefit (*Epistle* 1.5–6), unlike ignorant men who arrogate to themselves power that they do not have, who act disgracefully, are insulted, and then end in the wilderness (*Epistle* 1.10–11). He is self-sufficient, and does not beg from the masses (*Epistles* 1.2; 6.1), for he has ample resources in his friends.[46]

The Socratic epistles differ from other Cynic sources of the period in their emphasis on the circle of "friends."[47] Besides the financial assistance

---

[42]The letters of recommendation on behalf of political officials (pseudo-Socrates *Epistles* 3; 4) are designed to illustrate his support of good men.

[43]See A. J. Malherbe, " 'Gentle as a Nurse': The Cynic Background to 1 Thessalonians 2," *NovT* 12 (1970): 210–14. (= 35–48 in this volume); idem, "Medical Imagery" (= 121–36).

[44]For the criticism of resident philosophers in the context of harsh, wandering preachers, see Dio Chrysostom *Discourse* 32.8–11, and cf. Malherbe, "Gentle as a Nurse," 205–6 (= 38).

[45]For the Cynic's divine commission, cf. Dio Chrysostom *Discourse* 13.9, on which see J. L. Moles, "The Career and Conversion of Dio Chrysostom," *JHS* 98 (1978): 79–100, esp. 98–99, and *Discourse* 32.12, on which see E. Wilmes, "Beiträge zur Alexandrinerrede (Or. 32) des Dion Chrysostomos" (Diss. Bonn, 1970), 8-17.

[46]See Pseudo-Socrates *Epistles* 1.2–3; 2; 4; 6.8; 15.2; 19; 21; 22.1; 27.3–4; 28.2. 29.4.

[47]See Obens, "Qua aetate Socratis," 11–13, for a catalogue of references to the theme.

these friends render each other, they are pictured as in constant contact with each other, either in person,[48] or by means of letters, which are surrogates for their authors' physical presence (*Epistle* 18.1), and in which the philosophical discussion is continued.[49] The Socratics are made to represent differing Cynic positions, but their supposed contact with each other presents a picture of a school hammering out its differences in an attempt to come to some kind of harmony.

As the major representative of the milder Cynicism advocated in the letters, Aristippus illustrates their irenic tendency. As already noted, he commends Simon. He is further on good terms with Xenophon and other Socratics (*Epistle* 18), and the enmity between him and Plato is played down as jesting and a reconciliation is hinted at (*Epistle* 23.3). By selective use of the anecdotal tradition, rivalries are further played down and a harmonious picture is sketched. For example, although the tradition often records the austere Diogenes's criticisms of Plato, Diogenes does not appear in these letters, and even the less frequently attested opposition between Antisthenes and Plato is omitted, with Antisthenes left to rebuke only Aristippus.[50] The differences among members of the Academy after Plato's death are attributed to personal judgment and disposition (*Epistle* 4.2–3), and concern is expressed for the preservation and organization of the institution (*Epistles* 32; 33), yet the letters do not provide evidence for the institutionalization of Cynicism. The effort to bring Cynics into conversation with each other itself draws attention to their diversity, and there is no evidence that the authors are witnesses to organized Cynic schools. But there is at least an attempt made to mute their differences. The major confrontation that remains is between the harsh and the hedonistic Cynics, but attempts are made to ameliorate it.

The Cynics and Religion

No convincing generalization can be made about the Cynics' attitude toward religion. Modern opinions range from what is perhaps the classic one, that the Cynics were rationalists who had no patience with the supernatural or popular religion,[51] to one that describes them as conscious of a union with

---

[48]Cf. Pseudo-Socrates *Epistles* 9.4; 14.5–6; 22.1.
[49]Cf. Pseudo-Socrates *Epistles* 12; 27.5. For the seriousness with which the various types of literature are viewed, see *Epistles* 15.2–3; 18.2; 22.2. The literary catalogues are rejected, *memorabilia* are acceptable, but letters are preferred.
[50]See Swift Reginos, *Platonica,* 111–17, 148–49, for Diogenes, and 98-100 for Antisthenes.
[51]Represented by Gomperz, *Greek Thinkers,* 2.164; S. Dill, *Roman Society from Nero to Marcus Aurelius,* 2d ed. (London: Macmillan, 1905); W. Capelle, *Epiktet, Teles und Musonius: Wege zu glückseligem Leben,* Bibliothek der alten Welt (Zurich: Artemis, 1948), 15, 212-13.

God which empowered them.[52] A mediating view is that two strains can be identified, a positive one accompanied by a moderate view of mankind, and a skeptical one associated with rigorism.[53] The latter view, while it may find support in Oenomaus, runs aground on the fact that Demonax, known for his mildness, was decidedly cool toward religion,[54] and that Peregrinus, the major example of Cynic "mysticism," was known for his harshness.[55] Nevertheless, the Cynic epistles that reflect Cynicism of the austere type do tend toward a skeptical view,[56] and the Socratic epistles, while they do not make much of religion, do evidence a more positive attitude toward it. Thus, in the latter, Socrates offers a cock to Asclepius (*Epistle* 14.9), Xenophon builds a temple (*Epistle* 19), Socrates models himself upon God (*Epistle* 6.4)[57] and is divinely commissioned (*Epistle* 1.2,7). Still, religion is not at the center of the discussion and, as we have noted, where it does appear to justify Cynic behavior, it does so in a polemical context and is appealed to with the recognition that it may carry no weight with other Cynics.[58]

Conclusion

The considerable diversity of second-century Cynicism is still evident in the third, although the author of the Socratic epistles does attempt to play it down. Diogenes Laertius, who may have been more interested in biography than doxography, nevertheless notes that some Cynics still preferred the austere regimen of Diogenes.[59]

The evidence from Julian in the century that followed is more difficult to assess. His own austerity, susceptibility to religious mysticism, constant seeking for divine guidance, and the polemical nature of his addresses on the Cynics color his views to an inordinate degree.[60] Some facts, however, do emerge. The Cynics he opposes scorned religion, and Julian uses the

---

[52]Represented by J. Bernays, *Lucian und die Kyniker* (Berlin: Wilhelm Hertz, 1879); H. Rahn, "Die Frömmigkeit der Kyniker," *Paideuma* 7 (196): 280–92, who is dependent on Julian and Themistius.

[53]Gerhard, *Phoinix von Kolophon,* 79–83, 165–76, and idem, "Zur Legende," (n. 14 above), 394.

[54]See Lucian *Demonax* 11, 23, 27, 34, 37, and cf. Dudley, *A History of Cynicism,* 138.

[55]For his harshness, see Lucian *Demonax* 21; *Peregrinus* 17, 18, 19.

[56]See Malherbe, "Pseudo-Heraclitus *Epistle* 4," 45–51 (n. 10 above) which does not, however, do justice to the evidence of the Socratic epistles.

[57]Note also pseudo-Socrates *Epistle* 34.3, and for the modesty with which the assertion is made, cf. Julian *Oration* 7.235CD.

[58]For a similar apologetic use of the Pythia, see Julian *Oration* 7.211D–212A, and cf., H. Niehues-Pröbsting, *Der Kynismus des Diogenes und der Begriff des Zynismus* (Munich: W. Fink, 1979), 77–81.

[59]Diogenes Laertius *Lives of Eminent Philosophers* 6.104. Cf. Mejer, *Diogenes Laertius,* 3–4, 6.

[60]On his personality, see G. W. Bowersock, *Julian the Apostate* (Cambridge, Mass.: Harvard Univ. Press, 1978), 13–20, and on his attacks on the pseudo-Cynics, W. J. Malley, *Hellenism and Christianity* (Rome: Università Gregoriana Editrice, 1978), 144–55.

occasion to excoriate Oenomaus and present an interpretation of Diogenes as divinely guided, which may reflect his own predilections, but which is also part of the tradition.[61] Julian's own preference is evident when he complains that the Cynics ridiculed Diogenes for his austerity,[62] but demands that they exercise their *parrēsia* with charm and grace.[63] Julian could not tolerate Cynic criticism of his administration, which he viewed as subversion of the institutions of society.[64] Nonetheless, his tirade against Heracleius reveals that Cynics did attempt to present themselves at his court, and that they therefore were not anti-social in the manner of "Heraclitus" or "Diogenes."[65] Through Julian's invective glimpses are caught of rationalistic Cynics of the milder sort.

The fifth century knew Sallustius the Cynic, a man with whom Julian might have been better pleased. He was austere in his way of life, and, although not much is known of his religious outlook, he evidently shared Peregrinus's mysticism and practised divination.[66] In sum, Cynicism, which was essentially a way of life requiring no adherence to a canonical system of doctrine, continued to adapt itself to different viewpoints, and consequently retained the diversity which characterized it from early in its history.

---

[61]Julian *Orations* 6.199A; 7.209ABC, 210D–211B. (See notes 62 and 65 below for the divine commission.)
[62]Julian *Oration* 6.181A, 202D.
[63]Julian *Oration* 6.201BC. The characteristics of his models, Diogenes and Crates, differ from those of the letters attributed to them, and have much in common with Lucian's description of Demonax.
[64]Julian *Oration* 7.210C.
[65]Julian *Oration* 7.224C–226D.
[66]On Sallustius, see K. Praechter, "Salustios," PW 2d series, 1B (1920): 1967–70.

2

Mē Genoito
in the Diatribe
and Paul

Rudolf Bultmann's dissertation is still the best general description of diatribal style and remains the authority on the subject for most New Testament scholars.[1] Bultmann draws attention to the dialogical element in the diatribe in which a speaker or writer makes use of an imaginary interlocutor to ask questions of or raise objections to the arguments or affirmations that are made.[2] These responses are frequently stupid and are then summarily rejected by the speaker or writer in a number of ways, for example, by *oudamōs* ("by no means"),[3] *ou pantōs* ("not at all"),[4] *ou ma Dia* ("indeed not"),[5] or *minime* ("by no means").[6] The limited purpose of this study is to examine the way in which *mē genoito* ("by no means") is used to reject a response.

The impression gained from Bultmann is that *mē genoito* is widely used in the diatribal literature, usually thought to be represented in Greek by the *Discourses* of Epictetus, certain *Moralia* of Plutarch, various works of Philo, and by Bion, Teles, Musonius, Dio Chrysostom, Lucian, and Maximus of Tyre.[7] In fact, however, this particular rejection, as it appears as a response in a

---

[1]R. Bultmann, *Der Stil der paulinischen Predigt und die kynisch-stoische Diatribe,* FRLANT 13 (Göttingen: Vandenhoeck & Ruprecht, 1910).
[2]For a more extensive treatment, see S. K. Stowers, *The Diatribe and Paul's Letter to the Romans,* SBLDS 57 (Chico, Calif.: Scholars Press, 1981). See also now T. Schmeller, *Paulus und die "Diatribe": eine vergleichende Stilinterpretation,* NA N. F. 19 (Münster: Aschendorff, 1987).
[3]Dio Chrysostom *Discourses* 23.6; 26.6; Epictetus *Discourses* 1.6.13; 11.17,22. This study is based on Schenkl's text; the translations are indebted to W. A. Oldfather, *Epictetus: The Discourses as Reported by Arrian,* LCL (Cambridge, Mass.: Harvard University Press, 1925). All references are to the *Discourses.*
[4]Epictetus *Discourse* 4.8.2.
[5]Dio Chrysostom *Discourse* 14.14; Maximus of Tyre *Discourse* 6.1d (65,9 Hobein).
[6]Seneca *Epistles* 36.4; 60.3.
[7]*Der Stil der paulinischen Predigt,* 12 n. 1, 33 n. 4. See Stowers (*The Diatribe,* 48–75) for a discussion of the sources for the diatribe.

dialogue without being part of a larger sentence, is unique to Epictetus and Paul.[8]

Bultmann's interpretation of the diatribe is heavily dependent on Epictetus despite the latter's peculiar development of the style, and Bultmann makes his generalization about the use of *mē genoito* in the diatribe on the basis of Epictetus.[9] Bultmann is, furthermore, not as clear on the form of the rejection as one might wish.[10] There may therefore be merit in subjecting the way in which *mē genoito* is used by Epictetus and Paul to closer examination, especially since Bultmann draws conclusions about Paul's manner of argumentation from Paul's rejection of his interlocutor's objections. Attention will be given to the context in which the rejection is used, with special interest in the position of *mē genoito* in the argument, the introduction of the interlocutor's objection, the objection itself, the statement that follows *mē genoito,* and the latter's relation to the succeeding argument.

Mē Genoito in Context

As to its position, *mē genoito* in Epictetus frequently stands at the beginning of a new section of an argument (e.g., 1.10.7; 29.9), but much more frequently than it does in Paul it appears at the end of either a section of an argument or an entire diatribe to strengthen the argument or a particular affirmation (e.g., 1.1.13; 2.35; 5.10; 8.15; 3.1.44). In Paul it generally begins a new stage in an argument (Rom. 3:4, 6; 6:2, 15; 7:7, 13; 11:1, 11; 1 Cor. 6:15), although it does appear once (Rom. 3:31) at the end to strengthen an affirmation. For Paul it has primarily become a device by which he emphatically denies false inferences that could be (or were?) drawn from his theology, the correction of which he then proceeds to set forth.

The Introduction to the Objection

In a general description of the interlocutor in the pagan diatribe, Bultmann states that the words of the imaginary opponent as a rule are introduced by such short formulas as *phēsi* ("he says") and *all' erousin* ("but they will say"),

---

[8]In Epictetus, it is used in this manner in 1.1.13; 2.35; 5.10; 8.15; 9.32; 10.7; 11.23; 12.10; 19.7; 26.6; 28.19,24; 29.9; 2.8.2,26; 23.23; 3.1.42,44; 7.4; 23.13,25; 4.7.26; 8.26; 11.33,36. In Paul it appears in Rom. 3:4, 6, 31; 6:2, 15; 7:7, 13; 9:14; 11:1, 11; 1 Cor. 6:15; Gal. 2:17; 3:21. Galatians 6:14 and Luke 20:16 are not diatribal and will be left out of consideration. It does not appear in the representatives of the diatribe listed above.

[9]W. Capelle (*Epiktet, Teles und Musonius: Wege zu glückseligem Leben,* Bibliothek der alten Welt [Zurich: Artemis, 1948], 67–68) and Stowers (*The Diatribe,* 26–30, 53–58) discuss Epictetus's peculiar form of the diatribe.

[10]See Bultmann, *Der Stil der paulinischen Predigt,* 11 on the pagan diatribe, 66–68 on Paul.

although in lively discourse there may be no introduction at all.[11] He points out that Paul also introduces objections with such statements as *all' erei tis* ("but someone will say," 1 Cor. 15:35), *ereis oun* ("you will then say," Rom. 9:19; 11:19), and the characteristic *phēsi* (2 Cor. 10:10), which show that Paul knew the diatribal mode of expression.[12] Mostly, however, the objection is interjected as a question without any introductory formula. Bultmann goes on to claim that Paul did not completely take over the dialogical mode. The fiction of the interlocutor does not have for Paul the same force it had for the Greeks, and he therefore frequently does not formulate the objection in the direct words of the opponent, but in his own words, albeit in the sense of the opponent. For that the renderings *ti oun eroumen* ("What then shall we say?") and *alla erō* ("but I shall say") are characteristic, a fact which shows that Paul utilizes the diatribe to develop and present his thought in the form of statement and counterstatement.

Bultmann's definition of the quotation formulas as introductory formulas is too narrow and does not allow for a more comprehensive comparison. The characteristic, short questions which mark transitions in the argument and draw attention to what has been said function as introductions to the objections raised by the interlocutor, and should be included in a comparison of Epictetus and Paul.[13]

In Epictetus the false inferences rejected by *mē genoito* are mostly introduced by the interjection *ti oun* ("What then?"; e.g., 1.2.35; 8.14; 12.10; 2.23.23; 3.1.44) and the independent questions *epei ti dokeis* ("Otherwise, what do you think?"; 1.26.6); *ti dokeite* ("What do you think?"; 2.8.26; 4.8.26); and *ti autō legei* ("What does he say to him?"; 3.1.42). Very frequently there is no introduction to the false inference (e.g., 1.5.10; 11.23), on other occasions *oun* ("therefore," e.g., 1.9.32; 19.7; 2.8.2) and *ti eroumen* ("What shall we say?" 3.7.2) are part of the sentences containing the objections.

Like Epictetus, Paul uses *ti oun,* but does so only once (Rom. 6:15). *Ti eroumen* (Rom. 3:5) and *ti oun eroumen* ("What then shall we say?"; Rom. 6:1; 7:7; 9:14) are not part of the objections themselves, while *oun* (Rom. 3:31; 7:13; 1 Cor. 6:15; Gal. 3:21), *legō oun* ("Am I saying, then," Rom 11:1, 11) and *ara* ("then," Gal. 2:17) are part of the objections. *Ti gar* ("What then?") is used once (Rom. 3:3).

Bultmann's statements should thus be modified, at least with respect to the places where the objections call forth *mē genoito.* There Epictetus does not introduce the interlocutor's words with a quotation formula but, like Paul,

---

[11]Ibid., 10.
[12]Ibid. 12. *Phēsi* in 2 Cor. 10:10 is not diatribal; it introduces an assessment of Paul by real opponents.
[13]See *Der Stil der paulinischen Predigt,* 13–14, on transitions.

uses other formulas which set up the objections. It is not obvious that in these cases the interlocutor in Epictetus has more force than it does in Paul and, as his use of *ti eroumen* (3.7.2) indicates, he too can formulate the objection in his own words. Paul is very much like Epictetus, with the exception that he always has an introduction to the false conclusions. His introductions always contain causal particles or have causal force, thus connecting the false inference to what precedes. The impression thus gained, that Paul more securely fits the false inference into his argument, is only partly offset by the fact that when there are no introductions in Epictetus, the dialogical element is more pronounced than it is in Paul, and that it is designed to move the argument forward, whether it in fact succeeds in doing so or not.

The Objection

Bultmann points out that in the pagan diatribe the objection is frequently simply a rhetorical form the speaker uses to give greater clarity and emphasis to his thought.[14] On such occasions the objection may not be worth discussing but may be the absurd consequence the hearer draws from the speaker's words. In such cases the objection is introduced by *ti oun;* and slapped down by *mē genoito*. According to Bultmann, it is this diatribal use of the objection that is found in Paul.[15] The objections do not represent possible alternative views for Paul, but are absurdities. Sometimes objections expressing real opposing viewpoints do appear (e.g., Rom. 11:19; 1 Cor. 10:19?; 15:35), but almost always the imaginary opponent draws false inferences from Paul's viewpoint and, as in the diatribe, his objection is then forcefully rejected with *mē genoito*.

With respect to those objections which are followed by *mē genoito*, Bultmann is in general correct. However, while it is true that Paul in only two (Rom. 3:3; Gal. 3:21) of the thirteen passages under review formulates the objection in the words of the opponent, the difference from Epictetus should not be overstated. The majority of the objections in Epictetus do, formally at least, represent the opponent's view, but, in addition to 3.7.2, he elsewhere presents the objection in the first person, e.g., 1.10.7, *ti oun; egō legō, hoti aprakton esti to zōon; mē genoito* ("What then? Am I saying that he is an idle being? By no means!"; cf. 1.5.10). Furthermore, the objections in Epictetus and Paul are always in the form of rhetorical questions, which already points to their absurdity in both writers.

---

[14]Ibid., 10–11.
[15]Ibid., 67–68.

Statements Following *Mē Genoito*

Bultmann demonstrates that in the pagan diatribe the rejection of the objection could take place in different ways.[16] Frequently the retort is in the form of a counter-question. A calmer exposition could also follow, as it does especially in Seneca, Dio Chrysostom and Plutarch, but frequently the lively tone continues and the opponent is overwhelmed by a series of questions or exclamations. The opponent may also ask further questions, so that a regular dialogue ensues. Bultmann notes that Paul seldom answers objections with counter-questions (Rom. 9:19a-24), and that only Rom. 3:1-4, and 4:2 show the beginning of a dialogue.[17] Usually Paul slaps down the objection with *mē genoito* and then shows the objector his error either in a coherent statement and establishes his own viewpoint (Rom. 6:1; 7:7, 13; 9:14; 1 Cor. 15:35), or with a series of rhetorical questions or other rhetorical devices (Rom. 9:19-21; 1 Cor. 10:19.; 2 Cor. 12:16-18).

The short suppression of the opposing viewpoint clearly shows for Bultmann what is characteristic of Paul's way of thinking. In the diatribe false consequences are also rejected with *mē genoito,* but its predominance in Paul shows that here one has to do with something different. Paul reaches his propositions not by intellectual means but through experience and intuition. Thus in defending them he is not so much concerned to confirm them by intellectual considerations as he is to express the paradox of his propositions sharply and to guard against false ethical deductions. Nevertheless, he does use the form of the diatribe, and it is significant that most of the examples come from Romans, and that all appear in didactic contexts. Bultmann sees, then, on the one hand, far-reaching formal agreements which to a considerable degree also include an agreement in movement of thought, and on the other hand, a distinction between the thought of Paul and the Greek preacher.

Introductions

Insufficient attention has been given to Bultmann's observations that a coherent statement follows *mē genoito* in Paul, and more can be said about the form in which such statements occur. In all the places in Paul the rejection is supported by what immediately follows *mē genoito.* These supporting statements are affirmations introduced by *alla* ("but"; Rom. 3:31; 7:7, 13; 11:11) and *gar* ("for"; Rom. 9:15; 11:1-3; Gal. 2:18; 3:21), and by constructions characteristic of the diatribe: an imperative introduced by *de* ("but," omitted

---

[16]Ibid., 11.
[17]Ibid., 67–68.

by RSV; Rom. 3:4), rhetorical questions introduced by *pōs* ("how"; Rom. 3:6-7; 6:2-3), and *ouk oidate* ("do you not know?"; Rom. 6:16; 1 Cor. 6:16).[18] The supporting statements themselves contain quotations from or allusions to Scripture (Rom. 3:4; 7:7; 9:15; 11:11; 1 Cor. 6:16),[19] self-evident answers (Rom. 3:6; 6:2, 16; Gal. 2:18; 3:21) or contrary assertions (Rom. 3:31; 7:13). On one occasion Paul refers to his own case in substantiation of his rejection, but then goes on to quote Scripture (Rom. 11:1-2).

Theme

With the exception of Romans 3:31, which ends a section of an argument, and perhaps Galatians 2:18, it is characteristic of Paul that the support of *mē genoito* thus introduced provides the theme of the discussion that follows. This can be demonstrated by simply noting the important terms and/or their cognates in the succeeding sentences: Romans 3:4, *dikaioō* ("justify"), and *adikia* ("unrighteousness") and *dikaiosynē* ("righteousness") in v. 5; Rom. 3:6, *krinō* ("judge"), and *krinomai* ("am judged") (v. 7) and *krima* ("judgment") (v. 8); Romans 6:2, *apothnēskō* ("die"), and *thanatos* ("death") and *apothnēskō* in vv. 3, 4, 5, 7, 8, 10; Romans 6:16, *douloi* ("slaves") and *hypakoē* ("obedience"), and in vv. 17, 18, 19, 20, 22; Rom. 7:7, *dia nomou* ("through the law"), and *dia entolēs* ("through the commandment") in vv. 8 and 11; Romans 7:13, *katergazomai* ("work"), and in vv. 15, 17, 18, 20; Romans 9:15, *eleeō* ("have mercy"), and in vv. 16 and 18; Romans 11:1, *mē apōsato* ("did not reject") and *ouk apōsato* ("did not reject") in v. 2 and the corresponding *hypeleiphthēn* ("am left") in v. 3, *katelipon* ("have left," RSV: "have kept") in v. 4, and *leimma* ("remnant") in v. 5; Romans 11:11, *parazēlōsai* ("make jealous"), also in v. 14; 1 Corinthians 6:16, *ho kollōmenos* ("he who joins"), also in in v. 17; Galatians 3:22, *sygkleiō* ("consign"), also in v. 23 (RSV: "kept under restraint"). The suppression of the opposing viewpoint is thus not quite as short or abrupt as one might be led to believe by Bultmann, and we should do well to stress his observation that a coherent statement follows *mē genoito* in Paul.

Bultmann's brief description of the diatribal use of *mē genoito* leaves the impression that the exclamation marks the end of the matter under discussion.[20] A closer examination of Epictetus will clarify the matter and

---

[18]For imperatives, see *Der Stil der paulinischen Predigt*, 32–33; for *pōs*, Epictetus *Discourses* 3.22.77; 24.58; Dio Chrysostom *Discourse* 55.3; for *ouk oidate*, see *Der Stil der paulinischen Predigt*, 13.

[19]The 26th edition of Nestle-Aland, *Novum Testamentum Graece*, does not mark *parazēlōsai* in Rom. 11:11 as an allusion to Deut. 32:21 as previous editions did, but the quotation of the OT passage in Rom. 10:19 would argue that it should be so understood.

[20]*Der Stil der paulinischen Predigt*, 11 n. 4, 33.

enable us to judge the correctness of the distinction Bultmann draws between Paul and "the Greek preacher."

Unlike Paul, Epictetus does not always provide some substantiation for his rejection of the objection raised. This is especially the case when the form of the dialogue is strictly adhered to (e.g., 1.1.13; 26.6; 2.8.2; 23.23). But when Epictetus does support his rejections he is quite like Paul. The supporting statements are affirmations introduced by *alla* ("but": 1.28.24; 3.1.42, 44; 4.8.26–27) and *gar* ("for": 1.8.15; 12.10; cf. 4.8.26) but are also questions similarly introduced (*alla:* 1.10.7; *gar:* 2.8.26). He also uses the challenging questions and imperatives characteristic of the diatribe (1.29.9–10).[21] Epictetus is further similar to Paul in that his supporting statements may contain quotations of texts thought to have probative value (e.g., Homer *Iliad* 1.526 in 2.8.26) or be answers that are self-evidently true (e.g., 1.29.9) or be straightforward contrary assertions (e.g., 1.9.32). He also refers to himself to support his argument (1.2.36), and on one occasion, having done so, goes on to quote Plato *Apology* 17C as further confirmation (3.23.25).

Epictetus's support of his rejection may also provide the theme of the discussion that follows, but in this he is not nearly as consistent as Paul. One example of each type of supporting statement will illustrate his procedure in this regard.

In one instance, 2.8.26–27, Epictetus quotes *Iliad* 1.526 to substantiate his rejection. In the discussion that precedes, the question considered is whether the philosopher should affect a proud look *(ophrys)*. The objection is then raised:

"What do you think? *(ti dokeite;)* A proud look?" "By no means *(mē genoito)*! For *(gar)* the Zeus at Olympia does not affect a proud look, does he? On the contrary *(alla)*, his look is steady, as befits one who is about to say,
  No word of mine can be revoked or prove untrue *(Iliad* 1.526)."
"I will show you that I am of such character-faithful, reverent, noble, unperturbed."

Zeus provides the model for Epictetus, and to that extent the quotation determines the theme for what follows, the godlike demeanor of the philosopher.

Epictetus also advances what is self-evident to him to support his rejection of an objection. In 1.29.1–8, in discussing the Stoic's steadfastness, he claims that the Stoic should have no fear in the face of threat. Then, in 9–11 he records an objection:

"Do you philosophers, then *(oun)*, teach us to despise kings?"
"By no means *(mē genoito)*! Which one of us teaches you to dispute their claim

---

[21]M. Billerbeck, *Epiktet: Vom Kynismus,* Philosophia Antiqua 34 (Leiden: E. J. Brill, 1978), 94.

(antipoieisthai) to the things over which they have authority *(exousian)*? Take my
paltry body, take my property, take my reputation, take those who are with me.
If I persuade any to lay claim *(antipoieisthai)* to these things, let some man truly
accuse me."
"Yes, but I wish to control your judgments also."
"And who has given you this authority *(exousian)*?"

The rhetorical question following the rejection denies that Stoics dispute the
claim of kings to those things over which they have authority. Laying claim
(antipoieisthai) and authority *(exousia)* constitute the theme of what follows.
The sentence consisting of imperatives and the one following are self-evident
to the Stoic and are Epictetus's support for his denial.

   In 1.2 Epictetus refers to his own case to strengthen his rejection of an
objection. The subject of the diatribe is the question how the philosopher
may preserve his own character. Toward the end of the diatribe reference is
made to the greatness of Socrates.[22] But, it is pointed out, not all men share
his gifts. In 35–36 an objection is introduced and then rejected:

"What then? *(ti oun;)* Since *(epeidē)* I am without natural talent,
shall I for that reason stop being diligent?"
"By no means *(Mē genoito!)* Epictetus will not be superior to Socrates;
but if only I am not worse, that is enough for me."

In the few lines that continue to the end of the diatribe the theme of realizing
one's potential is continued.

Conclusion

Some conclusions can now be drawn. Paul's use of *mē genoito* does not have
a counterpart in the pagan diatribe in general but does in Epictetus. It may
therefore be the case that this way of rejecting an objection or false inference
is more characteristic of the type of schoolroom instruction in which Epictetus
engaged than street corner preaching.[23] Furthermore, this exclamation is part
of a larger form which is found frequently in Epictetus and always in Paul.
It would therefore appear that Paul had taken one way in which *mē genoito*
was put to use and used it exclusively in his argumentation.

   The larger form of which it is part does not mark the termination of an
argument, but rather a transition. It performs this function more consistently

---

[22]See K. Döring, *Exemplum Socratis: Studien zur Sokratesnachwirkung in der kynisch-stoischen
Popularphilosophie der frühen Kaiserzeit und im frühen Christentum,* Hermes Einzelschriften
42 (Wiesbaden: Franz Steiner, 1979), 43–79, for Epictetus's use of Socrates as a model, and in
the present connection, cf. 3.23, 25–26.
[23]Stowers, *The Diatribe,* 175–84, argues for the schoolroom as the social setting of Epictetus's
and other moral philosophers' diatribes.

in Paul than Epictetus. With one exception it always appears in Paul at the beginning of an argument, in Epictetus it does so only sometimes. Paul always makes clear grammatically that the objection is a false inference of what he has said, Epictetus does so only on occasion. Paul and Epictetus both state the objection as a rhetorical question to show it to be absurd. Paul always provides a reason for his rejection of the false conclusion, Epictetus does so only sometimes. With one exception, the reason Paul advances introduces the theme for the argument that immediately follows, in Epictetus it does so only occasionally.

The formal and functional agreements between Paul and Epictetus are thus more far-reaching than Bultmann demonstrated. Indeed, one may question, at least so far as the places where *mē genoito* is used, whether the distinction Bultmann maintains between "the Greek preacher" and Paul is valid. It would not appear that in those places Paul felt less need to confirm his propositions intellectually than Epictetus did or that he was more indebted to experience and intuition than the teacher of Nicopolis.

3

"Gentle as a Nurse":
The Cynic Background
to 1 Thessalonians 2

Paul's description of his Thessalonian ministry in 1 Thessalonians 2 has in recent years been variously interpreted. The discussion has revolved in part around the question whether vv. 1-12 are to be understood as an apology directed to a concrete situation in Thessalonica in the face of which Paul had to defend himself, or whether the language that seems to support such a view can be understood in another way.

A major statement of the latter option was made by Ernst von Dobschütz, who claimed that the "apology" reflects the mood of Paul at the time of writing rather than a strained relationship with the Thessalonians.[1] Martin Dibelius represented a somewhat similar view, but saw this as a favorite theme of Paul that he could have introduced without his having been forced to do so by circumstances in Thessalonica. Dibelius pointed out that it was necessary for Paul to distinguish himself from other preachers of his day without actually having been accused of being a charlatan. To illustrate his point he brought into the discussion descriptions of wandering Cynics.[2] More recently, Günther Bornkamm has lent his support to Dibelius.[3] Albert-Marie Denis does not specifically address himself to the problem, yet sees the main thrust of vv. 1-6 to be Paul's presentation of himself as the messianic prophet to the Gentiles.[4]

The most exhaustive recent treatment is that of Walter Schmithals, who argues forcefully that Paul is defending himself against specific charges that

---

[1]E. von Dobschütz, *Die Thessalonicherbriefe,* KEK 10 (Göttingen: Vandenhoeck & Ruprecht, 1909), 106–7.
[2]M. Dibelius, *An die Thessalonicher I.II. An die Philipper,* HNT 11, 3d ed. (Tübingen: J. C. B. Mohr [Paul Siebeck], 1937), 7–11.
[3]G. Bornkamm, "Faith and Reason in Paul," in *Early Christian Experience,* trans. P. L. Hammer (New York: Harper & Row, 1969), 45 n. 22.
[4]A.-M. Denis, "L'Apôtre Paul, 'prophète messianique' des Gentiles: Étude thématique de 1 Thess., II, 1-6," *ETL* 33 (1957): 245–318.

had been made against him.[5] Schmithals emphasizes that Paul's language in 1 Thessalonians 2 is in many respects similar to that of his Corinthian correspondence, and Schmithals claims that the same kind of Jewish Christian Gnostics are responsible for Paul's apologies in both groups of letters. He admits that there are parallels in 1 Thessalonians 2 to the descriptions of the Cynics cited by Dibelius, and accepts the necessity of genuine preachers having to distinguish themselves from the charlatans. However, he points out that there are no close verbal parallels to Paul in the material cited by Dibelius. More important to him, though, is that the form of Paul's description of his work in Thessalonica is of such a nature that it demands being viewed as an apology.[6] Schmithals is not explicit at this point, but what seems to make him think that Paul protests too much is Paul's antithetic statements which could be understood as denials of accusations:

> For you yourselves know, brethren, that our visit to you was *not* in vain *(kenē)*; *but* though we had already suffered and been shamefully treated *(hybristhentes)* at Philippi, as you know, we had courage in our God *(eparrēsiasametha)* to declare to you the gospel of God in the face of great opposition *(en pollō agōni)*. For our appeal does not spring from error *(ek planēs)* or uncleanness *(ex akatharsias)*, *nor* is it made with guile *(en dolō); but* just as we have been approved by God to be entrusted with the gospel, so we speak, *not* to please men, *but* to please God who tests our hearts. For we *never* used words of flattery *(kolakeias),* as you know, *or* a cloak for greed, as God is witness, *nor* did we seek glory *(doxan)* from men, *neither* from you *nor* from others, though we might have made demands *(dynamenoi en barei)* as apostles of Christ. *But* we were gentle *(ēpioi)* among you, like a nurse taking care of her own *(heautēs)* children. So, being affectionately desirous of you, we were ready to share with you *not only* the gospel of God but also our own selves, because you had become very dear to us (1 Thess. 2:1-8).[7]

This study seeks to contribute to the discussion by examining in greater depth the Cynic background posited by Dibelius. Attention will be directed to the diversity that existed among wandering preachers and among the Cynics themselves, and to the self-descriptions of serious-minded Cynic philosophers in this context.

---

[5]W. Schmithals, "The Historical Situation of the Thessalonian Epistles," in *Paul and the Gnostics,* trans. J. E. Steely (Nashville: Abingdon Press, 1972), 123–218. See now, R. Jewett, *The Thessalonian Correspondence: Pauline Rhetoric and Millenarian Piety* (Philadelphia: Fortress Press, 1986).

[6]von Dobschütz, *Die Thessalonicherbriefe,* 111.

[7]Cf. also W. Marxsen, "Auslegung von 1 Thess. 4, 13-18," *ZTK* 66 (1969): 24, who in this preliminary statement on the problem holds that one can speak of an apology in 1 Thess. 2:1-12, but of the Gospel, not of the apostle. He does, however, leave the matter open, and does not accept Schmithals's hypothesis. See now, at greater length, idem, *Der erste Brief an die Thessalonicher,* Zürcher Bibelkommentare 11.1 (Zurich: Theologischer Verlag, 1979), 22–25, 43–46.

Types of Philosophers

Given the situation described by such writers as Lucian of Samosata,[8] it is to be expected that the transient public speakers were viewed with suspicion.[9] It is understandable that the genuine philosophic missionary would want to distinguish himself from other types without his having explicitly been accused of acting like a particular type. A good illustration of how a wandering philosophic teacher of the better type described himself and his work is provided by Dio Chrysostom, the orator-turned-philosopher (A.D. 40–c. 120). Although Dio is in some ways atypical of the Cynics, his descriptions of these preachers are some of the most systematic available to us, and serve to illuminate our problem. In the proemia to four of his discourses, namely the Olympic discourse (*Discourse* 12), the discourse to Alexandria (*Discourse* 32), the first discourse to Tarsus (*Discourse* 33), and the discourse to Celaenae *Discourse* 35), he speaks of his relationship to his audience in a manner of interest to us.

These speeches come from a period in Dio's life after he had lived in exile and taught as a wandering Cynic.[10] Dio had been invited to deliver these addresses, and there is no question of his having to defend himself here against specific charges that he was a charlatan.[11] Nevertheless, he is aware of the suspicion of the crowd,[12] and he sets out to make clear what kind of preacher he in fact is. In doing so he distinguishes himself on the one hand from the sophists and rhetoricians, and on the other hand from the so-called Cynics. In examining his description of the ideal philosopher we shall concentrate on *Discourse* 32 while adducing material from his other discourses as well as from other Cynic sources to fill out the picture.[13] Although passing reference is occasionally made to this discourse in discussions of 1 Thessalonians 2, it has never been examined in detail in this connection.

---

[8]Cf. R. Helm, "Lucian und die Philosophenschulen," *Neue Jahrbuch für das klassische Altertum* 9 (1902): 351–69. C. P. Jones, *Culture and Society in Lucian* (Cambridge, Mass.: Harvard Univ. Press, 1986), 24–32.

[9]Cf. L. Friedlaender, *Darstellungen aus der Sittengeschichte Roms, in der Zeit von August bis Ausgang der Antonine* 8th ed. (Leipzig: S. Hirzel, 1910), 4.301–308, for the reactions of different classes of people to philosophers.

[10]For a useful discussion of Dio's life and works, see W. Elliger, *Dion Chrysostomos: Sämtliche Reden,* Bibliothek der alten Welt (Zurich: Artemis, 1967), VII-XLIV. For a dating of *Discourse* 32 under Vespasian, see C. P. Jones, "The Date of Dio of Prusa's Alexandrian Oration," *Historia* 22 (1973): 302–9, and for the traditional view, see J. F. Kindstrand, "The Date of Dio of Prusa's Alexandrian Oration—A Reply," *Historia* 27 (1978): 378–83, and n. 13 below. L. Lemarchand (*Dion de Pruse. Les Oeuvres d'avant l'exil* [Paris: J. de Gigord, 1926], 86–110) presents an independent view.

[11]On these discourses, see H. von Arnim, *Leben und Werke des Dio von Prusa* (Berlin: Weidmann, 1898), 438–39, 460-76; Elliger, *Dion Chrysostomos,* XVI.

[12]Cf. *Discourses* 12.1, 8-9, 15; 13.11; 34.1-3; 35.2, 5, 6.

[13]W. Weber, in *Hermes* 50(1915): 78–79, dates *Discourse* 32 between A.D. 108 and 112.

Resident Philosophers

The first type of philosopher Dio describes (*Discourse* 32.8) are the resident philosophers who "do not appear in public at all, and prefer not to run the risk, possibly because they despair of being able to improve the masses." He seems to have in mind men like Seneca and Cornutus, who were either members of large private households which they served as philosophic chaplains, or who were to be found at court.[14] These men, according to Dio, wish to maintain their dignity, and are useless *(anōpheleis)*. They are like make-believe athletes who refuse to enter the stadium to enter the contest of life.[15] The description of a Cynic's battles with hardships, human passions and men who are enslaved to them as a struggle or contest *(agōn)* is well known.[16] Another type of resident philosopher is the one who "exercizes his voice in what we call lecture-halls, having secured as hearers men who are his allies and can easily be managed by him" (32.8).[17] Evidently he has in mind philosophers like Musonius, Epictetus, and Demonax.[18]

Wandering Charlatans

The next type Dio mentions are the so-called Cynics who were to be found in great numbers in the city.[19] These are the hucksters Lucian satirizes so mercilessly. Dio describes them as a bastard and ignoble race of men. They have no knowledge whatsoever, he says, but adds with tongue in cheek,

> they must make a living ... Posting themselves at street corners, in alley-ways, and at temple-gates, they pass around the hat and deceive *(apatōsin)* lads and sailors and crowds of that sort by stringing together their puns *(skōmmata)* and philosophical commonplaces *(spermologian syneirontes)* and ribald jokes of the market place.[20]

---

[14]For the type, see von Arnim, *Leben und Werke des Dio von Prusa,* 4.445–46; Friedlaender, *Darstellungen aus der Sittengeschichte des Roms,* 335–36, 338–39; A. D. Nock, *Conversion: The Old and the New in Religion From Alexander the Great to Augustine of Hippo* (Oxford: Clarendon Press, 1933), 178–79, 296; Samuel Dill, *Roman Society from Nero to Marcus Aurelius,* 2d ed. (London: Macmillan, 1905), 289-333; J. N. Sevenster, *Paul and Seneca,* NovTSup 4 (Leiden: E. J. Brill, 1961), 15–18.

[15]*Discourse* 32.20–24. On *ōpheleia* as motivation of the Cynics, see G. A. Gerhard, *Phoinix von Kolophon* (Leipzig/Berlin: B. G. Teubner, 1909), 33–34, 36, 39.

[16]Cf. V. C. Pfitzner, *Paul and the Agon Motif,* NovTSup 16 (Leiden: E. J. Brill, 1967), 16–37; A. J. Malherbe, "The Beasts at Ephesus," *JBL* 87 (1968): 74–78. (= 79–89 in this volume).

[17]Nigrinus called the lecture halls *ergastēria* (workshops) and *kapēleia* (taverns); cf. Lucian *Nigrinus* 25.

[18]For this type, see von Arnim, *Leben und Werke des Dio von Prusa,* 446; Friedlaender, *Darstellungen aus der Sittengeschichte Roms,* 339.

[19]For the great number of Cynics abroad, see *Discourse* 72.4; Lucian *The Double Indictment* 6; *The Runaways* 3-5; Philo *Concerning Noah's Work as a Planter* 151.

[20]For Cynics in the streets and marketplaces, see Dio *Discourse* 77/78.34-35; Julian *Oration* 7.224AB; Lucian *Peregrinus* 3; Origen *Against Celsus* 3.50. For *syneirein,* see Dio *Discourse* 33.5, for *skōptein, skōmma, Discourses* 9.7; 32.22, 30; 33.10. For *spermologia,* see Acts 17:18; Plutarch *How to Tell a Flatterer from a Friend* 65B; Philostratus *Lives of the Sophists* 1.524 (cf. Philo's description of the sophists as *hoi logothērai, Moses* 2.212). On pleasing the crowd, see Dio *Discourses* 32.7; 35.8; 66.26.

From other descriptions of this type it appears that they deceived *(planān, apatān)* people by flattery *(kolakeuein, thōpeuein)* rather than speaking with the boldness and frankness of the true philosopher.[21] The result, Dio says, is that they achieve no good at all, but accustom thoughtless people to deride philosophers in general.[22] Such derision was commonly expressed in the charges that the Cynics were out for their own glory *(doxa)*, sensual gratification *(hēdonē)* and money *(chrēmata)*, the very things against which serious Cynics pitted themselves in their *agōn*.[23]

Orator-Philosophers

Dio then turns to excoriate a type of Cynic that was difficult to distinguish from rhetoricians (32.10).[24] To their hearers they made epideictic speeches or chanted verses of their own composition. Epideictic speech is described by ancient handbooks as rhetoric intended not for the sake of contest *(agon)*, but of demonstration.[25] Sophists who delivered such speeches felt no real involvement in the occasion on which they were delivered. Consequently, since they lacked substance and did not result in anything positive, they were described as vain or empty *(vanus, vacuus, inanis,* or *kenos)*.[26] Dio accuses the orator-philosophers of preaching for their own gain and glory. They have no desire to benefit their listeners; in fact, they corrupt them. It is like a physician who, instead of curing his patients, entertains them.[27]

Harsh Cynics

Dio knows of yet another type of Cynic who demands more of our attention. This type does speak with *parrēsia*, that boldness of the philosopher who

---

[21]*Apatē* is the more common of the two terms among the Cynics, but they can also be used interchangeably; cf. Dio Chrysostom *Discourse* 4.33, 35. For *planē*, cf. also W. Cronert, *Kolotes und Menedemus* (Munich: Muller, 1906), 36; Euripides *Rhadamanthus* Fragment 660 (3.176,8 Nauck), and Hippocrates's description of certain philosophers as *exapatai*, cf. *De victu* 24.8 (6.496 Littre). On deceit and flattery, cf. Dio Chrysostom *Discourse* 48.10 and O. Ribbeck, *Kolax* (Leipzig: Hirzel, 1883).

[22]For the reproach they brought on philosophy, see Lucian *The Runaways* 21; or *The Fisherman* 34; Julian *Oration* 7.225AB. On achieving no good because of a softened message, see Dio Chrysostom *Discourse* 33.10, 15.

[23]On the joining of *philodoxos, philēdonos,* and *philochrēmatos*, see Gerhard, *Phoinix von Kolophon*, 58–62, 87–88.

[24]Among them were the *kitharōdoi Kynikoi* (kithara-playing Cynics), a breed Dio considered a peculiarly Alexandrian phenomenon (cf. *Discourse* 32.62, 68). On his assessment of the rhetoricians, see *Discourses* 2.18; 4.35–39; 12.10; 33.1–6,23; 35.1, 9–10. For this type, see Friedlaender, *Darstellungen aus der Sittengeschichte*, 4.345-46.

[25]*Rhetorica ad Alexandrum* 1440b13. Cf. George Kennedy, *The Art of Persuasion in Greece* (Princeton: Princeton University Press, 1963), 152–54, 167. For *agōn* as a philosophical argument, see Sextus Empiricus *Against the Professors* 7.324; 11.19; Plutarch, *Progress in Virtue* 80B.

[26]Cf. Quintilian *Institutio oratoria* 12.16, 17, 73; Plutarch *That Epicurus Actually Makes a Pleasant Life Impossible* 1090A; Dio Chrysostom *Discourse* 31.30; Seneca, *Epistle* 114.16.

[27]For the Cynic as a physician of sick souls, see also Dio Chrysostom *Discourses* 32.17; 33.6–8, 44. Cf. K. Holl, "Die schriftstellerische Form des griechischen Heiligenlebens," *Neue Jarhbucher für das klassische Altertum* 19 (1912): 418.

has found true personal freedom, and who on the basis of this freedom strives to lay bare the shortcomings of his audience as the first step in improving them (*Discourse* 32.11).[28] The fault with the type of men Dio has in mind is that they display their boldness sparingly,[29]

> not in such a way as to fill your ears with it, nor for any length of time. No, they merely utter a phrase or two, and then, after railing *(loidorēsantes)* at you rather than teaching you, they make a hurried exit, anxious lest before they have finished you may raise an outcry and send them packing.

This type of speaker thus confused *loidoria* ("reviling") with *parrēsia* ("bold speech"). In Imperial times reviling, berating Cynics were such a common sight that the legendary figure of Timon the misanthrope was remembered as a Cynic.[30] Whether or how a philosopher's outspokenness should be tempered became an important topic of discussion.[31]

The Cynic, the morally free man, conceived it his right and duty to speak with *parrēsia* and to act as an example.[32] He did so because of his *philanthrōpia* ("love of humanity"), his desire to do good to all people.[33] As humane a person as Dio was convinced that it was necessary for the serious philosopher to be harsh when the occasion demanded it.[34] Dio himself spoke with *parrēsia*, but adapted his message to his hearers' needs,[35] and remained with them. Dio contrasts the genuine philosopher with the low-class Cynic:

> But as for himself, the man of whom I speak will strive to preserve his individuality in seemly fashion and with steadfastness, never deserting his post of duty, but always honoring and promoting virtue and sobriety and trying to lead all men thereto, partly by persuading and exhorting *(peithōn kai parakalōn)*, partly by abusing and reproaching *(loidoroumenos kai oneidizōn)*, in the hope that he may thereby rescue somebody from folly and low desires and intemperance and

---

[28]On *parrēsia,* see H. Schlier, s.v. *TDNT* 5 (1967): 871-86; esp. E. Peterson, "Zur Bedeutungsgeschichte von *parrēsia,*" *Reinhold Seeberg Festschrift* (Leipzig: D. W. Scholl, 1929): 283–297; Giuseppe Scarpat, *Parrhesia: Storia del termine e delle tradizioni in latino* (Brescia: Paideia, 1964).

[29]Note that in *Discourse* 33.6–8 Dio also moves from the example of the physician to discuss a limitation in *parrēsia.* Cf. also Epictetus, *Discourse* 3.23.30–38, who regards protreptic as the proper style of the philosopher in his lecture room, the *iatreion* ("hospital room") rather than, for example, epideictic.

[30]See F. Bertram, "Die Timonlegende. Eine Entwicklungsgeschichte des Misanthropentypus in der antiken Literatur" (Diss., Ruprecht-Karls-Universitat zu Heidelberg, 1906), 33 n. 1,38, 40–43. For the harshness of the Cynics, see especially Gerhard, *Phoinix von Kolophon,* 64–72, 165–68, and idem, "Zur Legende vom Kyniker Diogenes," *ARW* 15 (1912): 388–408.

[31]E.g., Plutarch, *How to Tell a Flatterer from a Friend,* 65F-74E.

[32]Cf. J. Bernays, *Lucian und die Kyniker* (Berlin: W. Hertz, 1879), 101–2; Lucian *Demonax* 3; Philo *Who is the Heir* 14; *On the Special Laws* 1.321.

[33]See J. Kaerst, *Geschichte der hellenistischen Zeitalters* (Leipzig/Berlin: B. G. Teubner, 1909), 2.118–120. Cf. Maximus of Tyre *Discourse* 14 (174,15–16 Hobein), "for the most philanthropic physician causes the greatest pain." For a modification of this view, which now seems to me too idealistic, see p. 18 above, which seeks to do justice to Cynic individualism.

[34]Cf. *Discourses* 32.19–24, 27,33; 33.7, 11–14.

[35]Cf. Maximus of Tyre, *Discourse* 1 *That a Philosopher's Discourse Is Adapted to Every Subject.*

soft living, taking him aside privately individually and also admonishing *(nou-thetōn)* them in groups every time he finds opportunity, with gentle words at times, at others harsh.[36]

Even when his listeners scorn him, "he is not vexed; on the contrary, he is kinder to each one than even a father or brothers or friends."[37] His concern is especially shown in the individual attention he gives.

The charlatans were also sometimes harsh, but for different reasons. They made up for the lack of content in their speeches by railing at the crowd, in this way hoping to secure its admiration.[38] They made a profession of abusiveness, considering shamelessness to be freedom, the incurring of hatred outspokenness, and avarice benevolence.[39] Naturally, they caused the *hybris* ("outrage, violence") of the crowd before too long and departed before they were attacked.[40] Their frankness was a cover for their cowardice and benefited no one.

Of special interest is the harshness of some Cynics which resulted from a pessimistic view of mankind. While all serious philosophers were conscious of the shortcomings of the masses,[41] few were as uncharitable as these men were.[42] They saw no hope of improving people except by the most abusive scolding. It was especially these men who were accused of misanthropy. Melancholy Heraclitus provided a perfect figure to whom letters from Imperial times representing this view of mankind could be ascribed. In pseudo-Heraclitus *Epistle* 7, he is represented as defending himself against the charge of misanthropy, for which the residents of Ephesus want to banish him from the city.[43] In response, he denies that he hates people; it is only their evil that

---

[36]*Discourse* 77/78.38.
[37]Discourse 77/78.42.
[38]Lucian *Philosophies for Sale* 10–11; Epictetus *Discourses* 2.22.28–30; 3.22.50–51; 4.8.34.
[39]Cf. Aelius Aristides, *Oration 3: To Plato: In Defense of the Four* 663–81 (511,16–519,19 Behr), Eng. trans. in *P. Aelius Aristides: The Complete Works,* trans. C. A. Behr (Leiden: E. J. Brill, 1986), 1.273–77. On this much discussed passage, see Bernays, *Lucian und die Kyniker,* 38, 100; Fried-laender, *Darstellungen aus der Sittengeschichte,* 4.306–308; and esp., E. Norden, "Beiträge zur Geschichte der griechischen Philosophie," *Jahrbücher für classische Philologie,* Supplementband 19, 2 (1893): 404–10, and A. Boulanger, *Aelius Aristide et la Sophistique dans la province d'Asie au IIe siècle de notre ère* (reprint, Paris: E. de Boccard, 1968), 249–56. See also p. 134 n.57 below.
[40]For the threat of the mob, see Dio Chrysostom *Discourses* 32.20, 24, 29, 74; 34.6; *Gnomologium Vaticanum* 352; pseudo-Diogenes *Epistle* 45.
[41]Cf. Dio Chrysostom *Discourse* 32.20–25, 27–28; Epictetus *Discourses* 1.18.3, 7, 9–11; 28.10–11; Plutarch *On the Fortune or the Virtue of Alexander 333BC;* Julian *Oration* 6.188D, 196D, 197B.
[42]Their low view of mankind appears most clearly in some of the Cynic letters, e.g., pseudo-Heraclitus *Epistles* 2; 4; 5; pseudo-Diogenes *Epistles* 27; 28; pseudo-Hippocrates *Epistle* 17.28, 43. On these letters, see R. Helm, *Lucian und Menipp* (Leipzig/Berlin: B. G. Teubner, 1906), 90–91; P. Wendland, "Philo und die kynisch-stoische Diatribe," in P. Wendland & O. Kern, *Beiträge zur Geschichte der griechischen Philosophie und Religion* (Berlin: George Reimer, 1895), 38–45; Gerhard, *Phoinix von Kolophon,* 67–68, 165–67, 170–76. See also, *The Cynic Epistles: A Study Edition,* ed. A. J. Malherbe, SBLSBS 12 (Missoula, Mont.: Scholars Press, 1977).
[43]See J. Bernays, *Die heraklitischen Briefe* (Berlin: Wilhelm Hertz, 1869).

he hates. That is what had robbed him of the divine gift of laughter. Even within the city he is not really a part of them, for he refuses to share their wickedness. Would that he could laugh, but, surrounded by enemies, and with the flagrant vices of mankind on every hand, he wonders how anyone could laugh. He will retain his dour visage even if it should mean his exile.

Gentle Philosophers

As can be expected, a reaction set in against the Cynic stress on the harshness of preaching.[44] It was now emphasized that at least as early as Crates Cynics had been known for their understanding of human nature and even for their gentleness at times.[45] The stress on the gentleness of Musonius,[46] Dio,[47] and Demonax[48] should be seen against this background. What is of particular interest to us is the way in which the different kinds of preaching were described.

A widespread gnomic statement clarified the difference between admonition and reviling:

> There is the greatest difference between admonition *(to nouthetein)* and reproach *(to oneidizein)*. For the former is gentle *(ēpion)* and amicable *(philon)*, the latter hard *(sklēron)* and outrageous *(hybristikon)*; the former corrects *(diorthoi)* those who err, the latter merely reproves *(elegchei)* them.[49]

Without denying the need for harshness when the occasion demands it, the value of admonition *(nouthesia)* was now affirmed.[50] The word *ēpios* ("gentle") is widely used as a synonym for *philanthrōpos,* the quality that the philosopher must have before he can speak with *parrēsia,*[51] and is used in the descriptions of the philosopher's speech. Thus an ancient characterization of Epictetus

---

[44]Cf. Gerhard, *Phoinix von Kolophon,* 39–45.

[45]See Plutarch *Table Talk* 632E; Julian *Oration* 6.201B, Crates "used to reprove them not harshly but with a charming manner." Cf. E. Weber, *De Dione Chrysostomo Cynicorum sectatore,* Leipziger Studien 10 (Leipzig: Hirschfeld, 1887), 211; Gerhard, *Phoinix von Kolophon,* 170–71; R. Hoïstad, *Cynic Hero and Cynic King* (Uppsala: Gleerup, 1948), 127-28.

[46]Cf. Cora E. Lutz, *Musonius Rufus: "The Roman Socrates,"* Yale Classical Studies 10 (New Haven, Conn.: Yale University Press, 1947), 29.

[47]Cf. Philostratus *Lives of the Sophists* 1.487; E. Weber, *De Dione Chrysostomo,* 220–21.

[48]Cf. K. Funk, "Untersuchungen über die Lucianische Vita Demonactis," *Philologus,* Supp.10 (1905–1907), 595–96.

[49]E.g., *Gnomologium Byzantinum* 59 (176 Wachsmuth); cf. also nos. 258, 259.

[50]Cf. Diogenes Laertius *Lives of Eminent Philosophers* 6.86; Dio Chrysostom *Discourse* 32.26–27. For the contrast between *loidoria (parrēsia)* and *nouthesia* see Plutarch *How to Profit By One's Enemies* 89B; *On Superstition* 168C; Dio Chrysostom *Discourse* 77/78.38. Weber, *De Dione Chrysostomo,* 208.

[51]E.g., Philo *The Sacrifices of Abel and Cain* 27; Hecataeus, according to Josephus *Against Apion* 1.186. See C. Spicq, "La philanthropie hellénistique, vertu divine et royale (à propos de Tit. III, 4)," *Studia Theologica* 12 (1958): 169–91, and "Benignité, mansuetudé, douceur, clémence," *RB* 54 (1947): 332.

says that as to his countenance he was solemn, in his association he was gentle *(ēpios),* and in his manner mild *(hēmeros).*[52]

It is not surprising that in ancient times the subject of gentleness should call to mind the figure of the nurse crooning over her wards. In addition to their physical attributes, the main qualification of nurses was that they were not to be irascible.[53] That people remembered their nurses in this way is illustrated by the large number of tomb inscriptions that describe nurses affectionately as being kind.[54] It became customary to contrast the harshness of a certain kind of *parrēsia* with gentle speech like that of a nurse who knows her charges.

Maximus of Tyre illustrates one such use. In a discourse in which he argues that the philosopher's speech must be adapted to every subject, he reveals a sympathetic view of man: The mass of men, the common herd, are naturally mild, but are difficult to persuade only because they have been fed with depraved nutriment. What they require is a musical shepherd who does not punish their disobedience with whip and spur.[55] Elsewhere, he elaborates on the contrasts he has in mind here. What is naturally adapted to mankind is "a certain musical and milder philosophy which might popularly allure and manage it, in the same manner as nurses charm through fabulous narrations the children committed to their care."[56] Maximus then states that he much prefers this treatment of the masses to the *parrēsia* of the philosophers. The word philosopher, he says, is hard or oppressive *(barys)* to the multitude. The philosophers would do well to follow the example of the ancient philosophers who clothed their philosophy in fables, just as physicians mix bitter medicines with sweet nutriment.[57]

Pseudo-Diogenes represents a completely different view of human nature and therefore of the way in which a philosopher should approach people.

---

[52]Moschion 3 (485 Schenkl).

[53]E.g., Soranus *Peri Gynaikeiōn* 32 (263–64 Rose); Oribasius (122, 3 Bussemaker-Daremberg); Favorinus according to Aulus Gellius *Attic Nights* 12.1.21; pseudo-Pythagoras *Epistle* 12. On the subject, see W. Braams, "Zur Geschichte des Ammenswesens im klassischen Altertum," *Jenaer medizin-historischer Beitrage* 5 (1913): 8. W. Schick, *Favorin Peri Paidōn Trophēs und die antike Erziehungslehre* (Leipzig: B. G. Teubner, 1912); E. Eichgrun, "Kallimachos und Apollonios Rhodios" (Diss., Berlin, 1961) 185–93.

[54]Cf. G. Herzog-Hauser, "Nutrix," PW 17.2 (1937): 1495.

[55]*Discourse* 1.3 (5,17–6.9 Hobein).

[56]*Discourse* 4.3 (43,16–19 Hobein). See also Julian *Oration* 7.204A. Julian, who holds that the Cynic's *parrēsia* should not be without a civilized mildness, rejects the use of myths, which nurses use. He may have used Dio Chrysostom as a source, cf. R. Asmus, *Julian und Dion Chrysostomus* (Tauberbischofsheim: Lang, 1895), although the similarities beween them could be due to the use of common sources.

[57]Cf. Diogenes *Fragment* 10 Mullach; Themistius *Oration* 5.63B; 24.302B; *Peri Aretēs* 18. See, however, Maximus of Tyre *Discourse* 25.5 (303,11–12 Hobein): A skilled physician may mix brief pleasure with the pain of the remedy, yet to impart pleasure is not the function of Asclepius but of cooks.

He sees gentleness as the method of the flatterer, or as showing ignorance of the true human condition.[58] His *Epistle* 29 appears to be a response to those Cynics who held that the philosopher should be gentle as a father or nurse: Those who associate with the masses do not understand with what vehemence the disease of evil has laid hold of the multitude. They have been gravely corrupted. It is now necessary to perform cautery and surgery and to use strong drugs on them. "But instead of submitting to such care, like children you have summoned to your sides mammies and nurses who say to you, 'Take the cup, my pet; show that you love me by pouring a little of the medicine and drinking it.' "[59]

Dio Chrysostom uses the figure of the nurse in an ambivalent manner. In *Discourse* 4.73-139 he describes a conversation between Alexander the Great and Diogenes. Diogenes is aware that Alexander despises him for the way in which he had been taking the king to task. In order to set him at ease, Diogenes then tells Alexander a fable, "just as nurses, after giving the children a whipping, tell them a story to comfort and please them." The purpose of the myth is to show that the passions are irrational and brutish.[60] A nurse is thus used with approval as an example of someone who understands human nature. In *Discourse* 33, however, a nurse is used to symbolize something of which Dio disapproves. In the proemium to this oration, Dio distinguishes himself from the flatterers who praise their hearers. He promises that he will speak with *parrēsia*, but cautions that he will not touch on all their ailments.[61] He will be the genuine physician who will help them, and he may subject them to abuse. In this he promises to follow the example of Socrates, who censured and rebuked his listeners, unlike the comic poets who

> flattered the assembled multitude as one flatters a master, tempering their mild snapping with a laugh, just as nurses, whenever it is necessary for their charges to drink something rather unpleasant, themselves smear the cup with honey before they hold it out to the children.[62]

What is common to both uses is that the figure of a nurse is used in connection with the amelioration of the philosopher's imperiousness.[63]

---

[58]E.g., *Epistle* 28. Cf. Bernays, *Lucian und die Kyniker,* 36, 96–98; Norden, "Beiträge zur Geschichte der griechischen Philosophie," 386–87, 395–410, on the harsh philosophers (n. 39 above).
[59]*Epistle* 29.4, 5.
[60]The myth is recounted in *Discourse* 5 (cf. 5.16).
[61]*Discourse* 33.7, 44. On the limitation of a subject, see Epictetus *Discourse* 1.29.30–31, 64; Musonius *Fragment* 1 (5,3–11 Hense). That this is a rhetorical cliche is argued by K. Thraede, "Untersuchungen zum Ursprung und zur Geschichte der christlichen Poesie I," *JAC* 4 (1961): 108–27.
[62]*Discourse* 33.10. On the comic poets' ineffective *parrēsia,* see Plutarch *How to Tell a Flatterer from a Friend* 68C.
[63]Epictetus mostly uses the figure of the nurse in a pejorative manner when he speaks of those who do not wish to advance in their philosophic understanding, cf., e.g., *Discourse* 2.16.25, 28, 39, 44.

Plutarch insists that *parrēsia*, like any other medicine, must be applied properly. Men need friends to speak to them frankly in times of good fortune. But in time of misfortune there is no need for a friend's *parrēsia* or for harsh words *(logōn baros echontōn)* or stinging reproof *(dēgmon)*.[64] It is intolerable for a sick man to be reminded of the causes of his illness. The very circumstances in which the unfortunate find themselves leave no room for *parrēsia*, but require gentleness and help. "When children fall down, the nurses do not rush up to berate them, but they take them up, wash them, and straighten their clothes and, after all this is done, then rebuke them and punish them."[65]

The Ideal Philosopher

We return to Dio's description of the Cynics. His criticisms of the various Cynics can be summarized as follows: Some did not really become involved in the struggle of life, either because they lacked the courage, or because their empty speeches were not designed to involve them in the situations to which they spoke. The common marketplace preachers are accused of error *(apatē, planē)*, flattery *(kolakeia)*, and preaching for reputation *(doxa)* and money *(chrēmata)*, and to satisfy their sensual appetites *(hēdonē)*. A special complaint is that the transients were sometimes brutally harsh rather than seeking to benefit their hearers. This harshness *(baros)*, we learn elsewhere, is justified by an insistence on the philosopher's *parrēsia* that would allow no gentleness *(ēpiotēs)* under the circumstances.

After describing the different Cynics, Dio characterizes the ideal Cynic in negative and antithetic formulations designed to distinguish him from them (32.11-12):

> But to find a man who with purity and without guile speaks with a philosopher's boldness *(katharōs kai adolōs parrēsiazomenon)*, not for the sake of glory *(mēte doxēs charin)*, nor making false pretensions for the sake of gain *(met' ep' argyriō)*, but *(all')* who stands ready out of good will and concern for his fellowman, if need be, to submit to ridicule and the uproar of the mob—to find such a man is not easy, but rather the good fortune of a very lucky city, so great is the dearth of noble, independent souls, and such the abundance of flatterers *(kolakōn)*, charlatans and sophists. In my own case I feel that I have chosen that role, not of my own volition, but by *(ouk' ap' . . . all' hypo)* the will of some deity. For

---

[64]*How to Tell a Flatterer from a Friend* 68A–70D. Plutarch uses *baros* in this kind of context almost as a synonym for *dēgmos*, cf. 59C, 72A. For *barys* used of the misanthropist, see Euripides *The Children of Hercules* 4 (cf. Gerhard, *Phoinix von Kolophon*, 31). For the biting character of Cynic speech, see Demetrius *On Style* 261, "every variety of Cynic speech reminds you of a dog that is ready to bite even as it fawns," and cf. Diogenes *Fragment* 35 Mullach; Plutarch *On Tranquillity of Mind* 468A, "By this gentle and philosophic argument he showed the Cynic's abuse to be idle yapping" (contrast 468C, *ēpios*).

[65]*How to Tell a Flatterer from a Friend* 69BC.

when divine providence is at work for men, the gods provide, not only good counsellors who need no urging, but also words that are appropriate and profitable to the listener.

Dio's insistence on the philosopher's boldness, and his statements on the philosopher's qualifications in negatives and antitheses, namely that he should speak without guile, not for the sake of glory or gain, but as one who has a concern for men, and in opposition to flatterers, charlatans, and sophists, is meaningful against the background he has sketched. It is natural for him to express himself in this manner even though a personal attack had not been made on him. Some of his other qualifications, however, deserve further attention.

He states that the philosopher must speak "with purity *(katharōs)* and without guile *(adolōs)*." *Katharōs* may mean "clearly," "plainly," and thus merely refer to clarity of expression.[66] It is probable, however, that it has greater significance. Elsewhere, Dio says that the Cynic must purify his mind by reason, trying to free it from the slavery to lusts and opinions. This purification is the fight for his own freedom, which is the basis for his *parrēsia*.[67] Epictetus also, in distinguishing the ideal Cynic from the charlatan, emphasizes that the Cynic must begin by purifying his own mind. It is the Cynic's conscience, his knowledge of his own purity and that he is a friend and servant of the gods, that allows him to speak with *parrēsia*.[68] Thus when Dio describes the true Cynic as *katharōs parrēsiazomenos*, he is referring to the Cynic's speaking with purity of mind, thus requiring that the frankness of such a man be based on true freedom, and he probably does so with the charlatans in mind who claimed to speak as philosophers, but who had not purified themselves.[69]

Again, Dio's emphasis on his divine commission is noteworthy.[70] The way in which the statement is formulated *(ouk . . . all',* "not . . . but") suggests that this qualification of the true Cynic is also given with the hucksters in mind. Epictetus too, when he describes the divine call of the Cynic, does so

---

[66]See J. C. G. Ernesti, *Lexicon Technologiae Graecorum Rhetoricae* (1795), s. v. "katharos."

[67]*Discourse* 77/78.40. Stated in a different manner, it is the Cynic's giving heed to the injunction *gnōthi sauton* ("know yourself"). See Plutarch's quotation of the Delphic command at the beginning of his tractate on *parrēsia, How to Tell a Flatterer from a Friend* 65F, cf. *Progress in Virtue* 81CD. This view is especially characteristic of Julian, cf. *Oration* 6.188A. True Cynic *parrēsia* is the verbal expression of inner *eleutheria* ("freedom"), and is nothing other than *eleutherostomein* ("to be free of speech"): O. Hense, "Bion bei Philon," *RhM* 48 (1892): 231. That this is also Dio's understanding of the true philosopher is clear from *Discourses* 4.57–58; 67; 80; cf. E. Weber, *De Dione Chrysostomo,* 141–53.

[68]*Discourse* 3.22.19, 93.

[69]Cf. *Discourse* 77/78.36-38, where the philosopher's *parrēsia* is described in antithesis to flatterers. Cf. also *Discourse* 51.4.

[70]Cf. *Discourses* 13; 32.21; 34.4–5.

by contrasting the crude charlatan with the man who had been sent by God.[71] That the Cynic could endure the *hybris* of the crowd proves his divine call.[72] It is possible, on the other hand, that Dio and Epictetus wanted to distinguish themselves from Cynics like Oenomaeus of Gadara, who did away with the reverence of the gods,[73] rather than from those masquerading under the Cynic cloak.

Paul and the Cynics

Paul's description of his Thessalonian ministry in 1 Thessalonians 2 is strikingly similar to the picture sketched by Dio, both in what is said and in the way in which it is formulated.

Dio says that some Cynics fear the *hybris* of the crowd and will not become involved in the *agōn* of life. The speech of some of them can be described as *kenos*. The true philosopher, on the contrary, faces the crowd with *parrēsia* because God gives him the courage. Paul says that although he had suffered and experienced violence *(hybristhentes)* in Philippi, his sojourn in Thessalonica was not empty *(kenē)*, but that he spoke boldly in God *(eparrēsiasametha en tō theō)* in a great struggle *(en pollō agōni)* (vv. 1, 2).

Dio says the charlatans deceive *(apatōsin)* their hearers and lead them in error *(planē)*. Paul says he did not preach out of error *(ouk ek planēs)* (v. 3).

Dio says the ideal philosopher must speak with purity of mind *(katharōs)* and without guile *(adolōs)*. Paul says he was not motivated by uncleanness *(ouk ex akatharsias)*, nor did he speak with guile *(oude en dolō)* (v. 4).

Dio says that the true philosopher will not preach for the sake of glory *(mēte doxēs charin)*, nor for personal gain *(mēt' ep' argyriō)*, nor as a flatterer *(kolakōn)*. Paul claims that he did not use a cloak for greed *(oute en prophasei pleonexias)*, nor did he seek glory from men *(oute zētountes ex anthrōpōn doxan)*, or flatter them *(oute . . . en logō kolakeias)* (vv. 5, 6).

Dio claims that he was divinely directed to speak. So does Paul (v. 4).

Dio emphasizes that the philosopher, in spite of personal danger, seeks to benefit his hearers by adapting his message to their situation, and being

---

[71]E.g., *Discourse* 3.22.2, 9–25, 50–61. For the same contrasting formulation in Dio, see *Discourses* 34.4; 45.1. Cf. Holl, "Die schriftstellerische Form des griechischen Heiligenlebens" (n. 27 above), 420 n. 3.

[72]Epictetus *Discourse* 1.24.1–10. Cf. Dio *Discourses* 9.9; 12.9; 32.21–22.

[73]Julian *Orations* 7.209AB; 6.199A. Cf. also pseudo-Crates *Epistle* 19; pseudo-Diogenes *Epistle* 7. On the differences in Cynic attitudes toward the gods, see R. Hirzel, *Der Dialog* (1895) 2.191 n. 3, and Gerhard, *Phoinix von Kolophon,* 80–81. The useful study by Helmut Rahn, "Die Frömmigkeit der Kyniker," *Paideuma* 7 (1960): 280–92, does not do justice to this diversity. See further on this subject, pp. 22–23 above.

kinder to them individually than even a father. He represents the view that the philosopher should not consistently be harsh *(barys),* but should on occasion be gentle *(ēpios)* as a nurse. Paul says that he was prepared to lay down his life for his converts (v. 8), that, like a father with his children, he worked with each one individually *(hena hekaston hymōn,* v. 10), and that, although as an apostle of Christ he could have been demanding of them, he was gentle as a nurse *(dynamenoi en barei . . . alla egenēthēmen ēpioi en mesō hymōn, hōs ean trophos thalpē ta heautēs tekna,* vv. 6-7).[74]

Conclusion

The similarities between Paul and Dio, and between Paul and Cynicism in general, can be extended, but these suffice to show that there are verbal and formal parallels between Paul and Dio that must be taken into account in any consideration of 1 Thessalonians 2. One is not obliged to suppose that Dio was responding to specific statements that had been made about him personally. In view of the different types of Cynics who were about, it had become desirable, when describing oneself as a philosopher, to do so in negative and antithetic terms. This is the context within which Paul describes his activity in Thessalonica. We cannot determine from his description that he is making a personal apology.

Two final cautions are in order. In the first place, to point out these striking similarities of language does not obviate the need to give serious attention to the exegetical problems of 1 Thessalonians 2 and elsewhere where the same subject is discussed. In the second place, to point out that Paul had the same practical concerns as Dio, and that he used the same language in dealing with them, does not imply that he understood these words in the same way Dio understood them. As we have seen, the Cynics, too, differed among themselves as to what they meant by the same language. The further step must be taken of coming to a clearer perception of the self-understanding(s) of the Cynics before investigating Paul's thinking on his ministry against this background. I have attempted to demonstrate that such an effort would be fruitful.

---

[74]Pedro Gutierrez, *La Paternité spirituelle selon Saint Paul,* ÉB (Paris: J. Gabalda, 1968) 87–117, does not seriously consider the possibility of the Cynic background of this passage. For the same *parrēsia-philia topos* elsewhere in Paul, see Philemon 8–9.

4

Exhortation
in 1 Thessalonians

It is generally recognized that 1 Thessalonians contains a good deal of moral exhortation. Chapters 4 and 5, which constitute almost one half of the letter, are clearly paraenetic. The paraenetic intention of the letter becomes an even more prominent feature, should one accept the claims that the point of the entire letter is found in 4:1-2 and 4:10b-12, and that 4:1—5:11 is the body of the letter,[1] and that all Pauline thanksgivings, in this case 1:2—3:13, have either explicitly or implicitly a paraenetic function.[2] In an earlier study I examined 1 Thessalonians against the background of ancient paraenesis, and concluded that the entire letter could be understood as paraenetic.[3] This study builds on that earlier one. The change from "paraenetic" to "exhortation" does not represent a change in my assessment of the letter; it is made in the hope that attention will focus on what is presented here rather than on terminology. Suffice it to say that the ancient use of "paraenetic" was broader than the modern, which is indebted to Martin Dibelius's concentration on the formal aspects of moral instruction.[4]

---

[1]C. J. Bjerkelund, *Parakalō: Form, Funktion und Sinn der parakalō-Sätze in die paulinischen Briefen,* Bibliotheca Theologica Norvegica 1 (Oslo: Oslo University, 1966), 134. For a recent assessment of the letter, see H. Boers, "The Form-Critical Study of Paul's Letters: I Thessalonians as a Case Study," *NTS* 22 (1976): 140–58.

[2]P. Schubert, *Form and Function of the Pauline Thanksgivings,* BZNW 20 (Berlin: Alfred Töpelmann, 1939), 16–20, 88–89.

[3]A. J. Malherbe "1 Thessalonians as a Paraenetic Letter," presented to the SBL Seminar on Paul in Los Angeles in 1972. The paper is incorporated in an essay, idem, "Hellenistic Moralists and the New Testament", to appear in *ANRW* 2.26. L. G. Perdue: "Paraenesis and the Epistle of James," *ZNW* 72 (1981): 241–56 esp. 242–46, provides an extensive summary of my discussion of paraenesis.

[4]For a detailed treatment of paraenesis, see B. Fiore, S.J., *The Function of Personal Example in the Socratic and Pastoral Epistles,* AnBib 105 (Rome: Biblical Institute Press, 1986). H. Koester: "1 Thessalonians—Experiment in Christian Writing," in *Continuity and Discontinuity in Church History: Essays Presented to George Huntston Williams on the Occasion of His 65th Birthday,* ed. F. F. Church and T. George (Leiden: E. J. Brill, 1979), 35, rejects the definition of the letter as paraenetic and suggests that it rather represents the protreptic letter. P. Hartlich, "De exhortationum a Graecis Romanisque scriptarum historia et indole," *Leipziger Studien* 11 (1889): 207–

Two recent studies have offered contrasting views of 1 Thessalonians. Edgar Krentz has drawn attention to the marked hellenistic character of the letter and claimed that the letter would readily have been understood by its readers as a document of the first century.[5] He thus stressed the letter's continuity with its environment. On the other hand, although Helmut Koester gave attention to the traditions Paul used, he emphasized Paul's accomplishment in creating something new.[6] I suggest that both are correct, but that more should be said: Paul adopts a manner of exhortation that most likely was familiar to his readers, and he uses popular philosophical traditions with which they can be expected to have been familiar, yet he does so in a way different from the philosophical preachers of his day. I thus share the interest of Elpidius Pax in Paul's manner of exhorting recent converts, but whereas Pax seeks to illuminate 1 Thessalonians with Jewish advice to converts, I draw attention to the Greco-Roman tradition of moral exhortation.[7]

In adducing material from this tradition I am not primarily interested in arguing that Paul drew directly from it, although there seems to be no good reason why he should not have done so. Similar use may possibly be found to have been made by other hellenistic Jews, and one suspects that Philo might offer evidence for this. My present concern, however, is with the application and modification of hortatory devices in this letter, which was written to recently converted Greeks. A concentration on this aspect of the letter may enable us to discern more clearly what would have been striking in it to its recipients.[8]

Hortatory Features

Before offering examples of the way in which Paul utilizes and modifies elements of that tradition, I shall identify some hortatory features that pervade the letter throughout.

In my earlier study I suggested that the letter was not apologetic, and argued that while chapters 4 and 5 are clearly paraenetic, the first three

---

336, had distinguished between paraenesis and protrepsis, but was refuted by T. C. Burgess, "Epideictic Literature," *Studies in Classical Philology* 3 (1902): 89–248, and his views were further modified by R. Vetschera, *Zur griechischen Paränese,* (Smichow/Prague: Rohlicek & Sievers, 1912).

[5]"1 Thessalonians: a Document of Roman Hellenism," paper presented to the SBL Seminar on the Thessalonian Correspondence in New York, 1979.

[6]"1 Thessalonians—Experiment in Christian Writing" (n. 4 above).

[7]"Beobachtungen zur Konvertitensprache im ersten Thessalonicherbrief," *Studii Biblici Franciscani Analecta* 21 (1971): 220–61, and "Konvertitenprobleme im ersten Thessalonicherbrief," *Bibel und Leben* 13 (1972): 24–37.

[8]For a similar interest, see N. Walter, "Christusglaube und heidnische Religiosität in paulinischen Gemeinden," *NTS* 25 (1979): 422–42.

chapters, which are autobiographical, already function paraenetically by laying the foundation for the specific advice that would follow in the second half of the letter. In arguing my case, I pointed to elements of paraenesis in ancient theory and practice, both rhetorical and epistolary, and showed that they were scattered throughout 1 Thessalonians. The conscious use of traditional material, frequently *topoi* on the moral life, has frequently been detailed, and will receive attention below. That what was said was not new is indicated by repeated use of such phrases as "even as you know" (1:5; 2:2, 5; 3:4), "as you know" (2:11) or simply "you know" (2:1; 3:3; 4:2; 5:2).[9] There is therefore no need to write or speak any further on the subject ("you have no need to have anyone write to you;" 4:9; 5:1).[10] It is enough to remind the readers, either implicitly by the use of "you know," or explicitly ("you remember," 2:9; "you remember us," 3:6) of the type of life they are to lead,[11] or perhaps to compliment them for already doing so and encouraging them to do so more and more ("just as you are doing," 4:1; "and indeed you do it," 4:10; "just as you are doing," 5:11; "that you do so more and more," 4:1, cf. 10).[12] A major part of ancient paraenesis was the offering of a model to be imitated ("you became imitators of us," 1:6, cf. 5:7; 2:14),[13] the delineation of which is done antithetically ("not . . . but," 2:1-8).[14]

To these features others can be added which are characteristic of hortatory speech. It is noteworthy, for example, that a wide range of hortatory terms occur in this short letter, and that they are scattered throughout the letter: *paraklēsis* ("appeal, exhortation"; 2:3), *parakalō* ("exhort"; 2:12; 3:2, 7; 4:1, 10, 18; 5:11, 14), *paramytheomai* ("comfort"; 2:12; 5:14), *(dia)martyromai* ("testify"; 2:12; 4:6), *stērizō* ("establish"; 3:2), *parangelia* ("instruction, precept"; 4:2), *parangellō* ("charge"; 4:11), *erōtaomai* ("beseech"; 5:12), *noutheteō* ("admonish"; 5:12,14), *antechomai* ("help"; 5:14), and *makrothymeomai* ("be patient"; 5:14). Most of these terms and their Latin equivalents appear as descriptions of different types of exhortation in the

[9]Cf. 4:6 ("as we told you before and charged you"); Isocrates *To Nicocles* 40 ("which things you too know"); Seneca *Epistle* 94.26 *(scis, scitis)*.

[10]Cf. Isocrates *To Philip* 105, "Therefore on this subject I think I need say nothing more"; Cicero *Letters to His Friends* 1.4.3; 2.4.2.

[11]Cf. Pliny *Epistle* 8.24.1, "The love I bear you obliges me to give you, not indeed a precept (for you are far from needing a preceptor), but a reminder that you should resolutely act up to the knowledge that you already have, or else improve it."

[12]Cf. Cicero *Letters to His Brother Quintus* 1.1.8; Seneca *Epistle* 25.4 *(ut facis);* 1.1 *(ita fac);* Cicero *Letters to His Friends* 6.10b.4 *(idque ut facias, etiam atque etiam te hortor);* Seneca *Epistle* 13.15; Ignatius *Romans* 2:1.

[13]Cf. Seneca *Epistles* 6.5–6; 11.9–10; 95.72.

[14]Cf. pseudo-Isocrates *To Demonicus* 9–11; Epictetus *Discourses* 2.12.14; 4.1.159–69; Lucian *Demonax* 3-8; Maximus of Tyre *Discourse* 25.1 (297,5–9 Hobein), 36.5 (420,5–423,13 Hobein).

Greek and Roman sources, and their use in 1 Thessalonians shows that Paul is concerned with a wide variety of types of exhortation.[15]

The philophronetic element in ancient letters, which sought to overcome the separation of writer and recipient, and in paraenetic letters provided the framework for the exhortation given, is also found in 1 Thessalonians.[16] Such letters were regarded as substitutes for their writers' presence, and intended to be exactly what the writer's conversation would have been had he been present.[17] The letters therefore speak at length about the writer and firmly establish his relations with his readers.[18] In 1 Thessalonians Paul also firmly cements his relations with his readers in a number of ways.[19] In addition to reminding them in various ways of his past relations with them, Paul modifies a convention of the friendly letter by substituting the expression "since we were bereft of you . . . in person not in heart" (2:17) for the "present/absent" cliche, and further heightens the emotional element by repeating his desire to see them in 3:6 (*epipothountes* ["longing"]) and 3:10 ("praying that we may see you face to face").[20] His personal relationship with them is still further

---

[15]Compare Seneca: Admonitory and preceptorial (paraenetic) speech, which is directed to particular situations (*Epistle* 94.1, 32, 35–36), consists of at least the following varieties: *consolatio, dissuasio, adhortatio, abiurgatio, laudatio* (*Epistle* 94.39), *admonitio* (*Epistle* 94.59; cf. 95.34, 65). On Seneca's psychagogy, see I. Hadot, *Seneca und die griechisch-römische Tradition der Seelenleitung,* Quellen und Studien zur Geschichte der Philosophie 13 (Berlin: Walter de Gruyter, 1969), here, esp. 8–9. See also Musonius *Fragment* 49 (130,9 Hense): *hortatur, monet, saudet, obiurgat.*

[16]On philophronesis in letters, see especially H. Koskenniemi, *Studien zur Idee und Phraseologie des griechischen Briefes bis 400 n. Chr.,* Annales Academiae Scientarum Fennicae, Series B, vol. 102.2 (Helsinki: Suomalainen Tiedeakatemia, 1956); K. Thraede, *Grundzüge griechisch-römischer Brieftopik,* Zetemata 48 (Munich: C. H. Beck, 1970).

[17]Cf. Seneca *Epistles* 6.5–6; 40.1; 75.1–7, and for the theory, see A. J. Malherbe, *Ancient Epistolary Theorists,* SBLSBS 19 (Atlanta: Scholars Press, 1988), 12–14.

[18]For the function of Seneca's "Selbstdarstellung" in his letters, see H. Cancik, *Untersuchungen zu Senecas epistulae morales,* Spudasmata 18 (Hildesheim: G. Olms, 1967), and Hadot, *Seneca und die griechisch-römische Tradition der Seelenleitung,* 174–76.

[19]*Pace* Koester, "1 Thessalonians" (n. 4 above), 36-37; idem, "Apostel und Gemeinde in den Briefen an die Thessalonicher," in *Kirche: Festschrift für Günther Bornkamm zum 75. Geburtstag,* ed. D. Lührmann and G. Strecker (Tübingen: J. C. B. Mohr [Paul Siebeck], 1980): 287-98.

[20]For the epistolary theory see Malherbe, *Ancient Epistolary Theorists,* 33: pseudo-Demetrius, *Epistolary Types* 1. The purpose of writing this type of letter is that the writers "think that nobody will refuse them when they write in a friendly manner, but will rather submit and heed what they are writing." The sample follows:

> Even though I have been separated from you for a long time, I suffer this in body only. For I can never forget you or the impeccable way we were raised together from childhood up. Knowing that I myself am genuinely concerned about your affairs, and that I have worked unstintingly for what is most advantageous to you, I have assumed that you, too, have the same opinion of me and will refuse me in nothing. You will do well, therefore, to give close attention to the members of my household lest they need anything, to assist them in whatever they might need, and to write to us about whatever you should choose.

On 1 Thess. 2:17; see Thraede, *Grundzüge,* 95–97. On *pothos* ("yearning") in letters, see Thraede's index and Koskenniemi, *Studien,* 174–75. On orphans, contrast Epictetus *Discourse* 3.24.14–16 which, according to R. Hoïstad, *Cynic Hero and Cynic King* (Uppsala: C. W. K. Gleerup, 1948), 62, is paraenetic.

stressed by the frequent use of personal pronouns, especially in conjunction with each other, for example, as they are strung together in 1:5-6: "among *you* for *your* sake. And *you* became imitators of *us* . . ."[21]

In describing his own work with the Thessalonians, Paul uses the images of nurse (2:7) and father (2:11-12) to convey his special concern for them. These images were current in his day to describe the special understanding of the moral philosopher who adapted his manner of exhortation to the condition of his hearers. Thus Plutarch, when giving instruction on the proper occasions on which to speak frankly, adduces the example of nurses: "When children fall down, the nurses do not rush up to berate them, but they take them up, wash them, and straighten their clothes, and, after all this is done, then rebuke them and punish them."[22] Paul intensifies the image by likening his behavior to that of a nurse toward her own children (*ta heautēs tekna*), not merely those under her charge.[23]

Paul moves from the image of the nurse (2:7-8) to refer to his giving of himself and his practice of self-support (2:9-10) before comparing himself to a father who exhorts his own children (2:11-12). His self-support is an example of his intention not to be burdensome or demanding (*en barei*, v. 7; *epibarēsai*, v. 9) of any of them *(tina hymōn)*,[24] but it may be introduced at this point as a natural transition to the image of father. That a desire for money had precedence over family relationships is an opinion well documented by ancient moralists of pessimistic bent. They thought that covetousness caused children to be hostile to their fathers to the point that they betrayed *(prodidontai)* them, and that parents in turn became more demanding *(baryteroi)* of their children.[25] Taking false oaths in the pursuit of wealth is also frequently condemned.[26] It is possible that Paul is aware of such statements and that he disavows any greed by reminding his readers that he had shared his own life

---

[21]Cf. also 1:2, 9; 2:6, 7, 8, 11, 17; 3:6, 12, where *hēmeis* ("we") and *hymeis* ("you") appear together.

[22]*How to Tell a Flatterer from a Friend* 69BC. Cf. Dio Chrysostom *Discourse* 4.74, and for a more detailed treatment, see A. J. Malherbe " 'Gentle as a Nurse': The Cynic Background to 1 Thess. 2," *NovT* 12 (1970), esp. 211–14 (= 43–45 in this volume).

[23]Cf. Plutarch *Consolation to His Wife* 609E: A mother's nursing of her own child is a sign of maternal love.

[24]That Paul's practice had much wider significance for him than this is argued successfully by R. F. Hock, *The Social Context of Paul's Ministry: Tentmaking and Apostleship* (Philadelphia: Fortress Press, 1980).

[25]The evidence is presented by G. A. Gerhard, *Phoinix von Kolophon* (Leipzig/Berlin, B. G. Teubner, 1909), 14–18. The reference alluded to here is Stobaeus *Anthology* 4.31.84 (5.764,2–5 and 765,12; Wachsmuth-Hense). *Prodidomi* appears in such contexts elsewhere, e.g., pseudo-Cebes *The Table* 40.3; pseudo-Crates *Epistle* 7.

[26]See Gerhard, *Phoinix von Kolophon,* 45–46, for the evidence. Cf., e.g., Theognis 199-200, "but if one shall win it unrighteously and unduly with a covetous heart, or by unrighteous seizure upon an oath . . ."

with them (2:8)[27] and that he had foregone the opportunity to be *barys* (2:8). He further calls not only on God as witness that he had acted "holy and righteous and blameless" toward the Thessalonians but first calls on the Thessalonians as witnesses to his claim.[28] He then calls to mind the various types of exhortation that he had applied (2:12). According to Lucian (*Demonax* 8), Demonax also, instead of being self-seeking, helped his friends by cautioning some, consoling others, reconciling brothers, making peace between husbands and wives, and so forth.

Of interest in this connection is the way in which Paul describes himself as father. It is possible that the original context of paraenesis was that of a father giving advice to his son,[29] but it had become common by Paul's time for the sage to exhort his listeners as their fathers, and to think of them as his children.[30] According to Dio Chrysostom (*Discourse* 77/78.41-42), despite the fact that some people deride the philosopher for, among other things, neglecting the opportunity to become rich, the philosopher believes that his fellow citizens, kinsmen and friends are more closely related and bound to him than others, and he is more kindly disposed to each *(hekastō)* of them than even a father or brothers or friends. This special relationship causes him not to hide anything from them, but to increase the intensity of his admonition *(nouthesia)* and exhortation *(parakeleusis)*.

Dio does not here describe the philosopher as a father, although he thinks of a relationship that transcends the natural. I refer to his statement

---

[27]Is it possible that *metadounai hymin . . . tas heautōn psychas* is meant to counter *prodidonai?* But see Dio Chrysostom *Discourse* 3.15, who never accepted money from those who would willingly give it, but rather shared *(metadidous)* the little he had with others. Cf. also Lucian *Nigrinus* 25–26; *Demonax* 8, 63, who shares a view that is more like that of Acts 20:34 than Paul himself, who speaks of giving himself. See Koester, "Thessalonians" (n. 4 above), 41–42; idem, "Apostel und Gemeinde" (n. 19 above), 290, for the argument that Paul's giving of himself to the Thessalonians who had become his *agapētoi* ("beloved") and fellow workers made him different from the philosopher, whose freedom would be violated by such a commitment. In general, I agree, but in view of the philosopher's motivations for preaching *(kēdemonia* ["solicitude"], *eunoia* ["goodwill"], *philanthrōpia* ["love of humanity"]) the matter should not be overstated. The issue was indeed of interest to philosophers like Dio Chrysostom. See the concern to retain one's individuality, below at n. 31.

[28]In 2:5 it is only God who is witness that he had not acted under a cloak of greed. Cf. Isocrates *Nicocles* 46, "you are my witnesses," in paraenesis.

[29]See J. Kroll, "Theognis-Interpretationen," *Philol.* Supp. 29(1936): 99. Cf. pseudo-Isocrates *To Demonicus* 9–11; Pliny *Epistle* 8.13.

[30]For Epicurus, see N. W. De Witt, *Epicurus and His Philosophy* (Minneapolis: Univ. of Minnesota Press, 1954), 99, 323; for Stoics, Epictetus *Discourse* 3.22.82; and for Pythagoreans, Iamblichus *Life of Pythagoras* 198 (*FVS* 1.471,20–28). The convention is also found in rhetoricians: Cf. Quintilian *Institutio oratoria* 2.2.5, who instructs that the teacher of rhetoric, who is to be a moral as well as rhetorical example, should adopt a parental attitude toward his students. P. Gutierrez (*La Paternité spirituelle selon Saint Paul*, ÉB [Paris: J. Gabalda, 1968], 29 n. 1 and 51–54) argues that the paternal image is not found in Greek didactic texts as it is in Jewish sources. The device appears frequently in the *Testaments of the Twelve Patriarchs*, e.g., *Testament of Simeon* 6.1; *Testament of Naphthali* 4.1; 8.1, etc.

because of the significance it attains when seen in the context of discussions of the philosopher's need to give attention to individuals and to vary his exhortation according to the condition he addresses. Earlier in the discourse (37–38) he had affirmed that the philosopher, while retaining his individuality, would lead people to virtue by adopting different means of persuasion, "partly by persuading *(peithōn)* and exhorting *(parakalōn),* partly by abusing *(loidoroumenos)* and reproaching *(oneidizōn)* . . . taking them aside privately one by one *(idia hekaston)* and also admonishing *(nouthetōn)* them in groups."[31] The desirability of individual and personalized instruction was widely recognized.[32] When Paul therefore reminds the Thessalonians that he had exhorted them individually *(hena hekaston)* and describes his exhortation as *paraklēsis* ("exhortation"), *paramythia* ("consolation"), and *martyria* ("charging"), he is claiming to have acted in so responsible a manner.[33] Paul, of course, differs from Dio in that his relationship to his converts as their father is different from Dio's philosopher to his public. According to 1 Corinthians 4:16-17, he begot his converts by means of the gospel and on that basis ("therefore") exhorted them to become imitators of him.[34] But such reflection on his spiritual paternity is absent from 1 Thessalonians 2:11-12, except to the degree that the goal of his exhortation is conduct worthy of God. As the *hōs* ("like") indicates, he uses the image by way of illustration, and his primary interest in using the image is, as it has been in vv. 7-10, to confirm his special relationship with them. The reflexive pronoun in "his own children" contributes to this as it did in "her own children" in v.7.

Paul's interest in exhortation in the letter is not confined to the various stylistic features that he adopts or to his reflection on his own pastoral method. The type of concern that he had exemplified was also to characterize the Thessalonians themselves, and is taken up especially in chapters 4 and 5. Thus, in each of the sections taking up specific matters, Paul mentions some aspects of the concern they should have for each other: 4:6, "that no man transgress and wrong his brother"; 4:9, "to love one another" (cf. 3:12); 4:18,

---

[31]Cf. also *Discourse* 13.31, on which see P. Desideri, *Dione di Prusa: Un intellettuale greco nell impero romano* (Messina/Florence: D'Anna, 1978), 24 n. 44. Examples of Dio's instruction to individuals have been preserved, e.g., *Discourses* 55; 56. Synesius (*Testimony Regarding Dio's Life and Writing* 1.11 [Treu; LCL edition of Dio Chrysostom, 5.375]) says that Dio admonished people of all stations *kath' hena kai athroous* ("singly and in groups").

[32]See especially Plutarch *On Listening to Lectures* 43E–44A; *How to Tell a Flatterer from a Friend* 70D-71D; Apollonius of Tyana *Epistle* 10 (addressed to Dio) and Philo *On the Decalogue* 36–39. On the Epicureans, see De Witt, *Epicurus* 94, and further on the subject, P. Rabbow, *Seelenführung: Methodik der Exerzitien in der Antike,* (Munich: Kösel-Verlag, 1954), 272–79, 317 n. 99, and Hadot, *Seneca und die griechisch-römische Tradition der Seelentleitung* (n. 15 above), 64–66.

[33]Cf. Acts 20:31. It is as difficult to classify or distinguish between the various types of exhortation mentioned by Paul as it is those mentioned by Seneca.

[34]Note the paraenetic elements in 1 Cor 4:14-21: antithesis ("not . . . but" [14, 15, 19, 20]); admonishing (14), fathers (16), exhortation (16), imitators (16), reminder (17).

"comfort one another"; 5:11, "comfort one another," and, of course 5:12-15. The mutual edification is further specified as having to take place *heis ton hena* (5:11), which is not simply equivalent to *allēlous* ("each other"), but is probably to be taken in the sense of *heis heni,* "person to person," as in Theocritus 22.65.[35] Finally, various types of exhortation and other actions as appropriate to persons with particular needs and to the community as a whole are mentioned in 5:14: "And we exhort you, brethren, admonish the idle *(noutheteite tous ataktous),* encourage the fainthearted *(paramytheisthe tous oligopsychous),* help the weak *(antechesthe tōn asthenōn),* be patient with them all *(makrothymeite pros pantas)."*[36]

Paul's Modification of the Tradition

Among the elements that Paul adopts from the hortatory tradition and modifies is his statement that the Thessalonians had become his imitators *(mimētai,* 1:6). Paul's use of the imitation motif is in line with contemporary paraenesis, but there are also noteworthy differences.[37] The use of the motif in exhortation is well known and requires little documentation,[38] but certain contrasts between Paul and his contemporaries should be noted.

---

[35]Cf. *anēr andri,* "man to man," in Maximus of Tyre *Discourse* 38.4 (443,5 Hobein). The equivalence to *allēlous* ("each other") is listed in BAGD s.v. 5.a. and BDF 247, 4, and the construction is described by the latter as dependent on a Semitic, especially Aramaic, model. The closest parallel in the NT is 1 Cor. 4:6, *heis hyper tou henos* ("one against another"). But there is no need not to do justice to the stress on the individual in the construction. Cf. 2 Thess. 1:3, "the love of every one of all of you *(henos hekastou pantōn hymōn)* for one another..."

[36]The practice of mutual edification in philosophical communities and Paul's advice and practice in relation to it call for exploration. For the practice, in addition to Rabbow (n. 32 above) and Hadot (n. 15 above), see H. G. Ingenkamp, *Plutarchs Schriften über die Heilung der Seele,* (Göttingen: Vandenhoeck & Ruprecht, 1971). For the practice among the Epicureans, see N. W. De Witt, "Organization and Procedure in Epicurean Groups," *CPh* 31(1936): 205-11, with the corrections by M. Gigante, "Philodème: Sur la liberté de parole," in *Acts du VIIIe Congrès, Assoc. Guillaume Budé* (Paris, 1969): 196-217, and further discussion of Philodemus by Rabbow, *Seelenführung,* 269-70, 276, and Hadot, *Seneca und die griechisch-römische Tradition der Seelenleitung* (n. 15 above), 64-65; A. J. Malherbe, *Paul and the Thessalonians: The Philosophical Tradition of Pastoral Care* (Philadelphia: Fortress Press, 1987), 61-94.

[37]See H.-H. Schade, *Apokalyptische Christologie bei Paulus: Studien zum Zusammenhang von Christologie und Eschatologie in die Paulusbriefen,* GTA 18 (Göttingen: Vandenhoeck & Ruprecht, 1981), 118-19, 123-26, for discussion of the most recent literature. Schade denies that the imitation motif has an ethical dimension. I maintain that its place in the autobiographical section of the letter, which already functions paraenetically, lends an ethical dimension to it.

[38]See, e.g. pseudo-Isocrates *To Demonicus* 11, 36; Seneca *Epistles* 11.9-10; 100.12; Pliny *Epistle* 8.13; Lucian *Nigrinus* 26; pseudo-Crates *Epistle* 19. Cf. the sample of the paraenetic letter provided by pseudo-Libanius *Epistolary Styles* 52 (75 Malherbe):

Always be an emulator *(zēlōtēs),* dear friend, of virtuous men. For it is better to be well spoken of when imitating good men than to be reproached by all men while following evil men.

Words and Deeds

While the philosophers did use the imitation motif, they were hesitant to call others to follow their own examples. In fact, there was a (lesser) hesitancy among them even to advance contemporary worthies as paradigms.[39] This diffidence is clearest in the Stoics.[40] Paul, in contrast, asserts that his readers had already become imitators of him and his associates and the Lord, the only place in his letters where he does so. By doing so here, Paul in good paraenetic fashion reminds them of the relationship which had existed between them, and which would undergird the advice that he is about to give. That he is interested in personal relationship rather than authority which flows from his apostleship, appears from his concentrated use of pronouns. Thus, while Paul's adoption of the imitation motif is in good hortatory style, the self-confidence with which he writes is extraordinary.

Contemporary Cynics, however, did make confident claims about their own accomplishments, sometimes comparing themselves with Heracles. Like Heracles, they asserted, they had been victorious in their labors *(ponoi)* and by enduring had attained the ideal.[41] On the basis of their own lives, they could then preach to others. That the philosopher's speech should conform to his deeds was a requirement not confined to Cynics,[42] but in their case it expressed their self-confidence. Lucian says of Demonax that it was the conformity of his life to his boldness of speech *(parrēsia)* that enabled him to point to himself as an example.[43] Cynics of more radical leaning claimed that the Cynic's superiority in his deeds was the basis for the harshness of his speech.[44] So, whereas the correspondence between a philosopher's speech

---

[39]On the use of historical examples, see G. C. Fiske, *Lucilius and Horace: A Study in the Classical Theory of Imitation,* University of Wisconsin Studies in Language and Literature 7 (Madison: Univ. of Wisconsin Press, 1970), 159–62. Recent examples are offered, e.g., by Teles *Fragment* 3 (23,12 Hense); Musonius *Fragment* 9 (49,12 Hense); Lucian *Demonax* 1–2, 7; Dio Chrysostom *Discourse* 7.81, 125–27, but are done so self-consciously and in contrast to normal practice. Cf. Seneca *Epistle* 83.13. Dio Chrysostom (*Discourse* 21.10–11) reflects the attitude, which is discussed by B. A. van Groningen, *In the Grip of the Past: Essay on an Aspect of Greek Thought* (Leiden: E. J. Brill, 1953), 6–12.

[40]See A. J. Malherbe, "Pseudo-Heraclitus, *Epistle* 4: The Divinization of the Wise Man," *JAC* 21 (1978): 55–56; idem, "Herakles," *RAC* 14 (1988): 560–62.

[41]Malherbe, "Pseudo-Heraclitus, *Epistle* 4," 58–59. See further J. T. Fitzgerald, *Cracks in an Earthen Vessel: An Examination of the Catalogues of Hardships in the Corinthian Correspondence,* SBLDS 99 (Atlanta: Scholars Press, 1988), 58.

[42]See, e.g., Seneca *Epistles* 108.35–37; cf. 6.5–6; Dio Chrysostom *Discourse* 70.6; Julian *Oration* 7.214BC; Lucian *Peregrinus* 19. For the application of the criterion, see R. Helm, *Lucian und Menipp* (Leipzig/Berlin: B. G. Teubner, 1906), 40–41, and see further, A. J. Festugière, "Lieux Communs littéraires et themes de folk-lore dans l' Hagiographie primitive," *Wiener Studien* 74 (1961): 140–42.

[43]*Demonax* 3. See M. Caster, *Lucien et la pensée religieuse de son temps* (Paris: Les Belles Lettres, 1937), 73–74.

[44]See pseudo-Crates *Epistles* 20; 21; pseudo-Diogenes *Epistles* 15; 27; 28; 29; pseudo-Heraclitus *Epistles* 4; 7.

and his conduct was generally regarded as an index to his trustworthiness, it was yet another way in which Cynics expressed their self-confidence and justified their demands that they be emulated.

Immediately before Paul refers to the Thessalonians as his imitators, he also mentions his speech (1:5). Paul's speech, however, is not compared with his deeds, which would have drawn attention to his trustworthiness as founded on his own accomplishments. Instead, he writes, "not only in word, but also in power and in the Holy Spirit and with full conviction," thus distinguishing himself from the philosopher by not stressing any particular deeds of his own but drawing attention to the way in which the gospel came to them. A philosopher would have said that *he* had come, "not in word only, but also in deed." Paul, on the contrary, does not draw attention to his accomplishments, but to his gospel, which he further describes as the gospel of God (2:2, 9) with which he had been entrusted (2:4), or as the word of the Lord (1:8) or of God (2:13). Furthermore, the gospel came to his readers in the Holy Spirit (1:5) and was received by them with joy of the Spirit (1:6). Attention is thus drawn, not to Paul's actions which underlie his confident expression, but to the way in which the gospel came to them and was received by them. It was not Paul's deeds nor his speech which gives him confidence, but God's election (cf. 1:4). The issue is neatly summarized in 2:13, "not as the word of men, but . . . the word of God, which is at work in you." Not Paul's action, but the Spirit's working, not, precisely, even his speech, but the gospel empowered by the Spirit. As that divine power, manifested in the gospel, was reflected in the lives of Paul and his associates, the Thessalonians became their emulators when they received the word.[45] The themes of imitation *(mimēsis)* and deed/word *(ergon/logon)* are thus utilized by Paul but are completely recast.

Paul's Frankness

Paul's modification of the hortatory tradition to describe himself as bearer of the divine message is further illustrated by his adaptation in chapter 2 of the description of the ideal philosopher and his exercise of frankness *(parrēsia)*. Elsewhere I have attempted to demonstrate that in the first half of the chapter Paul uses Cynic traditions about the ideal philosopher to describe his early ministry in Thessalonica.[46] The content as well as the form of what

---

[45]See J. H. Schütz, *Paul and the Anatomy of Apostolic Authority*, SNTSMS 26 (Cambridge: Cambridge Univ. Press, 1975), 126-27.

[46]See "Gentle as a Nurse" (n. 22 above; pp. 35–48 in this volume), concentrating on Dio Chrysostom *Discourse* 32.7–11. The discussion of *parrēsia* that follows is based on evidence in that essay. For suggested modifications of my argument, see Desideri, *Dione di Prusa*, 15–52, 172 (n. 31 above).

he says about himself have remarkable parallels in Dio Chrysostom's description of the ideal Cynic (*Discourse* 32.7-11). Here I wish to focus more narrowly on what he says about his *parrēsia*.

Originally a political term, by Paul's time *parrēsia* had come to be associated with the philosopher's freedom of speech which he exercised as a physician of men's souls. Having himself attained moral freedom, the philosopher felt compelled to turn others to it by harshly pointing out their shortcomings and holding up the fulfillment of human potential that the rational life would bring. As part of his self-commendation the Cynic would stress the harsh treatment that he had received from the mobs who would not listen to him. By emphasizing his courage under attack and his tenacity in preaching, the Cynic established his credentials as a preacher and expressed his intention to continue convicting the crowds of their sins.[47] Paul uses the themes of *hybris* ("shameful treatment") and *parrēsia* (2:1-2), but in a way different from the Cynics.

First, although he begins with a reference to his maltreatment in Philippi, his suffering is not put to the use it customarily was by Cynics. It does not serve to justify Paul's harsh *parrēsia*. On the contrary, using other *topoi*, Paul goes on to describe his ministry as gentle, like a nurse suckling her own children, and as understanding, like a father who gives individual attention to his own children as he exhorts them in different ways. The tradition of the philosopher's suffering is therefore used, but not to justify Paul's harsh demands. The relationship Paul shares with the Thessalonians is not based on his demonstration of his fortitude, but on his giving of himself on their behalf.[48]

Second, his freedom of speech does not have its source in anything that he has attained. He says, "we waxed bold in our God to speak to you the gospel of God" (2:2). While the moral philosopher was impelled by an awareness of his own moral freedom, acquired by reason and the application of his own will, to speak boldly to the human condition and demand its reformation, Paul regards his entire ministry, as to its origin, motivation, content, and method, as being directed by God. God grants him the boldness to speak, and what he says is not philosophical or rational analysis of the human condition, but the gospel of God. The traditions Paul uses in this chapter are primarily Cynic, although they are also found in other philosophers. But Paul's dependence on God for this speech is completely non-Cynic. The similarities to Stoicism have to be examined in greater detail than they have been or than I can on this occasion.

---

[47]Note the criticism of Bellerephon in pseudo-Socrates *Epistle* 1.12: He allowed himself to be driven out of the towns by the *hybris* of the people, and thus lost his *parrēsia*.
[48]Thus also Koester, "Apostel und Gemeinde" (n. 19 above), 290–91.

In the first part of the letter, then, Paul makes generous use of the hortatory traditions current in his own day but changes them to express his conception of himself as bearer of the divine message. The traditions were so common that one may assume that Paul's converts were familiar with them, and that his modifications of them would have been striking.

Paul's Practical Advice

The moral directions Paul gives in the latter half of the letter exhibit the same combination of the new and the old. I shall treat three examples from chapter 4 by way of illustration. Paul's reference to the instruction that he had given them, "for you know what precepts *(parangelias)* we gave you" (4:2), is in good paraenetic style. *Parangelia* is here equivalent to *praeceptum* or *parangelma,* a special precept of living addressed to a particular situation.[49] "You know" concentrates the memory on what the readers already know.[50] What is not customary in 4:1-2, of course, is Paul's specification of his exhortation as "in the Lord" and "through the Lord Jesus," and the requirement that the Thessalonians live "to please God." This combination of philosophical moral tradition and Christian religious or theological warrant also appears in what follows.

In 4:3-8, verses 4 and 6 have received most attention. It is not necessary for my immediate purpose to enter into a detailed discussion of these verses. The exegetical difficulties confront us in those verses which reflect traditional moral instruction, and our interpretation may be helped as we learn more about those traditions. Paul's advice on sex and greed might not have sounded so strange to someone who had heard the teaching of a philosopher like his contemporary Musonius Rufus. Musonius, in a discussion of sexual indulgence in and outside marriage, also writes of honor, lust, and wronging the man whose wife is taken in adultery.[51] But Paul's words would have had a sharper

---

[49]G. Milligan, *St. Paul's Epistles to the Thessalonians* (London: Macmillan, 1908), 47, already pointed to the equivalence of *parangelia* and *praeceptum.* For *praecepta* in paraenesis, see Seneca *Epistles* 94.1, 14, 32; 95.1, and M. Giusta, *I dossografi di etica* (Turin: G. Giappichelli, 1964) 1.162–63, 177–81. Aristotle *Nicomachean Ethics* 1104a7 uses *parangelia,* but *parangelma* was the more common term; see pseudo-Isocrates *To Demonicus* 44, and the titles of Plutarch's treatises *Gamika Parangelmata (Advice to Bride and Groom)* and *Politika Parangelmata (Precepts of Statecraft).* Instructive for 1 Thess. 4:1-2 is the snatch from Zeno, *tois parangelmasin hōs dei zēn . . . prosechein* ("to heed the precepts on how to live") (Stobaeus *Anthology* 4.106 [3.245 Wachsmuth-Hense] = *SVF* 1.238).

[50]See especially Seneca *Epistle* 94.25–26, and cf. notes 11 and 12.

[51]Musonius Rufus *Fragment* 12 (65,2-10 Hense). Krentz ("1 Thessalonians," 12-13; [n. 5 above]) also draws attention to Musonius. For the philosophical discussions of which Musonius's treatment is part, see O. L. Yarbrough, *Not Like the Gentiles: Marriage Rules in the Letters of Paul,* SBLDS 80 (Atlanta: Scholars Press, 1985), 31–63.

ring of familiarity if they were stripped of the motivational language in which his directions are couched.

In this passage, Paul stresses the motivation for the actions rather than the actions themselves. The pericope is framed by "sanctification" (vv. 3 and 7; cf. "Holy Spirit," v. 8), which forms an *inclusio,* thus indicating Paul's interest. As part of this stress, he further advances as motivations the knowledge of God, God's will and vengeance, and the Holy Spirit.

He must have had a reason for this extraordinary stress on the motivations for the Christian moral life, and I suggest that it is precisely this kind of motivation that in Paul's eyes and probably his readers' made his instruction different from the popular philosophical traditions he uses.

Whether morality had a close connection with religion in the Graeco-Roman world has been and continues to be debated.[52] That the discussion can continue would suggest that the connection, if it did exist, was not pronounced or essential. Philosophical writers did, of course, provide their ethics with a theoretical framework, but whether or precisely how religion informed the moral life is not always clear. In the eyes of Jews and Christians, at any rate, a major difference between their and pagan ethics, indeed a mark of their superiority, was that they always began with God. This is intoned most explicitly by the *Epistle of Aristeas* and by the Christian Apologists.[53] What was new in Christian teaching, according to A. D. Nock, was its motivation (fear of God, devotion to Jesus), and its claim to supply the power to satisfy its requirements.[54] This, I suggest, explains Paul's emphasis on motivation. He insists that Christian ethics be grounded in religion. Philosophical traditions are used, but without their preoccupation with the use of reason or the nature of character development. Paul is concerned with the sanctified rather than the rational life.

Something similar is found in 4:9-12, but not nearly to the same degree. Most elements of the advice would have sounded familiar.[55] *Hēsychia* (quiet

---

[52]See A. D. Nock, "Early Gentile Christianity and Its Hellenistic Background," in *Essays on Religion and the Ancient World,* ed. Z. Stewart (Cambridge, Mass.: Harvard University Press, 1972), 1.63–68; K. Prümm, *Religionsgeschichtliches Handbuch für den Raum der altchristlichen Umwelt: Hellenistisch–römische Geistesströmungen und Kulte mit Beachtung des Eigenlebens der Provinzen,* 2d ed. (Rome: Päpstliches Bibelanstalt, 1954), 322–27. A more nuanced view is that of H. W. G. Liebeschuetz, *Continuity and Change in Roman Religion* (Oxford: Clarendon Press, 1979). See also W. den Boer, *Private Morality in Greece and Rome* (Leiden: E. J. Brill, 1979).

[53]*Epistle of Aristeas* 132, 189, 200, 235; Aristides *Apology* 15; Theophilus *To Autolycus* 3.9, 15; Athenagoras *Embassy* 11; *Epistle of Diognetus* 6–7. On Lactantius, see Liebeschuetz, *Continuity and Change in Roman Religion,* 265–67, 271–75.

[54]A. D. Nock, *Conversion: The Old and the New in Religion from Alexander the Great to Augustine of Hippo* (Oxford: Clarendon Press, 1933), 218–20; cf. G. Wagner, *Pauline Baptism and the Pagan Mysteries* (London: Oliver & Boyd, 1967), 48.

[55]For what follows, see the more extensive discussion and the material collected in my "Hellenistic Moralists and the New Testament" (n. 3 above). See also Krentz, "I Thessalonians" (n. 5 above), 13–14.

living) was a well known *topos* in Paul's day;[56] *prassein ta idia* ("to mind one's own affairs") was a bit of advice already found in Plato and frequently after him;[57] manual labor was frequently discussed;[58] *euschēmosynē* ("decorum"), was a self-evident ideal to most philosophers, as was self-sufficiency.[59] The way in which these terms, frequently overlooked in exegesis, were used, may be illustrated by a line from pseudo-Musonius: "The true end of our being born into the world is to live orderly and with decorum *(tetagmenōs kai euschēmonōs),* our minds being furnished by nature with reason as overseer and guide for this purpose."[60] The social responsibility and demeanor that Paul inculcates have nothing extraordinary or surprising about them. Elsewhere I have suggested that Paul, in using these well-known *topoi,* may have had in mind preventing the Thessalonians from adopting social attitudes like those of the Epicureans.[61] The combination of the *topoi* on love and quietism point in that direction, as do certain details and the way Paul uses them. The traditions, then, are recognizable, but once again the Pauline edge is clearly evident.

To begin with, Paul does not speak of friendship or friends, but of brotherly love and brothers. He is familiar with the *topos* on friendship,[62] but he avoids the term as he does the description of Christians as friends. His reason for doing so may be that the terms carried connotations that were

---

[56]Some of the material was collected by F. Wilhelm, "Plutarch *Peri Hēsychias," RhM* 73 (1924): 466–82. For conditions in the first century which made withdrawal from active political involvement desirable, see R. MacMullen, *Enemies of the Roman Order: Treason, Unrest, and Alienation in the Empire* (Cambridge: Harvard Univ. Press, 1966), chapter 2, and cf. A. J. Festugière, *Personal Religion among the Greeks* (Berkeley and Los Angeles: University of California Press, 1954), chapter 4.

[57]*Republic* 6.496D, 4.433A; Dio Cassius *Roman History* 60.27.4. Note the influence of *Republic* 6.496CD (and also *Epistle* 7.325E and *Phaedo* 89D) in pseudo-Socrates *Epistle* 24, which also speaks of retirement. Cf. J. Sykutris, *Die Briefe des Sokrates und der Sokratiker,* Studien zur Geschichte und Kultur des Altertums 18/2 (Paderborn: Ferdinand Schöningh, 1933), 78-79.

[58]See Hock, *The Social Context of Paul's Ministry* (n. 24 above).

[59]On *euschēmosynē,* see Stobaeus *Anthology* 2.7.7a (2.80,10 Wachsmuth-Hense), 2.7.11e (2.97, 8 W-H) = (*SVF* 3.140, 502; Epictetus *Discourse* 3.22.2 *(aschēmonein).* On self-sufficiency, see A. N. M. Rich, "The Cynic Conception of AUTARKEIA," *Mnemosyne* Ser. 4.9 (1956): 23–29; R. Vischer, *Das einfache Leben: Wort–und motivgeschichtliche Untersuchungen zu einem Wertbegriff der antiken Literatur* (Göttingen: Vandenhoeck & Ruprecht, 1965), 60–87; K. Gaiser, "Das griechische Ideal der Autarkie," *Acta Philologica Aenipontana* 3, ed. R. von Muth (1976): 35-37.

[60]*Epistle to Pancratides* 2 (137,15-16 Hense), cf. 4 (138,15-18 Hense).

[61]*Social Aspects of Early Christianity,* 2d ed., enlarged (Philadelphia: Fortress Press, 1983), 25–27. I have attempted to situate the passage more precisely in the social context, which was informed by philosophical discussion and criticism of philosophers, in *Paul and the Thessalonians,* 95–107.

[62]See, e.g., H. D. Betz, *A Commentary of Paul's Letter to the Churches of Galatia,* Hermeneia (Philadelphia: Fortress Press, 1979), 221–33. To the bibliography on the *topos* provided by Betz should be added P. Marshall, *Enmity in Corinth: Social Conventions in Paul's Relations with the Corinthians,* WUNT Second Series 23 (Tübingen: J. C. B. Mohr [Paul Siebeck], 1987); J. C. Fraisse, *Philia: la notion d'amitié dans la philosophie antique* (Paris: J. Vrin, 1976); and J. M. Rist, "Epicurus on Friendship," *CPh* 75 (1980): 121–29.

too anthropocentric, and that he thought of Christian relationships as determined by God's call and not human virtues.[63] At any rate, he uses a term describing blood relationship to describe a spiritual one. Given the importance Paul attaches to love within the Christian community, it is not unlikely that the similarities to and differences from the discussions of friendship would have been obvious to his readers.

What does stand out is the way Paul introduces his exhortation. The Thessalonians, he says, have no need to be written to about brotherly love, for they have been taught by God to love one another. *Theodidaktoi* ("taught by God") is a Pauline coinage, and provides the reason for Christian love of the community. Paul's use of the word at this point takes on special significance if my suggestion that he has Epicureans in mind has any merit. Friendship was highly valued by the Epicureans, but they were criticized for their utilitarian view of it, viz. that it was prompted by need and was a means to happiness.[64] Stoics, on the contrary, thought of it as a divine gift, springing from nature,[65] and Plutarch, the Platonist, charged the Epicureans with being void of philanthropy and untouched by any spark of the divine.[66] By saying that love is divinely taught, Paul would thus tacitly be sharing Plutarch's criticism of the Epicureans. If one considers *theodidaktos* to be a conscious rejection of something that is *autodidaktos* ("self-taught"), or *adidaktos* ("untaught"), or of someone who is *autourgos tēs philosophias* ("a self-made philosopher"), the criticism becomes more pointed. Such words were frequently applied by themselves or others to philosophers who by reason developed the knowledge that is inherently or potentially in all people.[67] Epicurus above all others fostered the reputation that he was self-taught.[68] But even if it is thought a bit too much to speculate that Paul has Epicurus

---

[63]Thus J. N. Sevenster, "Waarom spreekt Paulus nooit van vrienden en vriendschap?" *NTT* 9 (1954/55): 356-63; see further, idem, *Paul and Seneca,* NovTSup 4 (Leiden: E. J. Brill, 1961), 174–80.
[64]E.g., Cicero *De finibus* 2.82–85.
[65]E.g., Cicero *De amicitia* 19–20, 27; Seneca *Epistle* 9.17. See G. Bohnenblust, "Beitrage zum *Topos Peri Philias,*" (Diss., Berlin, 1905), 7–8, 44.
[66]*That Epicurus Actually Makes a Pleasant Life Impossible* 1098DE.
[67]*Autodidaktos:* Diogenes, according to Stobaeus *Anthology* 4.32.11 (5.782,17–20; Wachsmuth-Hense), cf. 19; Juvenal *Satire* 13.19–22; Maximus of Tyre *Discourse* 10.5 (118,6–119,6 Hobein); 38.1 (438,5ff. Hobein); *adidaktos:* Julian *Orations* 6.183B; 7.209C; Dio Chrysostom *Discourse* 12.42, cf. Plutarch *Table-Talk* 673F; *Reply to Colotes* 1122E; Sextus Empiricus *Against the Professors* 9.96; *autourgos tēs philosophias:* Xenophon *Symposium* 1.5; Dio Chrysostom *Discourse* 1.9, 63 (cf. D. R. Dudley, *A History of Cynicism from Diogenes to the 6th Century* A.D. (London: Methuen, 1967), 150–52. For a rejection of my views and an emphasis on Philo as a source for understanding *theodidaktos,* see C. R. Roetzel, "*Theodidaktoi* and Handwork in Philo and 1 Thessalonians," in *L'Apôtre Paul: Personalité, style et conception,* ed. A. Vanhoye, BETL 73 (Louvain: Peeters, 1986), 324–31.
[68]Cf. Cicero *De finibus* 1.71. The material has been collected by E. Zeller, *Die Philosophie der Griechen,* 5th ed. (reprint, Darmstadt: Wissenschaftliche Buchgesellschaft, 1963), 3.1.374 n. 2, and discussed by A. J. Festugière, *Epicurus and His Gods* (Cambridge, Mass.: Harvard Univ. Press, 1956), 34.

or Epicureans in mind, his claim that Christians are taught by God to love one another is of a piece with the preceding theological motivations for Christian ethics.[69]

The last pericope to which I draw attention, 4:13-18, is of a different character. A major Pauline eschatological passage, it would appear to justify Helmut Koester's assessment, made in his discussion of the genre of the epistle: "In the case of the 'instructions' it is still possible to cite the philosophical and moral epistle as an analogy or parallel; but no analogies exist in letters of any kind for the eschatological admonitions which are found in 1 Thessalonians 4:13—5:11."[70] Koester is, of course, correct so far as the content of the eschatological material is concerned. But when it is observed that the eschatological statements function to comfort Paul's readers (4:18; 5:11), the absoluteness of his claim must be called into question. Paul is not providing eschatological instruction to inform his readers, but to console those who were grieving. In doing so, Paul's direction exhibits a number of similarities to themes found in the letter of consolation, a well known epistolary genre in antiquity.[71] To the Church Fathers, who knew the classical genres, this section of the letter appeared close to a consolatory epistle.[72]

Consolation was conceived of as belonging to paraenesis,[73] and the letter of consolation was discussed in epistolographic handbooks in terms that reflected its paraenetic character.[74] Philosophers, in particular, engaged in

---

[69]See Koester, "1 Thessalonians" (n. 4 above), 39, who draws attention to Philo. I disagree with him that *theodidaktoi* "emphasizes that the recipients are not dependent on the writer's instructions." There is an emphasis in the use of the term, but it is better explained in light of the emphasis in 4:1-8 as well as the traditions Paul uses here. Furthermore, the stress in chapters 1 and 2 on Paul as God's spokesman makes a distinction between God's word and aul's artificial. The formulation, "you have no need to have any one write you, for you yourselves have been taught by God," functions as a reminder of that instruction. Cf. 4:11, "as we charged you," in the same pericope, and 5:1-2, "you have no need to have anything written to you, for you yourselves know well," the latter of which must also refer to Paul's earlier insrucin

[70]"1 Thessalonians" (n. 4 above), 39.

[71]On consolation literature, see R. Kassel, *Untersuchungen zur griechischen und römischen Konsolationsliteratur* (Munich: C. H. Beck, 1958); R. C. Gregg, *Consolation Philosophy: Greek and Christian Paideia in Basil and the Two Gregories* (Cambridge, Mass./Philadelphia, Penn.: Patristic Foundation, 1975); Yves-Marie Duval, "Formes profanes et formes bibliques dans les oraisons funèbres de saint Ambrose," in *Christianisme et formes littéraires de l'antiquité tardive en occident,* Fondation Hardt, Entretiens 23 (Vandoeuvres/Genève, 1977), 235–301 (for bibliography).

[72]This appears, for example, from the way in which Theodoret (*In epistolam primam ad Thessalonicences commentarius* [PG 82.648]) comments on the passage. See also Gregg, *Consolation Philosophy,* 155–56.

[73]Cf. Theon *Progymnasmata* 3.117 Spengel, for whom consolation, judging by the length of his treatment, is a major example of protreptic. Protreptic and paraenesis were not yet distinguished at this time. See also the instruction of pseudo-Menander *Peri Epideiktikōn* 3.423–24 Spengel (= 160–64 Russell-Wilson), that the speech should begin with what is well known and end with an exhortation.

[74]Note the sample provided by pseudo-Demetrius *Epistolary Types* 5 (Malherbe, *Ancient Epistolary*

consolation in speeches, tractates, and letters.[75] These consolations, which have much in common with epitaphs, illustrate the consolatory character of 1 Thessalonians 4:13-18. For example, they minimize death by making it resemble sleep.[76] They call for grief to cease,[77] sometimes at the very beginning of the consolation,[78] which may be followed by recalling a teacher's words.[79] They complain that the deceased had been snatched away by death,[80] but take comfort in the hope that he is now dwelling with the gods and virtuous persons of the past,[81] and that he will be joined by those who are still alive,[82] over whom he has no advantage.[83]

In 4:13-18 Paul offers comfort to the Thessalonians who were grieving. He begins with their grief for those who had fallen asleep (v. 13), then uses various traditions to provide the reason ("for," v. 14) why they should not grieve, and on that basis ("therefore") directs them to comfort one another (v. 18). That what he says is similar to the consolatory themes I have identified

---

Theorists, 35):

> Since I happened not to be present to comfort *(parakalein)* you, I decided to do so by letter. Bear, then, what has happened as lightly as you can, and exhort yourself just as you would exhort someone else *(kathos allō parēnesas sautō paraineson)*. For you know *(epistasai)* that reason will make it easier for you to be relieved of your grief with the passage of time.

Cf. also Seneca *Epistle* 99.32, "These words I have written to you, not with the idea that you should expect a cure from me at such a late date—for it is clear to me that you have told yourself everything you will read in my letter. . ."

[75]See Dio Chrysostom *Discourses* 27.7–9; 28; 30; Plutarch *On Superstition* 168C; Julian *Oration* 7.223BC. Cf. K. Buresch, "Consolationum a graecis romanisque scriptarum historia critica" (Diss. Leipzig, 1886), 38.

[76]Cicero *Tusculan Disputations* 1.38.92; Plutarch *A Letter of Condolence to Apollonius* 107DEF. See I. Herkenrath, *Studien zu den griechischen Grabschriften* (Feldkirch, 1896), 21, 18; R. Lattimore, *Themes in Greek and Latin Epitaphs* (Urbana: Univ. of Illinois, 1962), 82–83; *Lucretius, Bk. III*, ed. and comm. E. J. Kenney (Cambridge, Mass: Cambridge Univ. Press, 1971), 207; B. P. Wallach, *Lucretius and Diatribe against the Fear of Death: De Rerum Natura* (Leiden: E. J. Brill, 1976), 59–61.

[77]Cf. G. Kaibel, *Epigrammata Graeca ex lapidibus contecta* (Berlin: G. Reimer, 1878), 345,3–4; Lattimore, *Themes in Greek and Latin Epitaphs*, 218, cf. 253 n. 299. For *mē lypēs* ("do not sorrow") and similar expressions on tombstones, see F. Preisigke, *Sammelbuch griechischer Urkunden aus Agypten* (Strassburg: K. J. Trubner, 1915), 3514, 3515, 3516, 5715, 5751, etc. These inscriptions are addressed to the deceased, but they would have a consolatory effect on the reader.

[78]E.g., Seneca *To Marcia on Consolation* 6.1–2.

[79]E.g., pseudo-Socrates *Epistle* 21.1–2; cf. Lucian *Nigrinus* 7.

[80]Cf. Plutarch *A Letter of Condolence to Apollonius* 117BC *(anarpazō, exarpazō,* "snatch up," "snatch away"). For *rapio* see Horace *Odes* 2.17.5; 4.2.21; Pliny *Natural History* 7.46; Ovid *Ex Ponto* 4.11.5 (in a consolation). For *eripio*, see Q. Curtius *History of Alexander* 10.5.10; Ammianus Marcellinus 30.5.18. On the other hand, *eripio* is also used for snatching someone from death, e.g., Cicero *Verrine Orations* 2.6.12; *On Divination* 2.25.

[81]Note the instruction of pseudo-Menander *Peri Epideiktikōn* 3.414,16–17; 3.421,16–17; Spengel (= 162, 176; Russell-Wilson); and for the practice, see Seneca *To Marcia on Consolation* 25.1; 26.3. Cf. Gregg, *Consolation Philosophy*, 180–81, 204, 208–9.

[82]Seneca *To Marcia on Consolation* 19.

[83]Plutarch *A Letter of Condolence to Apollonius* 113D.

would seem to be obvious, but there are also some obvious differences.[84] Whereas the consolations urge that reason limit the grief lest it become immoderate, for Paul it is the Christian hope, based on Christ's resurrection and coming, that makes comfort possible.[85] The traditions that he uses do not have their origin in the consolations, but the way they are made to function is not foreign to those consolations.

Conclusion

I have attempted to identify certain hortatory devices and terms used by Paul in writing to people who were most likely familiar with them. Paul's use of them demonstrates his continuity with the hortatory tradition, and reflects his pastoral method. At the same time, his use of the traditional hortatory material is marked by profound change as he reshapes the material to express his experience of God working in him, or sresses the theological and religious dimensions of ethics, or uses traditional Christian material to address issues also of concern to pagan consolers.

---

[84]One should do justice to Paul's emphasis that Christians will enjoy association with one another and the Lord in the eschaton (cf. "together with them" and "shall always be with the Lord" in 4:17 and "with him" in 5:11, and "God will bring with him" in 4:14). Paul's use of *harpazō* ("snatch") in v. 17, when seen in this context, represents a neat twist: Whereas the word usually denoted the separation from the living, Paul uses it to describe a snatching to association with the Lord and other Christians.

[85]Cf. Theodoret: We do not use *oikeioi logismoi* ("proper arguments"), but our teaching is derived from the word of the Lord (PG 82:648).

5

Paul
Hellenistic Philosopher
or Christian Pastor?

Modern interpreters have operated on the assumption that, like Tennyson's Ulysses, Paul was part of all that he had met, and that to understand him properly, it is necessary to view him in the cultural context in which he lived. As one might expect of him, however, Paul makes it difficult to decide precisely which context, the Jewish or the Greek, we should examine in order to understand his letters better. Born in Tarsus, an important hellenistic university city of the day, but educated on both the secondary and tertiary levels in Jerusalem (Acts 22:3), he was exposed to both, and interpreters have tended to view him from either a Greek or a Jewish perspective.[1] That Paul claims to have become all things to all people in order to save some (1 Cor. 9:19-23) indicates that he was aware of the need to adapt to particular contexts in which he found himself, and should caution us not to force everything he said or did into one mold. Here I wish to comment on the Greco-Roman side of Paul, without thereby implying that it offers us the keys to unlock all the mysteries surrounding this enigmatic figure.

Modern scholarship was not the first to discover Paul's indebtedness to Greek culture. His letters, even on a superficial level, have many affinities with the popular philosophy of his day, especially as it was represented by Stoicism and Cynicism. It does not surprise us that Tertullian, who was on the side of Jerusalem rather than Athens, referred to Seneca, the Stoic philosopher who served as chaplain to Nero, as "frequently our own."[2] Shortly afterward, an anonymous Christian, impressed by the similarities he saw between Paul and Seneca, composed a correspondence that was supposed

---

[1]The evidence is discussed by W. C. van Unnik, *Tarsus or Jerusalem: The City of Paul's Youth*, trans. G. Ogg (London: Epworth, 1962).
[2]Tertullian *De anima* 20.

to have taken place between the two.[3] No wonder, then, that Jerome, one hundred and fifty years after Tertullian, dropped Tertullian's qualifying "frequently," and referred to the Stoic simply as "our own Seneca."[4]

During the last hundred years, New Testament scholars have shown that many aspects of Paul's life and letters are illuminated when they are examined in the light of Greco-Roman culture. There can no longer be any doubt that Paul was thoroughly familiar with the teaching, methods of operation, and style of argumentation of the philosophers of the period, all of which he adopted and adapted to his own purposes. This is not to argue that he was a technical philosopher; neither were his philosophical contemporaries. The philosophers with whom Paul should be compared were not metaphysicians who specialized in systematizing abstractions, but, like Paul, were preachers and teachers who saw their main goal to be the reformation of the lives of people they encountered in a variety of contexts, ranging from the imperial court and the salons of the rich to the street corners.[5]

The points of similarity between Paul and his philosophic competitors may be stressed to the point that he is viewed as a type of hellenistic philosopher. In what follows I propose to note some of the similarities, but then to stress the function to which Paul put what he had received from the moral philosophers. That function is essentially pastoral, and Paul's adoption, and sometimes adaptation, of the philosophical tradition, reveal to us his awareness of the philosophic pastoral methods current in his day. By drawing attention to this function, I wish to sharpen the perspective from which the moral-philosophical material in Paul's letters is to be viewed. I select examples from his practice in establishing and shaping Christian communities, and the ways in which he adapted accepted means of persuasion to nurture his churches.[6]

---

[3]*New Testament Apocrypha,* ed. E. Hennecke and W. Schneemelcher (Philadelphia: Westminster Press, 1965), 2.133–41. Recent books on the correspondence are reviewed by Aldo Moda, "Seneca e il cristianesimo," *Henoch* 5 (1983): 93–109.

[4]Jerome *Against Jovinian* 1.49.

[5]See A. J. Malherbe, "Hellenistic Moralists and the New Testament," in *ANRW* 2.26 (forthcoming). Still classic discussions are L. Friedlaender, *Roman Life and Manners under the Early Empire,* trans. J. H. Freese (London: Routledge, n. d.), 3.214–18, and S. Dill, *Roman Society from Nero to Marcus Aurelius,* 2d ed. (London: Macmillan, 1905), 289–440. For a collection of texts illustrating the New Testament's indebtedness to the Greco-Roman moral philosophers, see Malherbe, *Moral Exhortation: A Greco-Roman Sourcebook,* Library of Early Christianity 4 (Philadelphia: Westminster Press, 1986).

[6]I have treated the subject at greater length in *Paul and the Thessalonians: The Philosophic Tradition of Pastoral Care* (Philadelphia: Fortress Press, 1987). See also my contribution, "New Testament (Traditions and Theology of Care)," in the *Dictionary of Pastoral Care and Counseling,* ed. R. J. Hunter et al. (Nashville: Abingdon Press, forthcoming).

The Founder of Churches

In his letters, Paul frequently refers to his initial preaching when he founded churches, and to the reception of his message.[7] Equally striking are his references to himself as an example which had either been followed by his converts, of which he reminds his readers, or which he offers for emulation.[8] In thus placing his own person at the very center of his teaching, Paul followed a procedure recommended by philosophers. Seneca illustrates the thinking in advice he gives to his friend Lucilius:

"Cherish some man of high character, and keep him ever before your eyes, living as if he were watching you, and ordering all your actions as if he beheld them." Such, my dear Lucilius, is the counsel of Epicurus; he has quite properly given us a guardian and attendant. We can get rid of most sins, if we have a witness who stands near us when we are likely to go wrong. The soul should have someone to respect—one by whose authority it may make even its inner shrine more hallowed. Happy is the man who can make others better, not merely when he is in their company, but even when he is in their thoughts! One who can so revere another, will soon be himself worthy of reverence. Choose therefore a Cato; or, if Cato seems too severe a model, choose some Laelius, a gentler spirit. Choose a master whose life, conversation, and soul-expressing face have satisfied you; picture him always to yourself as your protector and your pattern. For we must indeed have someone according to whom we may regulate our characters.[9]

Seneca has in mind more than an exemplification of moral virtues that are to be imitated; he is equally interested in the forming of a relationship which would contribute to a sense of security and the continuing spiritual cultivation of the imitator.

The context in which Paul taught was totally different from Nero's court, yet he followed the practice recommended by Seneca. As a maker of tents, Paul plied his trade in a workshop, probably within the setting of a household of artisans, and there offered his practice as an example to be imitated (cf. 2 Thess. 3:6-10). Some philosophers, too, were active in workshops, and took the opportunity to demonstrate their teaching by their practice. Musonius Rufus, another contemporary of Paul, worked the land during his exile, and illustrates how manual labor could be viewed by teachers like himself. He thought a philosopher's students would be benefited "by seeing him at work in the fields, demonstrating by his own labor the lesson which philosophy inculcates-that one should endure hardships, and suffer the pains of labor

---

[7] E.g., 1 Cor. 2:1-5; 3:6, 10; 4:15; 2 Cor. 1:18-25.; Gal. 4:12-15; Phil. 4:1-3; 1 Thess. 1:9—2:13.
[8] Cf. 1 Cor. 4:16; 11:1; Gal. 4:12; Phil. 3:17; 1 Thess. 1:6; 2 Thess. 3:7-9. See W. P. de Boer, *The Imitation of Paul: An Exegetical Study* (Kampen: Kok, 1962), and, for background to the New Testament use of personal examples, B. Fiore, S. J., *The Function of Personal Example in the Socratic and Pastoral Epistles,* AnBib 105 (Rome: Biblical Institute Press, 1986).
[9] Seneca *Epistle* 11.8-10.

with his own body, rather than depend on another for sustenance."[10] Paul, too, thought of manual labor as a hardship (cf. 1 Cor. 4:12), and also required that his converts work with their hands in order to be economically independent (cf. 1 Thess. 4:9-12). Recent investigation has demonstrated that his practice was informed by this Greek context rather than rabbinic custom.[11]

There are, however, sufficient differences between Paul and the philosophers to preclude our viewing him as a slavish, unreflective follower of current practice.[12] While some of the philosophers looked to the practice as an ideal, few actually followed it. Paul not only followed it, but his self-support was an integral part of his understanding of his apostleship. Called by God to be an apostle, he had no other choice than to heed the call, but he exercised his freedom in the manner in which he chose to preach: exultantly to offer the gospel free of charge (1 Cor. 9:15-19). Furthermore, in language one does not find in the philosophers, he describes his manual labor as a demonstration of his self-giving and love for his converts (2 Cor. 11:7-11; cf. 1 Thess. 2:9).

Paul was also more confident than the philosophers when he called on his converts to imitate him, and the nature of that confidence still further distinguishes him from them. Paul did not demand that his converts look to him as a paradigm of what one might accomplish through one's own effort, as the philosophers did. Writing to the Thessalonians, he reminds them of their initial encounter:

> our gospel came to you not only in word, but also in power and in the Holy Spirit and with full conviction. You know what kind of men we proved to be among you for your sake. And you became imitators of us and of the Lord, for you received the word in much affliction, with joy inspired by the Holy Spirit (1 Thess. 1:5-6).

Philosophers would have drawn attention to their own words and deeds; Paul draws attention to the gospel and the divine role in their conversion. It is only as divine power is exhibited in Paul's ministry that he becomes an example that is to be followed. Finally, Paul differs from the philosophers in his goal to form communities of believers rather than only bring about change in individuals. The communal dimension of self-support is evident in ensuring that within the community some are not burdened with the responsibility to support others (1 Thess. 2:9; cf. 2 Thess. 3:6-10), and that, when Christians in brotherly love work so as not to be dependent on others, they have the respect of outsiders (1 Thess. 4:9-12).

---

[10]Musonius Rufus *Fragment* 11.

[11]The subject has been discussed most fully by R. F. Hock, *The Social Context of Paul's Ministry: Tentmaking and Discipleship* (Philadelphia: Fortress Press, 1980).

[12]For further details, see A. J. Malherbe, "Exhortation in First Thessalonians," *NovT* 25 (1983): 238–56 (= 46–49 in this volume).

When he first formed churches, therefore, Paul made use of elements from the Greco-Roman philosophical moral tradition, but adapted them to express his theological understanding of his enterprise and to form communities of believers.

The Nurturer of Churches

By the first century A.D., moral philosophers had developed an extensive system of pastoral care which aimed, through character education, at the attainment of virtue and happiness. Paul made use of this tradition as he nurtured the churches he established. His first letter to the Thessalonians illustrates clearly this indebtedness as well as his modification of the tradition.

In 1 Thessalonians 2:1-12, Paul reminds his readers of his pastoral care when he had been with them, and does so in terms used in descriptions of the ideal philosopher. The items that he chooses to mention and the antithetic style he adopts find their counterparts in such descriptions as the one in Dio Chrysostom:

> But to find a man who with purity and without guile speaks with a philosopher's boldness, not for the sake of glory, nor making false pretensions for the sake of gain, but who stands ready out of good will and concern for his fellowman, if need be, to submit to ridicule and the uproar of the mob—to find such a man is not easy, but rather the good fortune of a very lucky city, so great is the dearth of noble, independent souls, and such the abundance of flatterers, charlatans and sophists. In my own case I feel that I have chosen that role, not of my own volition, but by the will of some deity. For when divine providence is at work for men, the gods provide, not only good counsellors who need no urging, but also words that are appropriate and profitable to the listener.[13]

But, once again, as there are similarities between Paul and such philosophers as Dio, so are there differences.

Basic to the philosophers' approach was the frankness with which they laid bare the shortcomings of their listeners. Convinced of their own moral attainment, which gave them the right, indeed the responsibility, to correct others, they were fearless in their denunciation of moral error. When they were opposed or reviled, they turned their maltreatment into self-commendation: their behavior in the face of opposition exhibited their refusal to give quarter to any sinner, and demonstrated their courage in continuing in their task. Paul uses the same technical language in describing his original preaching in Thessalonica: "though we had already suffered and been shamefully treated

---

[13]Dio Chrysostom *Discourse* 32.11–12. For a detailed discussion of the passage, see A. J. Malherbe, " 'Gentle as a Nurse': The Cynic Background to 1 Thess. 2," *NovT* 12 (1970): 203–17 (= 35–48 in this volume).

at Philippi, as you know, we waxed bold in our God to speak to you the gospel of God in the face of great opposition" (2:2). Here there is nothing of self-attainment, rather an awareness of God's power. What Paul engaged in was not a philosophical analysis of the human condition, but preaching God's gospel, and his boldness did not derive from his own moral freedom, but was engendered by God.

That Paul consciously worked with the philosophical traditions on the boldness of speech also appears from his use of the image of a wetnurse: "though we might have made demands as apostles of Christ, yet we were gentle among you, like a nurse suckling her own children" (2:6-7). In the first century, some Cynics, viewing the human condition as almost irredeemable, held that only the severest speech might have a salutary effect, and therefore flayed their audiences mercilessly. In response, philosophers of milder mien insisted that speakers should adapt their speech to the emotional conditions of their listeners, as nurses did: "When children fall down," according to Plutarch, "the nurses do not rush up to berate them, but pick them up, wash them, and straighten their clothes, and after all this is done, then rebuke and punish them."[14] Paul uses the same image, but again distances himself from philosophers like Plutarch by renouncing personal authority in pastoral care, and stating his reason for his demeanor: "So, crooning over you, we were ready to share with you not only the gospel of God but also our own selves, because you had become very dear to us" (2:8).

The philosophers' concern to adapt their teaching to the conditions of their listeners is further illustrated by Dio Chrysostom:

> But as for himself, the man of whom I speak will strive to preserve his individuality in seemly fashion and with steadfastness, never deserting his post of duty, but always honoring and promoting virtue and prudence and trying to lead men to them, on some occasions persuading and exhorting them, on others reviling and reproaching them ... sometimes taking an individual aside privately, at other times admonishing them in groups every time he finds a proper occasion, with gentle words at times, at others harsh.[15]

Paul followed the same method of modulating his instruction according to individual needs: "you know how, like a father with his children, we exhorted each individual one of you and charged you to lead a life worthy of God, who calls you into his own kingdom and glory" (2:11). Unlike Dio, Paul is not concerned with virtue and prudence, nor does he engage in abuse and reproach. Neither does he share Dio's fear that his individuality or integrity

---

[14]Plutarch *How to Tell a Flatterer from a Friend* 69BC.
[15]Dio Chrysostom *Discourse* 77/78.38. The most comprehensive treatment of ancient psychagogy is still P. Rabbow, *Seelenführung: Methodik der Exerzitien in der Antike* (Munich: Kösel-Verlag, 1954).

might be compromised, and the eschatological dimension that dominates his work is totally foreign to the philosopher. Nevertheless, the method Paul used was inherited from the philosophers, and he made it part of his own pastoral practice, only now it was informed by a different perception of self and task.

The rapid spread of Christianity should not be taken to mean that the new faith provided a haven from the turmoils of life. On the contrary, as 1 Thessalonians shows, conversion resulted in psychological trauma, discouragement, grief, uncertainty about the implications of the new faith for everyday life, and dislocation from the larger society. These conditions were exacerbated by the shortness of the periods during which Paul remained with his new converts. That the itinerant preacher would list as his chief apostolic hardship "the daily pressure upon me of my anxiety for all the churches" (2 Cor. 11:28) does not, then, surprise us.[16]

Paul prepared his converts for the hardships they would endure, and in this respect shared some things with Seneca. Seneca often writes on the proper, philosophic attitude toward hardships. He reflects two standard arguments from the long tradition of consolation literature.

> What, have you only at this moment learned that death is hanging over your head, at this moment exile, at this moment grief? You were born to these perils. Let us think of everything that can happen as something which will happen.[17]

They will happen because fate so decrees, and we can overcome them by anticipating them.[18] Paul evidently followed this advice, for he had told the Thessalonians that they should not be moved by their afflictions: "You yourselves know that this is to be our lot. For when we were with you, we told you beforehand that we were to suffer affliction; just as it has come to pass, and as you know" (3:3-4). Paul, of course, does not ascribe their experiences to impersonal fate; it is God who is in charge of their ultimate destiny, that is, their salvation through the Lord Jesus Christ (5:9). Nor does he desire Stoic impassivity; in fact, he shares their distress and affliction (3:7). What he does share with Seneca is a particular method of pastoral care.

Paul's Continuing Interest

Paul continued the nurture of his churches when he was separated from them. He accomplished this nurture by using intermediaries through whom

---

[16]On the Pauline hardships and the Greco-Roman background of their description and function, see J. T. Fitzgerald, *Cracks in an Earthen Vessel: An Examination of the Catalogues of Hardships in the Corinthian Correspondence*, SBLDS 99 (Atlanta: Scholars Press, 1988).
[17]Seneca *Epistle* 24.15.
[18]Seneca *Epistle* 91.4.

he maintained contact with the novices in the faith who might otherwise have felt abandoned, and through his letters. A letter was described in antiquity as one half of a dialogue, and was regarded as a substitute for one's presence.[19] Paul was familiar with ancient epistolary theory, especially with its requirement that the style of a letter be appropriate to the occasion and circumstance it addressed.[20] Recent research has demonstrated that Paul with sophistication and originality appropriated philosophical means of persuasion in his own pastoral care.[21] To illustrate how he did so, I again turn to 1 Thessalonians.

As to style, 1 Thessalonians is a paraenetic letter.[22] Paraenesis was a style of exhortation used to influence conduct rather than teach something new. It was, accordingly, used widely by moral philosophers who sought to modify the conduct of their audiences. Paraenesis stressed what was traditional, self-evidently good, and generally applicable. The stylistic devices used therefore sought to confirm the audience or readers in what they already knew by reminding them of it, complimenting them on what they had already accomplished and encouraging them to continue their practice, and offering models of virtue to be imitated. The assumption governing paraenesis was that a friendly relationship, frequently described as that between a father and his children, existed between the exhorter and the exhorted, which would set the tone and justify the advice.

Paul uses this style throughout 1 Thessalonians. He repeatedly impresses his readers with what they already know (1:5; 2:1-2, 5, 11; 3:3-4; 4:2; 5:2), and explicitly calls them to remembrance (2:9; 3:6). In paraenetic style he even says that there is really no need to write to them (4:9; 5:1), but compliments them for already doing what they should, and encourages them to do so more and more (4:1, 10; 5:11). He refers to the examples of the Judean churches (2:14) and the Thessalonians themselves (1:7), and claims that they had already become imitators of himself (1:6). The entire autobiographical sketch in the first three chapters functions as a paraenetic reminder and is paradigmatic. He uses the images of nurse (2:7), father (2:11), and orphan (2:17; RSV, "bereft") to describe his warm relationship with them, and in highly affective

---

[19]For ancient views of letters and letter writing, see A. J. Malherbe, *Ancient Epistolary Theorists,* SBLSBS 19 (Atlanta: Scholars Press, 1988).
[20]The most comprehensive discussion is by S. K. Stowers, *Letter Writing in Greco-Roman Antiquity,* Library of Early Christianity 5 (Philadelphia: Westminster Press, 1986). See also, J. L. White, *Light from Ancient Letters* (Philadelphia: Fortress Press, 1986).
[21]See, for example, S. K. Stowers, *The Diatribe and Paul's Letter to the Romans,* SBLDS 57 (Chico, Calif.: Scholars Press, 1981).
[22]The subject is treated extensively in A. J. Malherbe, "First Thessalonians as a Paraenetic Letter," presented to the SBL Seminar on Paul, 1972, and incorporated in "Hellenistic Moralists and the New Testament" (n. 5 above), on which L. G. Perdue, "Paraenesis and the Epistle of James," *ZNW* 72 (1981): 242–46, and D. W. Palmer, "Thanksgiving, Self-defence, and Exhortation in 1 Thessalonians 1–3," *Colloquium* [Australia] 14 (1981): 23–31, are dependent.

language expresses his concern for and identification with them in their tribulations (2:17—3:10).

Paul's use of these stylistic features makes 1 Thessalonians one of the best examples of ancient paraenetic letters. To appreciate Paul's genius, however, it is necessary to move beyond matters of style to the function of the letter, which is essentially pastoral. Paul wrote to a small group of neophyte Christians who were in "tribulation," that is, they were experiencing difficulties in redefining themselves socially, were uncertain about details of the Christian life, and felt abandoned by Paul and isolated in the world. Paul uses the paraenetic style to build their confidence.

His affective language and the images used to describe himself express his sense of the bond he feels with them. His repeated use of the paraenetic "as you know" makes the point that, despite their newness in the faith, they already are possessors of Christian tradition, and his encouragement to continue in what they are doing draws attention to their achievement rather than their shortcomings. As he had modulated his nurture when he was with them, so does he in the letter, where he exhorts (2:12; 4:10), charges (2:12; 4:6), commands (4:2, 11), and beseeches (5:12) them, and offers a basis for their consolation (4:18; 5:11). Paul has clearly used the paraenetic style to create the first Christian pastoral letter, which also happens to be the earliest piece of Christian literature we possess.

The Nurturing Church

Paul thought that, in addition to his own efforts, his congregations' concern for each member was necessary to the nurture of the church. It is striking how a communal concern pervades a letter like 1 Thessalonians. Every item of conduct that Paul takes up in the latter half of the letter is communal in nature. Transgression in marriage is described as fraud of a Christian brother (4:6), social responsibility is inculcated in a context provided by brotherly love (4:9–12), and Paul provides information on the parousia so that the grieving Thessalonians might comfort each other (4:13–18). He then becomes more explicit:

> Therefore, exhort and build one another up, one on one, as indeed you are doing. But we beseech you, brethren, to respect those who labor among you, who care for you in the Lord, and admonish you, and to esteem them very highly in love because of their work. Be at peace among yourselves. And we exhort you, brethren, admonish the disorderly, comfort the discouraged, help the weak, be patient with all. Beware lest someone repays evil with evil; rather, seek each other's good and that of all.[23]

---

[23] 1 Thess. 5:11-15.

A close comparison of the pastoral care Paul requires of the Thessalonians with his own reveals that theirs is to be an extension of his.

This description of communal soul-care has parallels among certain philosophers. The philosophers who have so far come under consideration in this essay were concerned with individuals rather than communities, but the Epicureans formed communities that in many respects were similar to Christian congregations.[24] They were governed by detailed instructions on how admonition within the community was to be given and received.[25] Recipients of the admonitions were instructed on how to cultivate a proper disposition toward those who did the admonishing, to have the desire to be improved, and on the importance of maintaining harmony. Those delivering the admonition were directed to speak without bitterness, and always to have the goal of benefiting others by taking into consideration the different natures of people and adjusting their admonition accordingly, fully aware that excessive sharpness might result in retaliation.

Paul's directions stress the same elements. His understanding of the Thessalonian community, however, differs radically from the Epicureans' understanding of theirs, and this understanding of Paul's places his comments on the church's pastoral care in a different light. The church of the Thessalonians is "in God" (1:1), that is, it was created by God, who calls them "into his own kingdom and glory" (2:12). It is an eschatological community which Paul hopes he will boast of when Christ returns (2:19), and it will not be destroyed by death (3:11-13; 4:14-15, 17). In the letter, this language, which distinguishes Christians from the Epicureans, "reinforces the sense of uniqueness and solidarity of the community."[26]

Conclusion

I return to the question in the title of this chapter: Was Paul a hellenistic philosopher or a Christian pastor? It may well be the case that, when Paul is viewed as a theologian, the hellenistic elements do not lie at the center of his thinking but provide the means by which he conducts his argument. But when he and others discuss his ministry, it is extraordinary to what degree

---

[24]Although overstated, much of the material adduced by N. W. De Witt, *St. Paul and Epicurus* (Minneapolis: Univ. of Minnesota, 1964), is relevant.

[25]See N. W. De Witt, "Organization and Procedure in Epicurean Groups," *CPh* 31 (1936): 205–11, and the qualifications by M. Gigante, "Philodème: Sur la liberté de parole," *Actes du VIIIe Congrès, Assoc. Guillaume Budé* (Paris, 1969): 196–217. The primary source discussed is the work on frankness by Philodemus: see *Philodemus Peri Parrēsias*, ed. A. Olivieri (Leipzig: B. G. Teubner, 1914).

[26]W. A. Meeks, "Social Functions of Apocalyptic Language in Pauline Christianity," in *Apocalypticism in the Mediterranean World and the Near East*, ed. D. Hellholm (Tübingen: J. C. B. Mohr [Paul Siebeck], 1983): 694.

the categories and language are derived from the Greeks.[27] The same is also true when Paul is viewed as pastor. Paul is so familiar with the rich Greek traditions of pastoral care, and uses them in so unstudied a fashion, that it would be wrong to think that he only superficially mined the lode for his own purposes. He is more consistent and unconscious in his appropriation of the pastoral tradition than most of his pagan contemporaries. Like Ulysses, he had in fact become part of what he had met. At the same time, his apostolic self-understanding and theology so completely informed his pastoral care that the antithesis in the title is false. As to his method of pastoral care, Paul is at once hellenistic and Christian.

---

[27]See, e.g., H. D. Betz, *Der Apostel Paulus und die sokratische Tradition: Eine Exegetische Untersuchung zu seiner Apologie 2 Korinther 10–13,* BHT 45 (Tübingen: J. C. B. Mohr [Paul Siebeck], 1972); A. J. Malherbe, "Antisthenes and Odysseus, and Paul at War," *HTR* 76 (1983): 143–73 (=91–119 in this volume).

6

The Beasts at
Ephesus

Paul's statement in 1 Corinthians 15:32, that he had fought with beasts at Ephesus has long been a notorious *crux interpretum*. *Ethēriomachēsa* ("I fought with beasts") can be understood in either a literal or figurative sense.[1] When taken literally, the expression is usually thought to refer to a struggle with wild animals in the arena at Ephesus.[2] When understood figuratively, the expression is most frequently understood to refer to Paul's battle with his opponents at Ephesus.[3]

There are problems in connection with both interpretations, as the extensive literature dealing with the verse shows. One of the objections to taking *ethēriomachēsa* figuratively is that, if Paul is here referring to his struggle with opponents of his ministry, he is using a very unusual expression for what was to him a very usual experience. Despite the fact that the figurative use elsewhere is not unknown, such a use of the verb without any further qualification sounds unusual.[4] Nevertheless, the figurative understanding has

---

[1]See the summary of the issues by Robert E. Osborne, "Paul and the Wild Beasts," *JBL* 85 (1966): 225–28. For the literal understanding, see W. Michaelis, *Die Datierung des Philipperbriefes* (Gütersloh: Bertelsmann, 1933), 44–49; for the figurative meaning, see J. Schmid, *Zeit und Ort der paulinischen Gefangenschaftsbriefe* (Freiburg: Herder, 1931), 38.

[2]For literal fighting with beasts, see Diodorus Siculus *Library of History* 3.43.7; Josephus *The Jewish War* 7.38. If *ei ... ethēriomachēsa* ("if ... I fought with beasts") is taken as a contrary to fact condition (e.g., by Michaelis, *Die Datierung*, 44–49), Paul is referring only to the possibility of his fighting with wild beasts. Such a reading might suggest that he was imprisoned in Ephesus and that he was in danger of being thrown to the beasts. Cf. G. S. Duncan, *St. Paul's Ephesian Ministry: A Reconstruction* (New York: Charles Scribner's Sons, 1930), 126–31.

[3]The passages most frequently referred to for the figurative meaning are Ignatius *Romans* 5.1; Appian *The Civil Wars* 2.61; Philo *Moses* 1.43-44. Schmid, *Zeit und Ort*, 59 n. 5, adds PRylands 1.15,7; Vettius Valens *Anthology* 2.40 (resp. 129,33 and 130,21 in Kroll), and Plutarch *Can Virtue be Taught?* 439.

[4]Thus Schmid, *Zeit und Ort*, 41; J. Weiss, *Der erste Korintherbrief*, KEK 5 (Göttingen: Vandenhoeck & Ruprecht, 1910), 365; C. R. Bowen, "I Fought with Beasts at Ephesus," *JBL* 42 (1923): 66–67, "when Paul uses the term without explanation, I submit that these simple words could not have been understood otherwise than literally by the readers at Corinth ... It is true that ancient authors sometimes compare wild men with wild beasts, but there is no evidence (outside the words we are considering) that *thēriomachein* without explanation was ever used as such a figure ... The verb had really no other use than the specific reference to the combats in the arena."

generally prevailed because of the problems a literal interpretation would raise for Paul's standing as a Roman citizen. Roman citizens might in serious cases be so condemned, but then lost their citizenship. Paul's later appeal to Caesar (Acts 25:11) would indicate that he was still a citizen at that time and that he had therefore not been thrown to the beasts.

I am interested in determining whether the idea of fighting with beasts in a figurative sense is indeed as unusual as has been maintained. Whereas earlier discussions have centered mostly on the implications of Roman law for the interpretation of the passage and on the historical circumstances of Paul's work in Ephesus, I will examine literary evidence that has not been brought into the discussion.

Diatribe Style

Commentators on 1 Corinthians 15:29-34 have noted in passing that some characteristics of the diatribe, used especially by Cynics and Stoics, are found in this passage. Closer examination of this section in which *ethēriomachēsa* appears reveals that the language and style of the diatribe are concentrated here to an unusually high degree.

1. The style is simple, like that of the diatribe.[5] The sentences are short and simply constructed. They are similar in construction, are of substantially equal length, and are paratactic in nature with almost no connectives. They are frequently in the form of rhetorical questions and sometimes make use of transitional formulae such as *epei ti* ("otherwise," v. 29) and *ti kai hēmeis* ("and why are we?" v. 30) which are common in the diatribe.[6]

2. Imperatives are used as in the diatribe. The hortatory subjunctive (v. 32) is used with the force of the ironic imperative so much loved in the diatribe.[7] Serious imperatives (*mē planāsthe* ["do not be deceived"], v. 33; *eknēpsate* ["come to your right mind"], v. 34) of verbs common in the diatribe are placed at the end of the unit where they would be found in the diatribe.[8]

---

[5]Cf. R. Bultmann, *Der Stil der paulinischen Predigt und die kynisch-stoische Diatribe,* FRLANT 13 (Göttingen: Vandenhoeck & Ruprecht, 1910), 17–19. See the more recent studies of the diatribe by S. K. Stowers (*The Diatribe and Paul's Letters to the Romans,* SBLDS 57 Chico, Calif.: Scholars Press, 1981); idem, "The Diatribe," in *Greco-Roman Literature and the New Testament,* ed. D. E. Aune, SBLSBS 21 (Atlanta: Scholars Press, 1988), 73–83; T. Schmeller, *Paulus und die "Diatribe": eine vergleichende Stilinterpretation,* NA N.F. 19 (Münster: Aschendorff, 1987).
[6]Cf. Epictetus *Discourses* 2.16.11; 1.16.3; 1.18.11; Bultmann, *Stil der paulinischen Predigt,* 55.
[7]Cf. Epictetus *Discourse* 3.26.12.
[8]Cf. Bultmann, *Stil der paulinischen Predigt,* 32–33. For *mē planāsthe,* see Epictetus *Discourse* 4.6.23.

3. Related to the imperatives are the exclamations which heighten the explosive character of the diatribe. *Ti moi to ophelos* ("what do I gain?") (v. 32) has such force.[9] So does *ne* ("I protest"), the particle of strong affirmation which occurs only here in the New Testament, but is frequent in the diatribe.[10]

4. The hardships expressed by *kindyneuomen* ("we are in peril," v. 30), *apothnēskō* ("I die," v. 31) and *ethēriomachēsa* ("I fought with beasts," v. 32) represent the so-called *peristasis* catalogue of the diatribe, the lists of hardships faced by the wise man.[11]

5. The diatribe abounds with quotations, especially from Homer, Euripides, Menander, and Philemon.[12] Frequently quotations appear at the end of a section as the one from Menander in verse 33 does. The quotation from Menander's *Thais* has the proverbial character that was a feature of many quotations in the diatribe. This is the only quotation from pagans in an undisputed letter of Paul. In his reticence to quote from them Paul is markedly different from Philo, who delights in such quotations.[13] The quotation here should therefore be regarded as significant. It need not suggest that Paul had any extensive knowledge of Greek literature. Menander's writings were highly regarded in Paul's day,[14] and were frequently suggested as excellent reading for the aspiring rhetorician.[15] It is likely that Paul's contact with Greek literature took place on this level.

6. The whole discussion is conducted as an *argumentum ad hominem,* as is frequent in the diatribe. This is seen in the use of the ironic imperative,

---

[9]Cf. Bultmann, *Stil der paulinischen Predigt,* 33, 86–87.

[10]Cf. Epictetus *Discourse* 2.20.29; A. Bonhoffer, *Epiktet und das Neue Testament* RGVV 10 (Giessen: Alfred Töpelmann, 1911), 143.

[11]Epictetus *Discourse* 1.24.1, "It is hardships which show what men are." Cf. Bultmann, *Stil der paulinischen Predigt,* 19–20, 71–72. For dying daily, see Seneca *Epistle* 24.20; Athenaeus *The Deipnosophists* 12.552B; *Philo Against Flaccus* 175. *Kindyneuein* ("to be in danger") and *apothnēskein* ("to die") are used together in Epictetus *Discourse* 2.19.24. For the lists of hardships in the moral philosophers and Paul, see J. T. Fitzgerald *Cracks in an Earthen Vessel: An Examination of the Catalogues of Hardships in the Corinthian Correspondence,* SBLDS 99 (Atlanta: Scholars Press, 1988).

[12]Bultmann, *Stil der paulinischen Predigt,* 43–46. On the use of the poets in moral teaching in general, see G. A. Gerhard, *Phoinix von Kolophon* (Leipzig/Berlin: B. G. Teubner, 1909), 228–84.

[13]Cf. K. L. Schmidt, "Der Apostel Paulus und die antike Welt," *Vorträge der Bibliothek Warburg, Vorträge 1924–25,* 45 (= *Das Paulusbild in der neueren Forschung,* ed. K. H. Rengstorff [Darmstadt: Wissenschaftliche Buchgesellschaft, 1964]: 223).

[14]Cf. Plutarch *Table-Talk* 712D; *Summary of a Comparison between Aristophanes and Menander* 854AB. For early Christian knowledge of Menander, see R. M. Grant, "Early Christianity and Greek Comic Poetry," *CPh* 60 (1965): 157–60.

[15]See Quintilian *Institutio oratoria* 10.1.69-70; Dio Chrysostom *Discourse* 18.6-7; Ausonius *Epistle* 22, *To Nepos.* Further on the subject, see A. J. Malherbe, *Social Aspects of Early Christianity,* 2d ed., enlarged (Philadelphia: Fortress Press, 1983), 41–45.

but is expressed most clearly in the concluding statement of the section (v. 34): *pros entropēn hymin lalō* ("I say this to your shame").[16]

It has long been established that Paul uses the style of the diatribe in his letters. Whether his adoption of this style was by direct appropriation from pagan examples or whether it was mediated to him by the hellenistic synagogue need not detain us here.[17] What is important for our purpose is that the immediate context in which *thēriomachein* occurs has obvious, even unusual (for Paul), contacts with the diatribe, which represents the moral preaching of the Roman empire.[18] It is appropriate, then, to examine the moral literature of this period for any light it may shed on the meaning of *thēriomachein*.

The Passions as Beasts

At least as early as Plato human passions and the pleasures of the flesh are described as beasts that fight against man.[19] That these warring passions should be subdued by the wise man in pre-Christian times became part of the teaching in philosophical schools and gymnasia.[20] But it was the Cynics and Stoics who first developed a complete picture of the struggle of the sage.[21] The terminology of the arena became part of the language of the diatribe and other moral writings,[22] and it was especially in the Cynic heroes Heracles and Diogenes that the ideal struggle was seen to have taken place.

Heracles was the most important of the Cynic patrons.[23] His hardiness had caught the imagination of the hellenistic period and he came to exemplify the person who is in control of himself and is truly independent. As fighter

---

[16]R. M. Grant ("Hellenistic Elements in 1 Corinthians," in *Early Christian Origins: Studies in Honor of Harold R. Willoughby*, ed. A. Wikgren [Chicago: Quadrangle Books, 1961]: 61) suggests that the word "shameful" in 1 Corinthians reflects conventional moral judgments. He does not refer to 1 Cor. 6:5 or 15:32.

[17]See below, notes 64–72.

[18]For the diatribe and moral preaching in the Empire, see P. Wendland, *Die hellenistisch-römische Kultur: in ihren Beziehungen zu Judentum und Christentum. Die urchristlichen Literaturformen*, 3d ed., HNT 1 (Tübingen: J. B. Mohr [Paul Siebeck], 1912), 75–96, 353–58.

[19]Cf. *Republic* 589A-B; *Phaedo* 66C, 83B; *Protagoras* 352D, 355B.

[20]For the place of philosophy in hellenistic education, see H. I. Marrou, *A History of Education in Antiquity* (New York: Mentor, 1964), 282–95. For its role in moral formation and the social settings in which it was taught, see A. J. Malherbe, *Moral Exhortation: A Greco-Roman Sourcebook*, Library of Early Christianity 4 (Philadelphia: Westminster Press, 1986), 30–47, 23–29, respectively. For the preaching itself, see idem, *Paul and the Thessalonians: The Philosophic Tradition of Pastoral Care* (Philadelphia: Fortress Press, 1987), 21–28.

[21]See now V. C. Pfitzner, *Paul and the Agon Motif*, NovTSup 16 (Leiden: E. J. Brill, 1967), esp. 16–37. The author does not relate his findings to 1 Cor. 15:32; cf. 76 n. 1.

[22]Cf. Epictetus *Discourse* 2.18.22-23; Seneca *Epistle* 80.2–3.

[23]See D. R. Dudley, *A History of Cynicism* (London: Methuen, 1937), 13; J. Bernays, *Lucian und die Kyniker* (Berlin: W. Hertz, 1879), 22; A. J. Malherbe, "Pseudo-Heraclitus, Epistle 4: The Divinization of the Wise Man," *JAC* 21 (1978): 42–64; idem, "Herakles," *RAC* 14 (1988): 560–62.

of beasts he had been called *thēroktonos* ("killer of wild beasts"),[24] and of greater interest to us, he was also called *thēriomachos* ("fighter of wild beasts").[25] The moralists of the first and second centuries A.D. still refer to his labors,[26] but Heracles was now seen as the savior of people, not merely because he had defended them against the wild beasts, but because in his example he continued to show them how to conquer themselves and also to be victorious over the tyrants who oppress them.[27] These hellenistic descriptions of Heracles, and also of Diogenes, provide the background for understanding Paul's statement in 1 Corinthians 15:32-34.

Heracles the glutton was a familiar figure in the fourth century B.C.,[28] and it is clear that this unflattering tradition continued.[29] Yet a favorable portrayal of Heracles was known by the time of Antisthenes, who is considered by Diogenes Laertius (*Lives of Eminent Philosophers* 1.15; 6.13) to have been the founder of the Cynic sect.[30] Dio Chrysostom tells us that Heracles purified himself of the *hēdonai* ("pleasures"), which are the beasts, and that this is what is meant by his taming the earth.[31] The Cynic has Heracles as his model and is himself a soldier fighting against pleasures, thus seeking to purify his own life.[32]

Diogenes also fought with these beasts and was compared to Heracles.[33] For Diogenes the struggle against pleasures was fiercer and greater than that against other hardships.[34] Pleasure's onslaught is subtle, "it deceives and casts

---

[24]Tegea, *IG* v (2), 91.

[25]Lucian *Lexiphanes* 19.

[26]E.g., Epictetus *Discourse* 1.6.32; Dio Chrysostom *Discourse* 63.6. Pfitzner (*Paul and the Agon Motif,* 29) overstates the case when he says, "They strove to remove the popular opinions held concerning Hercules and his great feats by asserting that those men erred who thought that he had fought against beasts, for the beasts were allegorized as the vices of men the hero sought to extirpate in his global wanderings."

[27]Cf. Dio Chrysostom *Discourse* 1.84. For the idealization of Heracles in Greek literature of the Roman Age, see R. Höïstad, *Cynic Hero and Cynic King* (Uppsala: C. W. K. Gleerup, 1948), 50–73; G. K. Galinsky, *The Herakles Theme: The Adaptations of the Hero in Literature from Homer to the Twentieth Century* (Totowa, New Jersey: Rowman and Littlefield, 1972); A. J. Malherbe, "Herakles" (n. 23 above), 559–67.

[28]Cf. Euripides *Alcestis* 788-802; Aristophanes *Birds* 1574–1693. On the early Heracles as a glutton, see A. J. Toynbee, *A Study of History* (London: Oxford Univ. Press), 6.466–67.

[29]Cf. Athenaeus *The Deipnosophists* 12.512E.

[30]Dudley, *A History of Cynicism,* 13. Other writers considered Diogenes the founder; see below, p. 97 n. 35.

[31]*Discourse* 5.22–23. Cf. E. Weber, *De Dione Chrysostomo Cynicorum sectatore,* Leipziger Studien 10 (Leipzig: Hirschfeld, 1887), 253-55; Louis Francois, *Essai sur Dion Chrysostome, philosophe et moraliste cynique et stoïcien* (Paris: Librairie Delagrave, 1921), 165–71.

[32]Lucian *Philosophies for Sale* 8. For the philosophers' use of military imagery, see A. J. Malherbe, "Antisthenes and Odysseus, and Paul at War," *HTR* 76 (1983): 143–73 (= 91–119 in this volume).

[33]Dio Chrysostom *Discourse* 8.26–28.

[34]Dio Chrysostom *Discourse* 8.20. Behind this lies an ancient tradition, according to K. Hahn, *De Dionis Chrysostomi: orationibus, quae inscribuntur Diogenes (V, VIII, IX, X)* (Frankfurt: J. G. Steinhaeusser, 1896), 41. Cf. also *Discourse* 9.12, *to pantōn amachōtaton thērion* ("the most redoubtable beast of all").

a spell with baneful drugs, just as Homer says Circe drugged the comrades of Odysseus, and some forthwith became swine, some wolves, and some other kinds of beasts."[35] Pleasure drives the victim into a sort of sty and pens him up; henceforth the victim goes on living as a pig or wolf.[36]

The Cynic's struggle was not conceived of as only an inward one. Men who live shameful lives, especially those who dishonor philosophy by their lives, are shameless beasts *(anaischynta thēria)*, and Heracles was supposed to have been sent to exterminate them.[37] In this vein Lucian under the alias of *Parrēsia* (Frankness) announces, before he engages the philosophers, that he is about to enter battle with no ordinary beasts.[38] They act like dogs that bite and devour one another.[39] Although Lucian did not hold any philosophical school in high esteem,[40] it is nevertheless clear that for him Heracles is especially concerned with the Epicureans who speak for *Hedonē* (Pleasure) who makes people live a bestial life.[41]

Plutarch represents the widespread antipathy of the period to the Epicureans. In his polemical writings against them he uses the language we have been considering. In his *Against Colotes,* Colotes, perhaps smarting under the charge that his sect lived like wild beasts,[42] states that it was a lack of proper laws that would result in leading the life of savage beasts. Plutarch counters that life would become savage, unsocial, and bestial not merely because of the absence of laws, but because of the Epicurean philosophy, particularly its "doctrines inciting men to pleasure." For Plutarch, "this is the life of brutes, because brute beasts know nothing better nor more honest than pleasure."[43]

In hellenistic literature the libertinistic life popularly, if unjustly, associated with the philosophy of Epicurus is frequently summarized as *esthiein*

---

[35]Dio Chrysostom *Discourse* 8.21. For this allegorization of *Odyssey* 10.236, see further, Plutarch *Advice to Bride and Groom* 139A. It may also be behind Lucian *The Double Indictment* 21. Cf. also Hahn, *De Dionis Chrysostomi,* for other occurrences.

[36]Dio Chrysostom *Discourse* 8.24-26.

[37]Lucian *The Runaways* 19, 23. Cf. Epictetus *Discourse* 1.6.32. The Cynics were themselves compared with animals, but this comparison is most frequently considered apt because of their viciousness and harshness; cf. Gerhard, *Phoinix von Kolophon,* 37–39.

[38]*The Fisherman* 17.

[39]*The Fisherman* 36; cf. *Philosophies for Sale* 10.

[40]Cf. W. Schmid and O. Stählin, *Geschichte der griechischen Literatur* (Munich: C. H. Beck, 1924), 2.2.712-14. Also see M. Caster, *Lucien et la pensée religieuse de son temps* (Paris: Les Belles Lettres, 1937), 9-122; and C. P. Jones, *Culture and Society in Lucian* (Cambridge, Mass.: Harvard Univ. Press, 1986), 24–32.

[41]E.g., *The Double Indictment* 20; *The Runaways* 19.

[42]For the Epicurean assertion that the first impulse of all living animals is toward pleasure, see *Fragment* 398 Usener. Usener (lxx) thinks that the pseudo-Plutarchean *Beasts are Rational (Gryllus)* was directed against Epicureans who lived liked animals. For later discussion and modification of this view, see A. Philippson, "Polystratos' Schrift uber die grundlose Verachtung der Volksmeinung," *Neue Jahrbücher fur das klassische Altertum* 23 (1909): 506.

[43]*Reply to Colotes* 1108D, 1124E-1125C; cf. *That Epicurus Actually Makes a Pleasant Life Impossible* 1089C.

kai pinein ("to eat and drink").[44] In Plutarch's anti-Epicurean writings this becomes a formula for the sensual life.[45] This description of the profligate life seems to have entered the Greek world as a description of Sardanapalus, the most well-known figure of oriental antiquity among the Greeks.[46] According to a tradition well-known in hellenistic times, this wealthy seventh-century Assyrian was the founder of Tarsus,[47] and his grave was supposed to have been in Anchiale, fourteen miles from the city.[48] On the grave was an inscription reading *esthie, pine, paize* ("eat, drink, play").[49] Chrysippus adds that a fuller statement by Sardanapalus appeared on the tomb, part of which read "knowing full well that thou art but mortal, indulge thy desire, find joy in thy feasts. Dead, thou shalt have no delight."[50] According to the Epicureans, of course, there is no afterlife and one's moral life should therefore be lived totally within the perspective of the present life.[51] By New Testament times Sardanapalus had become the stock figure used by Cynics for the kind of man who has been led astray by pleasure.[52] Consequently, it is not uncommon to find Heracles contrasted to Sardanapalus, the Epicurean *par excellence*.[53]

Our investigation thus seems to lead to the conclusion that Paul's use of *thēriomachein* ultimately comes from language used by the moralists of his day to describe the wise man's struggle against hedonism. His quotation from Isa. 22:13, "Let us eat and drink, for tomorrow we die," in this context would be reminiscent of the slogan attributed to the Epicureans and reflects the contemporary anti-Epicurean bias. The suspicion that Paul does have in mind some kind of Epicureanism has been expressed by some commentators,[54]

---

[44]See the references in J. J. Wettstein, *Novum Testamentum Graecum* (Amsterdam: Dommer, 1752), 2.169.

[45]E.g., *That Epicurus Actually Makes a Pleasant Life Impossible* 1098C, 1100D; *Reply to Colotes* 1125D.

[46]See E. Maass, *Orpheus: Untersuchungen zur griechischen, römischen, altchristlichen Jenseits-dichtung und Religion* (reprint, Aalen: Scientia Verlag, 1974), 209–13; F. H. Weissbach, "Sardanapal," PW 1A (1920): Jenseitsdichtung und Religion, 2436–75. Cf. the vast collection of references in J. E. B. Mayor's note on Juvenal *Satire* 10.362 (*Thirteen Satires of Juvenal* [London: Macmillan, 1880], 178–79).

[47]Cf. Weissbach, "Sardanapal," 2466–70; H. Böhlig, *Die Geisteskultur von Tarsus mit Beruck-sichtigung der paulinischen Schriften,* FRLANT 19 (Göttingen: Vandenhoeck & Ruprecht, 1913), 12–13.

[48]Cf. W. M. Ramsay, *The Cities of St. Paul* (London: Hodder & Stoughton, 1907), 132–35.

[49]This form of the inscription is given, among others, by Athenaeus *The Deipnosophists* 12.530B; Strabo *Geography* 14.5.9. Instead of *paize,* some of the authors in the tradition have *ocheue* ("copulate") or *aphrodisiaze* ("have intercourse"). Cf. the discussion in Weissbach, "Sardanapal," 2443-48.

[50]According to Athenaeus *The Deipnosophists* 8.336AB.

[51]Cf. *Fragments* 336–41, 396-97 Usener.

[52]Dudley, *A History of Cynicism,* 155; Gerhard, *Phoinix von Kolophon,* 181–90.

[53]E.g., Cleomedes *De motu circulari corporum caelestium* 2.1.91-92; Juvenal *Satire* 10.360–62; Plutarch *Against the Stoics on Common Conceptions* 1065C. For the contrast between Diogenes and Sardanapalus, see Maximus of Tyre *Discourses* 1.9; 32.9.

[54]E.g., Wettstein, *Novum Testamentum Graecum,* 2.169, who calls the quotation from Isa. 22:13 an *Epicureorum vox.* Also, E.-B. Allo, *Saint Paul: Prémiere épitre aux Corinthiens,* 2d ed., ÉB (Paris: J. Gabalda, 1956), 417.

but, so far as I can ascertain, has never been pursued carefully. It is not our purpose here to determine the view of the resurrection either held by the Corinthians or ascribed to them by Paul.[55] At this point we are only concerned to determine the meaning of the language he uses.

After the quotation from Menander[56] in verse 33 Paul concludes this part of his argument and again uses terms found in anti-Epicurean polemic: *eknēpsate dikaiōs* ("come to your right mind," v. 34). The view that pleasure is like a drug[57] or like wine[58] was not applied exclusively to Epicureans, but it could obviously be pressed into service against them in a special way. Epicurus answers the accusation that the end of his philosophy is sensuality by asserting that pleasure as he conceives of it is sober reasoning. In his letter to Menoeceus a number of calumnies against him are answered.[59] People, he says, attribute these views to him either because they are ignorant,[60] prejudiced, or wish to misrepresent him. Pleasure is *nēphōn logismos* ("sober reasoning") which investigates every choice and avoidance.[61] The greatest good is *phronēsis* ("prudence"), which is more precious even than philosophy, for all other virtues spring from it. It teaches that a life of pleasure must be a life lived *phronimōs kai kalōs kai dikaiōs* ("prudently and nobly and justly").[62] The idea of justice is an important element in Epicurus's thinking, and its appearance with *nēphōn logismōs* is not accidental.[63] If this background can be posited, *eknēpsate dikaiōs* may come from an ironic demand made of Epicureans that they sober up in a just manner.

Hellenistic Judaism

Paul need not have been directly dependent on such anti-Epicurean discussions for the language he uses. Nevertheless, it is not immediately obvious why he could not have derived this particular style of expression from the

---

[55]For a summary of the discussion, see J. C. Hurd, *The Origin of 1 Corinthians* (London: SPCK, 1965), 195–200.

[56]Menander himself had been a fellow student of Epicurus at Athens.

[57]See notes 35 and 36.

[58]Cf. Dio Chrysostom *Discourses* 30; 36; 39.

[59]Diogenes Laertius *Lives of Eminent Philosophers* 10.131-32.

[60]This may itself be a slap at the accusation that Epicurus was ignorant and an enemy of all learning. Cf. A. J. Festugière, *Epicurus and His Gods,* trans. C. W. Chilton (Cambridge, Mass.: Harvard Univ. Press, 1956), 33-36.

[61]Cf. Plutarch *Against Colotes* 1123F, "if men not sodden with drink or under the influence of drugs and out of their minds, but sober *(nēphontes),* and in perfect health, writing books on truth and norms and standards of judgment. . . ."

[62]Cf. Diogenes Laertius *Lives of Eminent Philosophers* 10.140.

[63]Note its recurrence in the *Kyria Doxai (Principal Doctrines)* (Diogenes Laertius *Lives of Eminent Philosophers* 10.140, 144, 150–53), and the polemic in Plutarch *Reply to Colotes* 1124D-1125A.

philosophers in the marketplace, whose common property it was.[64] Even a familiarity on his part with the contrast between Heracles and Sardanapalus is not impossible. In one of his discourses to Tarsus, Dio Chrysostom calls Heracles the founder of the city and refers to the Tarsians' custom of constructing a funeral pyre in Heracles' honor.[65] If Paul did not actually grow up in Tarsus,[66] he nevertheless did spend a number of years there during which he could have learned the traditions associated with the city (Gal. 1:21-22; cf. Acts 9:30ff.). Without wishing to press it too far, we may note that in an earlier discussion of immorality in 1 Corinthians (10:7) Paul, again using an Old Testament passage, describes immorality as *phagein, pein,* and *paizein* ("eating, drinking, playing"), a striking parallel to the inscription said to have been on Sardanapalus's grave.

It is also possible that Paul was dependent on hellenistic Judaism, not only for the use of the diatribe,[67] but also for the manner of his discussion in 1 Corinthians 15:32-34. Philo describes the pleasures as serpents: They are like the serpents in the wilderness (Num. 21:6).[68] Again, the serpent of Eve is the symbol of pleasure that attacks the reasoning faculty *(logismos)* in us, and its enjoyment leads to the ruin of understanding.[69] The Epicurean element is also present in Wisdom 2:6, "Let us enjoy the good things that exist," which also is reminiscent of Isaiah 22:13. Although the people whom the author of Wisdom had in mind may not have been Epicureans,[70] it is likely that they had been influenced by a superficial knowledge of Greek (Epicurean) thought. The views attributed to them may reflect Old Testament passages, but these allusions are of such a nature that they could express the ideas of pleasure-loving Greeks.[71] The habit of calling a philosophical or religious opponent an Epicurean, or of describing him in Epicurean terms, is not unknown in

---

[64]The hesitancy of Pfitzner *(Paul and the Agon Motif,* 3) to take this possibility seriously is not well founded.

[65]*Discourse* 33.47.

[66]So W. C. van Unnik *(Tarsus or Jerusalem: The City of Paul's Youth,* trans. G. Ogg [London: Epworth, 1962]), who has not met with complete approval; cf. N. Turner, *Grammatical Insights into the New Testament* (Edinburgh: T. & T. Clark, 1965), 83–85.

[67]For the "agon motif" in hellenistic Judaism, see Pfitzner, *Paul and the Agon Motif,* 38–72; for the influence of the diatribe on the hellenistic synagogue preaching, see H. Thyen, *Der Stil der jüdisch-hellenistischen Homilie,* FRLANT 47 (Göttingen: Vandenhoeck & Ruprecht, 1955).

[68]*Allegorical Interpretation* 2.77 (cf. 72–73, 74, 81, 84, 87–89). Cf. Paul's treatment of the same event (Num. 21:6) in 1 Cor. 10.

[69]*On Husbandry* 108; cf. 97 with *Allegorical Interpretation* 2.72-75.

[70]That they were Epicureans is argued by A. Dupont-Sommer, "Les 'impies' du Livre de la Sagesse sont-il des Epicuriens?" *RHR* 111(1935): 90–109. For a contrary view, see J. Fichtner, "Die Stellung der Sapientia Salomonis in der Literatur- und Geistesgeschichte ihrer Zeit," *ZNW* 36 (1937): 113–32.

[71]Thus P. Heinisch, *Das Buch der Weisheit* Exegetisches Handbuch zum Alten Testament 24 (Münster: Aschendorff, 1912), 40–42.

pagan, Jewish, or Christian literature.[72] Paul's appropriation of his language is in this tradition.

Conclusion

Regardless of the avenue by which Paul was introduced to this mode of expression, he appropriated it in no artificial way. It became part of his own style. The question still has to be addressed, however, as to what Paul refers to when he says "What do I gain if, humanly speaking, I fought with beasts at Ephesus?" Fighting with beasts in a figurative sense was, as we have seen, not an uncommon description of the sage's struggle. Such a figurative understanding of *thēriomachein* in this context appears to be the correct one. The Cynic hero was said to fight with beasts when he subdued his own passions as well as his hedonistic opponents. Paul describes his self-control with an athletic metaphor in 1 Corinthians 9:24-27.[73] It may be part of his intention to include the idea of self-control in 1 Corinthians 15:32 as well. However, "in Ephesus" leaves the impression that Paul has a more particular circumstance in mind which was known to his readers.

In 1 Corinthians 16:8-9 Paul states his intention to remain in Ephesus because a door had been opened for him, and that he has many adversaries. It is not possible to determine with absolute certainty who these adversaries were,[74] but they may very well have been the beasts with whom he had fought.[75] In 1 Corinthians 15 Paul is arguing against people who denied the future resurrection of the body in favor of a present one in the spirit.[76] For them eschatology had been radically realized.[77] They were already experiencing the blessings of the eschaton (cf. 1 Cor. 4:8; 15:19). Their morality was not governed by any futuristic hope. In the face of this Paul insists that the

---

[72]See R. Jungkuntz, "Fathers, Heretics and Epicureans," *JEH* 17 (1966): 3–10.

[73]The *gar* ("for," omitted in the RSV) in 10:1 relates this figure closely to 10:1-13. That it is simply a loose conjunctive (so Pfitzner, *Paul and the Agon Motif,* 83) is unlikely.

[74]Cf. Schmid, *Zeit und Ort,* 38. If Romans 16 was indeed written to Ephesus (W. Michaelis, *Einleitung in das Neue Testament,* 3d ed. [Bern: Berchtold Haller, 1961], 160–64), Paul's warning in Rom. 16:17-20 may provide a clue to the character of these men. For a description of them as Jewish-Christian Gnostics, see W. Schmithals, *Paul and the Gnostics,* trans. J. E. Steely (Nashville: Abingdon Press, 1972), 219–38.

[75]The description of heretics as beasts is not unusual; cf. Phil. 3:2; Acts 20:29; Titus 2:12; Ignatius *Ephesians* 7.1; *Smyrnaeans* 4.1.

[76]Cf. E. Haenchen, "Gnosis. II. Gnosis und NT," *RGG,* 3d ed. (1958): 2.1653; H. von Soden, "Sacrament and Ethics in Paul," in W. A. Meeks, *The Writings of St. Paul* (New York: W. W. Norton, 1972): 257–68; J. Schniewind, "Die Leugner der Auferstehung in Korinth," *Nachgelassene Reden und Aufsätze* (Berlin: Alfred Töpelmann, 1952): 110-39. E. Lövestam ("Über die neutestamentliche Aufforderung zur Nüchternheit," *ST* 12 [1958]: 83–84) suggests that *eknēpsate* ("come to your right mind") and *agnōsia* ("no knowledge") betray the gnostic character of the heretics, but that Paul uses the terms here in his own way.

[77]For a discussion of this kind of eschatological outlook and its influence on morality, see W. L. Lane, "1 Tim. 4:1-3. An Early Instance of Over-Realized Eschatology," *NTS* 11 (1964): 164–67.

Christian's moral life must be lived with a view toward the resurrection of the body (cf. 1 Cor. 6:12-14). In Ephesus he had opposed evil persons, for association with them corrupts (cf. 1 Cor. 5:6-13). If there were no resurrection of the body, his struggle at Ephesus had been in vain. It would have been a struggle on a merely human level *(kata anthrōpon)*, without a hope of resurrection.[78] The Corinthians, familiar with Paul's experiences, would readily see the application to their own situation.

---

[78]For this understanding of *kata anthrōpon*, see BAGD, *s.v.* "anthrōpos," 1.b.; J. Hering, *The First Epistle of Saint Paul to the Corinthians,* trans. A. W. Heathcote and P. J. Allcock (London: Epworth, 1962), 171; Schmid, *Zeit und Ort,* 43 n. 2. A similar use of *kata anthrōpon* is found in 1 Cor. 3:3-4, where the Corinthians' conduct is said to show that they live as mere humans, rather than as people governed by the Spirit. Cf. Kümmel's note on 3:4 in H. Lietzmann-W. Kümmel, *An die Korinther 1–2,* 4th ed., HNT 9 (Göttingen: Vandenhoeck & Ruprecht, 1949), 171.

7

Antisthenes and Odysseus, and Paul at War

Paul's use of military imagery in 2 Corinthians 10:3-6 deserves closer attention than it has received. Moffatt's translation vividly reflects the descriptions of ancient sieges which underlie Paul's statements:

> I do live in the flesh, but I do not make war as the flesh does; the weapons of my warfare are not weapons of the flesh, but divinely strong to demolish fortresses—I demolish theories and any rampart thrown up to resist the knowledge of God. I take every project prisoner to make it obey Christ, I am prepared to court-martial anyone who remains insubordinate, once your submission is complete.

Most commentators have been content to list parallel expressions, but have rarely examined at any depth the literary or philosophical traditions that may have influenced Paul.[1]

Proverbs, Philo, and Paul

Proverbs 21:22 (LXX), "A wise man assaults fortified cities *(ochyras),* and demolishes the fortification *(katheilen to ochyrōma)* in which the ungodly trusted *(epepoitheisan),*" is frequently simply cited,[2] suggested as a passage

---

[1]Albrecht Oepke's article on "hoplon" (*TDNT* 5 [1968]:292–94) and Otto Bauernfeind's on "stra-teuomai" (*TDNT* 7 [1971]: 701–13) are singularly unhelpful. The Stoic parallels to the Pauline use of the military metaphor, especially those in Seneca, have frequently been noted. See J. N. Sevenster, *Paul and Seneca,* NovTSup 4 (Leiden: E. J. Brill, 1961), 156 n. 2. But 2 Cor. 10:3-6 is usually neglected or entirely omitted from discussion. Sevenster approaches the subject from the virtue of bravery and denies that Paul has anything in common with Seneca.

[2]C. F. G. Heinrici, *Das zweite Sendschreiben des Apostel Paulus an die Korinther* (Berlin: W. Hertz, 1887), 417 n. 2; J. H. Bernard, "The Second Epistle to the Corinthians," in W. Robertson Nicoll, ed., *The Expositor's Greek Testament* (London: Hodder & Stoughton, n. d.), 3.95.

to which Paul alludes;[3] or is claimed to be the basis of his thought.[4] Paul's reference to confidence *(tē pepoithēsei)* in verse 2 and his claim to demolish fortresses *(kathairesin ochyrōmatōn)* in verse 4 have strengthened the suspicion that this passage loomed large in his thinking. Both Paul and Proverbs do have in mind a fortified city which is attacked, but sieges were so common in antiquity, and the terminology of siegecraft so widespread, that the sharing of these few words hardly constitutes proof of dependence.[5]

Paul's description of his attack is much more detailed than that of Proverbs. In addition to the general statement that he has weapons to demolish fortifications *(pros kathairesin ochyrōmatōn),* he views his attack as part of a campaign *(strateuometha, strateia),* refers to the special nature of his weapons, draws attention to a particular defensive measure—a rampart that is thrown up *(hypsōma apairomenon)*—threatens to take every thought *(noēma)* captive, and claims that he is prepared *(en hetoimō echein)* to punish every disobedience. Certain of these details call for special comment. This is the only place where *ochyrōma* appears in the New Testament. Its nonliteral use in the LXX (cf. Lam. 2:2), especially Proverbs 21:22, has led scholars to surmise that the Old Testament provided Paul with the image. The word was widely used, however, for military fortifications,[6] so that an appeal to the Old Testament must be supported by other evidence. Paul's description of one feature of the defensive fortification as a "raised rampart" *(hypsōma epairomenon)* also belongs to the military science of siegecraft. John Chrysostom identified *hypsōma* with *pyrgōma,* a defensive tower,[7] but it has been objected that *hypsōma* with this meaning cannot be found in Greek usage.[8] The word *hypsos* for a tall defensive structure, however, is frequently found, for example, in the directions of Aeneas Tacticus *(On the Defense of Fortified Positions* 32.2) to "throw up in opposition wooden towers or other high

[3]A. Plummer, *A Critical and Exegetical Commentary on the Second Epistle of St. Paul to the Corinthians,* ICC (Edinburgh: T. & T. Clark, 1915), 276; H. Windisch, *Der zweite Korintherbrief,* KEK 6 (Göttingen: Vandenhoeck & Ruprecht, 1924), 297; H. Lietzmann-W. G. Kümmel, *An die Korinther 1–2,* HNT 9 (Tübingen: J. C. B. Mohr [Paul Siebeck], 1949), 208; P. E. Hughes, *Paul's Second Epistle to the Corinthians,* NICNT (Grand Rapids: Wm. B. Eerdmans, 1962), 351 n. 7; C. K. Barrett, *A Commentary on the Second Epistle to the Corinthians,* HNTC (New York: Harper & Row, 1973), 251. Less confident is A. Schlatter, *Paulus, der Bote Jesu: Eine Deutung seiner Briefe an die Korinther* (Stuttgart: Calwer, 1934), 615 n. 9.
[4]Bauernfeind, "strateuomai," 710.
[5]See A. W. Lawrence, *Greek Aims in Fortification* (Oxford: Clarendon Press, 1979), in general, and for a list of accounts of attack and defense, 53–66.
[6]See Xenophon *Hellenica* 3.2.3; Polybius *The Histories* 4.6.3, and for the papyri, J. H. Moulton and G. Milligan, *The Vocabulary of the Greek Testament* (London: Hodder & Stoughton, 1929), 470.
[7]*In epistolam secundam ad Corinthios,* Homily 21 (PG 61.543), where he also states that Paul continues the metaphor in order to express the thought better.
[8]Thus Lietzmann-Kümmel, *An die Korinther,* 141; Barrett, *Second Corinthians,* 252. Werner Straub *(Die Bildsprache des Apostels Paulus* [Tübingen: J. C. B. Mohr [Paul Siebeck, 1937], 92) questions whether *hypsōma* still belongs to the image.

structures" *(antaeiresthai pyrgous xylinous ē alla hypsē).*[9] Paul's use of the less usual *hypsōma* may have been suggested by *ochyrōma* and *noēma,* and is in any case an example of his play on nouns which end in -*ma* which, according to BDF 488.3 (p. 259), belongs "to the dainties of the Hell. artists of style." Paul's claim to be prepared to punish is also stated in a phrase *(en hetoimō echontes)* used of military preparedness.[10] The imagery of siegecraft that Paul uses, therefore, was so common that there is not sufficient reason to think that he had Prov. 21:22 in mind.[11]

Philo also makes extensive use of the image of the siege and applies it to the personal lives of individuals. For example, according to him, those persons "who take refuge in virtue, as in an indestructible and impregnable fortress *(akathaireton kai erymnotaton teichos)* disregard the darts and arrows aimed at them by the passions that stalk them."[12] Stated otherwise, reason *(logos)* is a weapon against the passions; thus Moses was given a reasoning faculty *(logismos)* to engage in a campaign on behalf of virtue *(strateia hyper aretēs).* If the passions are not fought, they will storm the citadel of the soul and lay siege to it.[13]

Philo's *On the Confusion of Tongues* (128–31) has been regarded as particularly relevant to the interpretation of 2 Corinthians 10:3-6. The basis for this section is 107–14: Philo takes Genesis 11:4, "Come let us build for ourselves a city and a tower whose top shall reach to heaven," as his point of departure. In addition to ordinary cities, he says, the lawgiver thinks there are ones men carry about established in their souls. The fool's mind summons as allies and co-workers the senses and passions to help build and fortify the city, which has a tower as a citadel, a most secure palace *(basileion ochyrotaton)* for the tyrant vice. The tower "seeks to rise to the regions of celestial things with the arguments of impiety and godlessness in its van."

In 128–31 Philo describes the battle with the cities so constructed and provides a further interpretation of the cities and the tower. The cities had

---

[9]Cf. 40.1; Thucydides *History of the Peloponnesian War* 1.90.3; 1.91.1; 2.75.6.

[10]For *en hetoimō echein,* see Polybius *The Histories* 2.34.2; Philo *On the Embassy to Gaius* 259; without *echein,* Dionysius of Halicarnassus *The Roman Antiquities* 8.17.1; 9.35.6; 9.12.14.

[11]It is equally unnecessary to seek the origin of Paul's use in a particular campaign or in Paul's own past. A. P. Stanley (*The Epistles of St. Paul to the Corinthians* [London: Murray, 1858], 516) suggests that Paul may have had in mind the campaign of Pompey against Mithridates and the Pirates. Bauernfeind ("strateuomai," 711 n. 37) asserts that Paul "did not borrow directly from the usage of Roman troops and their commanders," and suggests that the language may very well have come from "Paul's past as a Pharisee, if not strict zealot."

[12]*Every Good Man is Free* 151.

[13]*Allegorical Interpretation* 3.113-14; 2.91. Cf. *On Dreams* 2.82: *eulabeia* ("caution") is to man what a wall is to a city. In *On Dreams* 1.103, *logos* is described as a weapon of defense. In it man has a most strong redoubt and impregnable fortress *(megiston eryma kai phrouran akathaireton).* The LCL translators note (5.350-51 n. b.) the difficulty of distinguishing between "reason" and "speech" as the meaning of *logos,* and compromise with "rational speech" or "rational speech and thought." See further, n. 50.

been fortified to menace *(epeteichisan)* the unhappy souls. Taking his clue from Judges 8:8-9, 17, Philo interprets the tower to signify a turning away from God. Built through the persuasiveness of arguments, its purpose was to divert and deflect the mind from honoring God. Justice, however, demolishes these structures. Gideon always stands prepared *(aei . . . eutrepistai)* to demolish this stronghold *(pros ge tēn tou ochyrōmatos toutou kathairesin),* able to do so by virtue of the strength he had received to demolish every argument that would persuade the mind to turn away from holiness *(kathairesein panta logon apostrephein dianoian hosiotētos anapeithonta).* The similarity to 2 Corinthians 10:4, *pros kathairesin ochyrōmatōn* ("to demolish fortresses"), was so striking to Hans Windisch that he was almost tempted to find a literary connection between Paul and Philo, but he decided that they both proceeded from Proverbs 21:22. He thought the perspective and terminology of the conflict between philosophers and sophists, which clearly stand out in Philo, were used by Paul in his battle against the Corinthian gnosis.[14]

What Philo shares with Proverbs 21:22 is essentially that the fortifications were built by the ungodly. However, Philo's point of departure appears to have been Judges 8, which he embellished with the military imagery that was common and which he frequently uses elsewhere in his writings. One would conclude that this is a case of literary dependence only by relying on a narrowly focused use of the concordances. The similarities between Paul and Philo, however, are more striking. They both develop the imagery in greater detail than Proverbs and use it in their descriptions of religious psychology. For example, they both refer to preparedness for battle, the ability to undertake it, the struggle as a campaign *(strateia),* and introduce the intellect *(logismos;* for Philo, also *logos* and *dianoia)* into their discussions.

There are, nevertheless, substantial differences between the ways the military imagery is used in 2 Corinthians 10:3-6 and in *On the Confusion of Tongues.* To begin with, while the nature of the fortifications seems similar, their purposes are different. The structures Paul attacks are defensive in nature, but for Philo the cities Gideon attacks are offensive in purpose. *Epiteichizein* describes the building of a walled city that would serve as a base for sorties to menace or secure an area.[15]

---

[14]Windisch, *Der zweite Korintherbrief,* 297. He is followed by H. D. Betz, *(Der Apostel Paulus und die sokratische Tradition: Eine exegetische Untersuchung zu seiner "Apologie" 2 Korinther 10–13* BHT 45 Tübingen: J. C. B. Mohr [Paul Siebeck, 1972], 68, 140–41), who stresses the antisophistic use of the image. It should be noted that references to this passage from Philo had been made long before Windisch, but had not really been put to fruitful use in interpreting 2 Cor. 10:4. Cf. J. J. Wettstein, *Novum Testamentum Graecum* (Amsterdam: Dommer, 1752), 2.203; H. St. John Thackeray, *The Relation of St. Paul to Contemporary Jewish Thought* (London: Macmillan, 1900), 239.

[15]In addition to the references provided by LSJ 664, see est. Y. Garlan, *Recherches de poliorcétique grecque* (Athens: École Francaise, 1974), 33–38. For Philo, see Andre Pelletier, "Les passions a l'assault de l'âme d'après Philon," *REG* 78 (1965): 52–60.

In Philo it is the unhappy soul who is at the mercy of the citadel of vice. More importantly, Philo and Paul differ in their presentation of the contestants' relation to the fortifications. In *On the Confusion of Tongues* it is the sophistic elements that make use of the fortifications in their attacks on the intellect. Philo can speak of the rational faculties as armament and the struggle for virtue as a campaign, but he does not do so in the passage that has been used to interpret Paul's use of the imagery. For Paul, on the other hand, it is not sophistries but the cognitive element which is related to the fortifications. The *logismoi,* which are the reasoning faculties[16] and not sophistries,[17] constitute the defensive measures, the fortifications *(ochyrōmata),* and the rampart raised *(hypsōma epairomenon)* against the attack by the knowledge of God, and what is taken captive is every thought *(noēma),* which is made to obey Christ. Thus, while Paul shares some details with *On the Confusion of Tongues* 128–31, he differs from it not only in the functions of the fortifications, but also in the fact that the issues at stake are cognitive and volitional rather than sophistic. One is therefore not justified in asserting that Windisch had demonstrated the antisophistic origin of the imagery Paul uses.[18] In this particular passage Philo utilizes the imagery in an anti-sophistic manner, but it is also clear from the passages outside *On the Confusion of Tongues* alluded to above, as well as references to Epictetus that Windisch provides, that there is a philosophical background to the imagery.

Antisthenes and the Philosopher's Armament

Paul and other early Christians were not unique in using martial imagery.[19] It was used in a transferred sense by all kinds of persons including philosophers, adherents of the mystery cults, and orators.[20] Johannes Leipoldt may

---

[16]As it does in Philo, e.g., see n. 13. See further Leisegang's index. H. W. Heidland ("logizomai," *TDNT* 4 [1967]: 287) is correct in his judgment that the philosophical term is in view here. See further below.

[17]Thus Plummer, *Second Corinthians,* 276; Lietzmann-Kümmel, *An die Korinther,* 141. Cf. also Betz, *Der Apostel Paulus,* 68, 121. For *logizesthai* as a slogan in the Corinthian discussion, see D. Georgi, *The Opponents of Paul in Second Corinthians* (Philadelphia: Fortress Press, 1986), 228–32, 235–36.

[18]Thus Betz *(Der Apostel Paulus,* 68), who does, however, recognize the difficulty of the passage.

[19]For the usage elsewhere in the Pauline literature: 1 Thess. 5:8; 2 Cor. 2:14; Col. 2:15; Eph. 6:14-17. On the use in the New Testament and other early Christian literature, in addition to Bauernfeind, "strateuomai," and Oepke, "hoplon," see A. Harnack, *Militia Christi: Die christliche Religion und der Soldatenstand in den ersten drei Jahrhunderten* (reprint, Darmstadt: Wissenschaftliche Buchgesellschaft, 1963); C. Schneider, *Geistesgeschichte des antiken Christentums* (Munich: C. H. Beck, 1954), 1.705–7; J. Leipoldt, "Das Bild vom Kriege in der griechischen Welt," in *Gott und die Götter. Festgabe für Erich Fascher zum 60. Geburtstag,* ed. G. Delling et al (Berlin: Evangelische Verlaganstalt, 1958), 16–30; C. Spicq, *Saint Paul: Les Épitres pastorales,* 4th ed., ÉB (Paris: J. Gabalda, 1969), 1.350-51.

[20]For the mystery cults, see F. Cumont, *The Oriental Religions in Roman Paganism,* 3d ed.

be overstating the matter somewhat with his claim that the application of the imagery to the personal lives of individuals is essentially Greek and not Jewish in origin, and that this is the source of the Christian use but he is on the mark in so far as 2 Corinthians 10:1-6 is concerned.[21] The imagery that Paul uses here is part of a tradition that goes back at least to the fifth and fourth centuries B.C. The following discussion will be concerned not so much with the ultimate origin of the imagery as with one tradition which appears to lie behind 2 Corinthians 10:1-6.

It is not clear who first used martial imagery to describe the spiritual or intellectual struggle of individuals.[22] For our purposes it suffices to note that the custom had attained currency by the time of Socrates' immediate followers.[23] The increased usage of the imagery was at least partly due to the Idealization of the Spartans, which can be explained by the political conditions and ideology of the period.[24] Spartans on principle rejected the efficacy of fortifications.[25] Their attitude is contained in lacanic apophthegms attributed to various Spartans, beginning with Lycurgus and Theopompus, but especially to generals from the end of the sixth and beginning of the fifth centuries. The attribution of the same or similar statements to different persons makes it difficult to be certain that any one of them did in fact say what he is claimed to have said. What is important, however, is that the attitude expressed was taken to be Spartian and that it enjoyed wide circulation for centuries.

The Spartans held that a city is well fortified when it is surrounded by brave men.[26] Such men are, in effect, its walls,[27] and the virtue of its inhabitants provides sufficient fortification.[28] Spartans contemptuously charged that cities fortified in "the ordinary manner were places for women to dwell in.[29] These

---

(reprint, New York: Dover, 1956), 213 n. 6; R. Reitzenstein, *Die hellenistische Mysterienreligionen nach ihren Grundgedanken und Wirkung,* 3d ed. (reprint, Darmstadt: Wissenschaftliche Buchgesellschaft, 1956), 192-97; S. G. Griffiths, *Apuleius of Madauros: The Isis Book (Metamorphoses, Book XI),* EPRO 39 (Leiden: E. J. Brill, 1975), 254–55.

[21]Leipoldt, "Das Bild vom Kriege," 22. He argues that, while Paul uses Jewish language, he adapts it. Leipoldt does not mention 2 Cor. 10:3-6.

[22]For Heraclitus, see Leipoldt, "Das Bild vom Kriege," 17–18; for Pythagoras as Socrates's source, see H. Emonds, "Christlicher Kriegsdienst. Der Topos der militia spiritualis in der antiken Philosophie," reprinted in Harnack, *Militia Christi,* 131–62; see 137–41.

[23]E.g., in Plato *Apology* 28D-29A; *Phaedo* 62D. For other references, see Leipoldt, "Das Bild vom Kriege," (n. 19 above) 16–18.

[24]See Garlan, *Recherches de poliorcétique grecque,* 91–103.

[25]Garlan, *Recherches de poliorcétique grecque,* 98–99.

[26]Plutarch *Lycurgus* 19.4.

[27]Plutarch *Sayings of Spartans* 217E, 228E.

[28]Plutarch *Sayings of Spartans* 210E.

[29]Plutarch *Sayings of Kings and Commanders* 190E; *Sayings of Spartans* 212E, 215D, 230C. Cf. 228DE: Lycurgus forbade attacks on walled places so that brave men might not die at the hands of a woman, child, or any such person.

sentiments recur with regularity for centuries, most frequently, but not always, identified with the Spartans, and they appear in all kinds of literature. In addition to Plutarch, who collected many of the apophthegms, such popular phllosophers as Epictetus and Dio Chrysostom registered their admiration for these ideas of the Spartans,[30] and the apophthegms found their way into gnomologies.[31] The popularity that the apophthegms enjoyed is illustrated by their use in rhetorical exercises and in orations.[32] That the Spartan ideas should then appear without any attribution in the works of historians and in Christian literature is only to be expected.[33]

While other philosophers admired the Spartans, the Cynics had a special affinity for them, and Cynics may have figured importantly in the transmission of the apophthegms attributed to Spartans.[34] Antisthenes and Diogenes, each of whom was regarded in antiquity (as in modern times) as the founder of the school,[35] are represented in the doxographic tradition as admiring the Spartans.[36] Of special significance for us in the present context is Antisthenes, who adopted and elaborated the Spartan view of moral armament, thus initiating the development of a theme that would continue to occupy philosophers, Stoics, and Cynics in particular.

According to a number of fragments representing his thought, Antisthenes applied the image of the fortified city to the sage's soul. In a statement preserved by Epiphanius he is said to have affirmed that one should not be envious of others' vices (or what they regard as shameful), for while cities' walls are ineffectual against a traitor within, the soul's walls are unshakable

[30]Epictetus *Fragments* 39; 61 (487, 491 Schenkl); Dio Chrysostom *Discourses* 1.31; 22.2; 80.4. On Dio's admiration for Sparta, see P. Desideri, *Dione di Prusa: Un intelletuale greco nell' impero romano* (Messina/Florence: D'Anna, 1978), 248 n. 40, 463 n. 13a. Cf. also Philostratus *Life of Apollonius of Tyana* 1.38.
[31]*Gnomologium Vaticanum* 69 (32 Sternbach). For the passages in Stobaeus, see the apparatus in Sternbach and in Schenkl.
[32]For exercises, see Seneca *Suasoriae* 2.3.14; Philostratus *Lives of the Sophists* 1.514; cf. 2.584. See also Menander Rhetor *Peri Epideiktikōn* 3.381,11; Spengel (= 100 Russell-Wilson). For the use in practice, see Aelius Aristides *Oration* 26.79; Maximus of Tyre *Discourse* 32.10. Note the rejection of Plato *Republic* 6.496D in Maximus of Tyre *Discourse* 10.10 (195,13-19; Hobein).
[33]E.g., in Polybius *The Histories* 9.10.1 and pseudo-Justin *Exhortation to the Greeks* 3.
[34]On the idealization of Sparta, see F. Ollier, *Le Mirage spartiate* 1 (Paris: É. de Boccard, 1933), 2 (Paris: Les Belles Lettres, 1943). For the philosophers in general, see 1.195–440; for the Cynics, 2.21–54. On the latter, cf. G. A. Gerhard, *Phoinix von Kolophon* (Leipzig-Berlin: B. G. Teubner, 1909), 252.
[35]Cf. Julian *Oration* 6.187C, and see n. 122. Cf. pseudo-Crates *Epistle* 6: Antisthenes began doing philosophy, Diogenes brought it to perfection. For an account of the modern debate, see R. Hoïstad, *Cynic Hero and Cynic King* (Uppsala: C. W. K. Gleerup, 1948), 5–21. See further p. 83 above.
[36]Diogenes: Diogenes Laertius *Lives of Eminent Philosophers* 6.27, 39, 59. Antisthenes: Diogenes Laertius *Lives of Eminent Philosophers* 6.2.; cf. Plutarch *Lycurgus* 30; *Fragment* 195 Caizzi; cf. Aristotle *The Art of Rhetoric* 3.10.1411a24.

and cannot be broken down.[37] While he here stresses inner security, Antisthenes also recognized the importance of associating with persons of moral excellence. Elsewhere he directs:

> Make allies of men who are at once brave and just. Virtue is a weapon that cannot be taken away *(anaphaireton hoplon hē aretē)*. It is better to be with a handful of good men fighting against the bad, than with hosts of bad men against a handful of good men.[38]

Nevertheless, what is essential here is that the sage's association is to be with others like him, that is, persons who possess virtue which cannot be lost.[39] It is the virtuous man's prudence *(phronēsis)* that has a firm base *(asaleuton)*.[40] Thus Antisthenes affirmed,

> Prudence *(phronēsis)* is a most secure stronghold, for it does not crumble nor is it betrayed. We must build walls of defense with our own impregnable reasonings *(analōtois logismois)*.[41]

Here for the first time we have Paul's imagery in which the reasoning faculties *(logismos, phronēsis)* function in the inner fortification of a person. The image becomes common, and we shall trace it as it was used by Stoics and Cynics. Before doing so, however, it will be profitable to observe how Antisthenes applied this concern with moral armament to his interpretation of Odysseus. Odysseus came to represent a certain type of moral philosopher, and Antisthenes' brief for him is not without interest to the reader of 1 and 2 Corinthians.

The Sophists, among them Antisthenes' teacher Gorgias, had attacked Odysseus for being unscrupulous. Antisthenes defended him in two sophistic speeches and in a statement preserved in the Homeric scholia. The speeches

---

[37]Epiphanius *Panarion* 3.26 *(Fragment* 90 Caizzi).
[38]Diogenes Laertius *Lives of Eminent Philosophers* 6.12 *(Fragment* 71 Caizzi). On the need of friends for correction, see Plutarch *How to Profit by One's Enemies* 89B *(Fragment* 77 Caizzi); the same sentiment is attributed to Diogenes in Plutarch *How to Tell a Flatterer from a Friend* 74C; *Progress in Virtue* 82A. For rejection of the Cynic view that virtue cannot be lost, see Xenophon *Memorabilia* 1.2.19.
[39]Diogenes Laertius *Lives of Eminent Philosophers* 6.105: the philosopher is a friend to someone like him *(philos tō homoiō)*.
[40]According to Philo *Every Good Man is Free* 28. Cf. Stobaeus *Anthology* 3.14.19 (3.474,10-13 Wachsmuth-Hense).
[41]Diogenes Laertius *Lives of Eminent Philosophers* 6.13 *(Fragment* 88 Caizzi); cf. Hesychius Milesius *De viris illustribus* 7. The translations of the second line differ. R. D. Hicks in LCL translates, "Walls of defense must be constructed in our impregnable reasonings." L. Pacquet, *(Les Cyniques grecques: Fragments et témoignages,* Collection philosophia 4 [Ottawa: Université d'Ottawa, 1975], 40) renders it "Il faut edifier dans nos âmes des remparts inexpungables." F. Decleva Caizzi ("La tradizione antisteno-cinica in Epitteto," *Scuole socratiche minore,* ed. G. Giannantoni, Pubbl. del centro di studio per la storia della storiografia filosofica 4 [Bologna, 1977]: 113) correctly translates it "Occorre erigere un muro con i propri raggionamenti inespugnabili," and justifies this rendering (n. 76) by referring to Aeschylus *The Libation-Bearers* 613, where *en logois* means "with speech."

represent two types of persons. They treat the "tension between the straight-forward and honorable Ajax, who is alien to all intrigues, compromises, or innovations, on the one hand, and the crafty Odysseus on the other, the man who always comes off best by his inventiveness, adaptability and shameless-ness."[42] Antithenes' Odysseus is the prototype of one kind of Cynic who becomes well known in later centuries. The setting for the two speeches is the contest of Ajax and Odysseus for Achilles' arms, and the contest is inter-preted as being about virtue.[43]

In the *Ajax* the speaker is represented as brave and forthright. He insists that he is a man of deeds and not words. War is not to judged by words which will not benefit anyone in battle. He had come to Troy willingly, was always arrayed foremost in battle, and was alone, without the protection of a wall. His actions are proof that he deserves to receive the armor. It is the wrong people who are presuming to be judges of virtue. Odysseus, Ajax says, is a man of words. He is cowardly and would not dare *(tolmēseie)* use Achilles' weapons. His participation in the battle was underhanded, for he put on rags and sneaked into Troy. He acts in secret and willingly suffers ill treatment, even to the point of being flogged, if he might thereby gain *(kerdainein)* something.

Odysseus is made to reply in a longer speech. The *Odysseus* is directed not only to Ajax, but to all the other heroes, because Odysseus claims that he has done the expedition more good than all of them put together. Ajax is ignorant, but the poor fellow cannot help it. Is he really so brave? After all, he is protected by his famous shield, a veritable wall made of seven bulls' hides. Compared with Ajax, Odysseus is unarmed. He does not rush the enemies' walls but enters their city stealthily and overpowers them from within with their own weapons. "I know what is on the inside and what the enemies' condition is, and not because I send someone else to spy the situation out. In the same way that steersmen look out night and day how to save *(sōsousi)* the sailors so do I myself and I save *(sōzō)* both you and all the other men." All the dangers that Odysseus endured were for their benefit. He flees no danger nor would he dare *(etolmōn)* strive for reputation, even were he a slave, poor man or flogged. He had no weapons given him for battle, yet is constantly prepared, night and day, to fight any individual or group. While Ajax is snoring, Odysseus is saving him—the only weapons over

[42]Hoïstad, *Cynic Hero and Cynic King,* 94–102, here 96. Other commentators on the speeches: Decleva Caizzi, "La tradizione antistenico-cinica in Epitetto," 90–91; W. B. Stanford, *The Ulysses Theme,* 2d ed. (Ann Arbor: Univ. of Michigan, 1976), 96–99.

[43]The texts followed are those of Caizzi: *Fragments* 14 *(Ajax)* and 15 *(Odysseus).* See, now, *Socraticorum reliquiae,* ed. G. Giannantoni (Rome: Edizioni dell' Ateneo, 1983), 2.339–43, for the most recent critical text; 3.231–37 (1985) for discussion, and H. D. Rankin, *Antisthenes Sokratikos* (Amsterdam: Hakkert, 1986), 155–71, for translation and comment.

which he disposes being the servile ones *(douloprepē hopla)* of the rags he wears. Ajax makes the mistake of equating physical strength with bravery. One day a poet skilled in discerning virtue will come and portray Odysseus as enduring, rich in counsel, resourceful, city-sacking, and as the one who alone sacked Troy.

As Ragnar Höistad has shown, Antisthenes used the speeches as a means of propaganda for his conception of the virtuous man.[44] His enthusiasm for Odysseus had to be defended. In the sixth century, Theognis *(Elegy* 213–18) had eulogized Odysseus:

> O heart, present a different tinge of character to every friend, blending your mood with that of each. Emulate the complex polypus that always takes the appearance of the adjacent rock. Cleverness is better than inflexibility.

Stanford's comment is apropos and recognizes the similarity to Paul's self-description in 1 Corinthians 9:19-23:

> Here one recognizes a special aspect of Odysseus's traditional versatility and resourcefulness—the Pauline quality of being all things to all men. But as this poet phrases it, and in its wider context of political spite and rancour, the eulogy has a distinctly unpleasant flavour. Its tone is machiavellian, rather than Homeric or apostolic . . . we are faced here with one of the fundamental ambiguities in Odysseus's character. The border between adaptability and hypocrisy is easily crossed. Theognis had to make very little distortion to transform Odysseus's versatility into this despicable opportunism. Soon, when Pindar, Sophocles, and Euripides reconsider the matter, Odysseus will pay dearly for Theognis's admiration.[45]

Antisthenes spoke to these calumnies. According to a scholion on the first line of Homer's *Odyssey,* "Tell me, Muse, of the *polytropic* man," Antisthenes attempted to absolve his hero of the charges of duplicity by interpreting the ambiguous *polytropos* to refer to Odysseus's skill in adapting his figures of speech ("tropes") rather than understanding it in the pejorative ethical sense of "often changing one's character, hence unstable, unprincipled, unscrupulous." Even Pythagoras, he says, taught his disciples to speak to children

---

[44]Whether he was allegorizing or not has been debated. See R. Höistad, "Was Antisthenes an Allegorist?" *Eranos* 49 (1951):16–30; J. Tate, "Antisthenes Was Not an Allegorist," *Eranos* 51 (1953): 14–22; cf. R. Laurenti, "L'iponoia di Antistene," *Revista critica di storia della Filosofia* 17 (1962): 123–32.

[45]Stanford, *The Ulysses Theme,* 91, and for discussion of the scholion that follows, 99. The scholion is printed as *Fragment* 51 in Caizzi. For the debate over the meaning of *polytropos,* see T. Kakridis, "Die Bedeutung von *polytropos* in der Odyssee," *Glotta* 11 (1921): 288–91; P. Linde, "Homerische Selbsterläuterungen," *Glotta* 13 (1924): 223–24. On Antisthenes's interpretation, see also E. Norden, "Beiträge zur Geschichte der griechischen Philosophie," *Jahrbücher für classische Philologie,* Suppl. 19.2 (1893): 394–95; A. Rostagni, "Un nuovo capitolo della retorica e della sophistica," *Studi italiani di filologia classica* 2 (1922): 150–59; G. A. Kennedy, "Ancient Disputes over Rhetoric in Homer," *AJP* 78 (1957):27–28; Decleva Caizzi, "La tradizione antistenico-cinica," 103.

in childlike terms, to women in womanlike terms, to governors in govern-
mental terms, and to ephebes in ephebic terms.

In sum, Antisthenes used the military imagery in two different ways. On
the one hand, the rational faculties are the wise man's fortifications. However,
the imagery changes when applied to Odysseus, the prototype of the virtuous
man who seeks to benefit others. Odysseus willingly accepts ill treatment and
adapts himself and his speech to changing circumstances in order to gain the
good and save people. The only weapons he has are the servile rags he wears.
These three items—the philosopher's intellectual armament, the philosopher's garb, and Odysseus as sage—continued to interest writers of the following centuries.

The Fortification of the Wise Man

Military imagery to describe the sage's life became popular especially among
Stoics, and particularly in the early Empire. Seneca's dictum, *vivere militare
est* ("life is a battle") expressed the view of many.[46] As a general commands
his army, so does the divine the universe,[47] and the wise man takes care to
occupy the post assigned him.[48] He perceives the divine and the cosmic
scheme of things, and his position within it, through reason *(logismos)*.[49]
Reason has been given to him as a weapon. Just as animals received from
nature their several means of defense, so man has received reason.[50] With it
as his weapon he overcomes all misfortune.[51] The popularity of the imagery,
particularly that of the impregnable fortress, around the middle of the first
century A.D., is evident in Epictetus and especially Seneca, and its use illu-
minates 2 Corinthians 10:3-6.[52]

---

[46]*Epistle* 96.5; cf. Epictetus *Discourse* 3.24.31,34.

[47]Pseudo-Aristotle *On the Cosmos* 6.400b8-9, on which see W. Capelle, "Schrift von der Welt,"
Neue Jahrbuch für das klassische Altertum 15(1905): 558 n. 6 for other references.

[48]Epictetus *Discourses* 1.9.16,24; 3.1.19; cf. 3.13.14; 3.24.99-100; 3.26.29. He swears allegiance to
God and does not complain: 1.14.15; cf. 1.29.29. For Seneca, see Emonds, "Christlicher Kriegsdienst" (n. 22 above), 143–48.

[49]Pseudo-Aristotle *On the Cosmos* 6.399a32.

[50]Cf. Plutarch *Chance* 98DE; Maximus of Tyre *Discourse* 20.6 (249,1-9 Hobein); cf. 31.4 (365,14-
15 Hobein); Pseudo-Phocylides 128. The notion is widespread, not only among Stoics, although
they seem to have found it particularly apt. In its more popular use, it is speech that is said to
distinguish man from the beasts, but it is not always possible to decide which meaning *logos*
has in any particular context (cf. n. 13 above). On some occasions such words as *phronēsis* and
logismos provide clarity. On the topic, see S. O. Dickerman, *De argumentis quibusdam apud
Xenophontem, Platonem, Aristotelem obviis et structura hominis et animalium petitis* (Halle:
Wichan & Burkhardt, 1909); A. S. Pease, *M. Tulli Ciceronis De Natura Deorum* (Cambridge,
Mass.: Harvard Univ. Press, 1958), 2.875–76; P. W. van der Horst, *The Sentences of Pseudo-
Phocylides,* SVTP 4 (Leiden: E. J. Brill, 1978), 199–201.

[51]Menander *Sententiae* 515 (63 Jaekel); cf. 582, 621 (66, 69 Jaekel).

[52]For a few generations earlier, see Horace *Epistle* 1.1.60 and *Satire* 2.3.296–97, the latter referring
to the Stoic Stertinius giving his convert Damasippus the Stoic precepts as weapons.

For Epictetus, the philosopher's thoughts are his protection.[53] In his depiction of the true Cynic, who represents for him the philosophical ideal, the philosopher's self-respect *(aidōs)* a concept central to Epictetus's view of the philosopher, constitutes his fortification.[54] The Cynic must be adorned on every side with self-respect as other men are with walls, doors, and doorkeepers.[55] His authority to censure others does not derive—like that of kings and tyrants—from weapons and bodyguards, but from his conscience and a purified mind.[56] His is an inner protection; as a public man he is not hidden by walls and protective curtains.[57]

Seneca provides much more elaborate examples of the way in which the imagery of the fortified city was used to describe the philosopher's security.[58] He shares the Stoic confidence that the wise man withstands every attack and cannot be injured.[59] The sage is fortified against all possible inroads, is alert, and will not retreat from misfortunes.[60] Bravery is his impregnable fortress; surrounded by it he can hold out from anxiety during life's siege, for he uses his own strength as weapons.[61] To be victorious, he must toughen his mind.[62] The Stoic should recognize that he can raise no wall against Fortune that she cannot take by storm. He should therefore strengthen his inner defenses; if they be safe, he can be attacked, but never captured,[63] for it is the power of the mind to be unconquerable.[64] He therefore girds himself about with philosophy, an impregnable wall that Fortune cannot breach to get at the independent soul who stands on unassailable ground.[65] The wise man may be bound to his body, but he is an absentee so far as his better self is concerned, and he concentrates his thoughts on lofty things *(cogitationes suas ad sublima intendit)*.[66] Virtue alone can attain to that height from which no force can drag it.[67] In short, as Seneca says of Stilpo's greatness of soul:

> though beneath the hand of that destroyer of so many cities fortifications shaken by the battering ram may totter, and high towers *(turrium altitudinem)* under-

---

[53]*Discourse* 4.6.14.
[54]On *aidōs* in Epictetus, see B. L. Hijmans, *ASKESIS: Notes on Epictetus' Educational System* (Assen: Van Gorcum, 1959), 27–30; M. Billerbeck, *Epiktet: Vom Kynismos,* Philosophia Antiqua 34 (Leiden: E. J. Brill, 1978), 67–68.
[55]*Discourses* 4.8.33; cf. 4.3.7.
[56]*Discourse* 3.22.13-19, 94-95. Cf. Dio Chrysostom *Discourse* 77/78.40.
[57]*Discourse* 3.22.14-16; cf. Marcus Aurelius *To Himself* 3.7.16.
[58]See Emonds, "Christlicher Kriegsdienst," 152–54, who attributes Seneca's fondness for the metaphor to his teacher Quintus Sextius. Cf. W. Ganss, "Das Bild des Weisen bei Seneca" (Diss., Freiburg: Gutenberg, 1952), 43-47; Sevenster, *Paul and Seneca,* 156–62.
[59]*De constantia sapientis* 3.4-5; *De beneficiis* 5.2.3-4.
[60]*Epistles* 59.6-8; cf. 64.3-4.
[61]*Epistle* 113.27-28.
[62]*Epistle* 51.5-6.
[63]*Epistle* 74.19.
[64]*De vita beata* 4.2.
[65]*Epistle* 82.5
[66]*Epistle* 65.18.
[67]*De vita beata* 15.5.

mined by tunnels and secret saps may sink in sudden downfall, and earthworks rise to match the loftiest citadel *(editissimas arces)*, yet no war-engines can be devised that will shake the firm-fixed soul.[68]

The perfect man,

full of virtues human and divine, can lose nothing. His goods are girt by strong and insurmountable defenses ... The walls which guard the wise man are safe from both flame and assault, they provide no means of entrance, are lofty *(excelsa)*, impregnable, godlike.[69]

The self-sufficient Stoic sage, secure in the high fortifications of his reason and trusting in his own weaponry, is very much like the objects of Paul's attack.

The Philosopher's Dress as Armament

Antisthenes's other use of military imagery to describe the philosopher's dress *(schēma)* also appears in the later philosophers.[70] The threadbare cloak worn without a tunic, together with a staff and a wallet, came to be associated especially with the long-haired and -bearded Cynics and were important to them with respect to both their practice and their self-understanding. They could claim that their garb was not so unusual, since the statues of male deities, when they were clad at all, wore only a cloak.[71] Nevertheless, their garb did draw attention to them, and Cynics of the serious sort made use of the opportunity to instruct the audiences created in response to their dress.[72] In a *captatio benevolentiae* to such an audience, Dio Chrysostom says that by being drawn to him by his garb they honor philosophy, which itself is voiceless and without boldness of speech *(aparrēsiastos)*.[73] They know that a man who has this appearance has prepared himself

---

[68]*De constantia sapientis* 6.4.

[69]*De constantia sapientis* 6.8.

[70]See J. Geffcken, *Kynika und Verwandtes* (Heidelberg: Winter, 1909), 53–58; E. Schuppe, "Tribon," PW 6A (1937): 2415–19, esp. 2417; H. D. Betz, *Lukian von Samosata und das Neue Testament*, TU 76 (Berlin: Akademie-Verlag, 1961), 133 n. 3; idem, *Der Apostel Paulus*, 47–53; B. R. Voss, "Die Keule der Kyniker," *Hermes* 95 (1967): 124-25; W. Liefeld, "The Wandering Preacher as a Social Figure in the Roman Empire" (Diss., Columbia University, 1967, 146ff., 167ff.; J. F. Kindstrand, *Bion of Borysthenes: A Collection of the Fragments with Introduction and Commentary*, Studia Graeca Upsaliensis 11 (Uppsala: Almqvist & Wiksell, 1976), 161–63.

[71]Dio Chrysostom *Discourse* 72.5; pseudo-Lucian *The Cynic* 20.

[72]Dio Chrysostom *Discourse* 34.2; 35.2-3.

[73]Dio Chrysostom *Discourse* 12.9; cf. 72.16. On the philosopher's *parrēsia*, see A. J. Malherbe, " 'Gentle as a Nurse': The Cynic Background to 1 Thess. 2," *NovT* 12 (1970): 203–17 (= 35–48 in this volume).

to admonish them and put them to the test and not to flatter or to spare any of them, but, on the contrary, ... to reprove them to the best of his ability by his words, and to show what sort of persons they are.[74]

Thus, while the garb identifies him as a philosopher, it is also associated with personal challenge that more often than not met with rejection.[75]

Lucian's view that many Cynics dressed in the way they did only to make themselves more conspicuous was true of many,[76] and even persons who favored the ideal were put off by Cynics' boasting about their garb.[77] But the serious Cynics, to whom we shall return later, boasted about their dress because they attached far greater significance to it. To them, taking up the garb was not simply a means of attracting an audience, but a deliberate act to demonstrate that the simplicity of soul for which they strived found expression in their way of life.[78] The Cynic assumed the dress at his "conversion" as part of his self-examination and self-discipline.[79] As he takes the "short cut to happiness," the practical life of virtue, and shuns the circuitous route of doctrine and intellectual speculation,[80] he dons the garb to assist him in stripping to essentials in his new life. His dress is his armament in the campaign he now conducts.[81] A gift from the gods,[82] these weapons aid him in a number of ways. They separate him from the multitude and its values and drive him to rely on his inner self, where his security lies.[83] They show that he is opposed to popular opinion and is in a campaign against the appearances which war against life.[84] Taken up for the sake of frugality, the weapons are effective in driving away from him lovers of pleasures, and they aid him in exercising simplicity in spirit and everyday life.[85] In short, they demonstrate him to be a person who places the highest value on the exercise of his own free will.

These Cynics are like Antisthenes' Odysseus in that their lowly garb is described as weapons. Unlike him, however, their dress does not enable them

---

[74]Dio Chrysostom *Discourse* 72.9. The entire oration deals with the philosopher's garb. The crowds approach him with suspicion (7), active dislike (9), or curiosity (10–11).

[75]E.g., Dio Chrysostom *Discourses* 32.20,24,29,74; 34.6; *Gnomologium Vaticanum* 352 (135 Sternbach); pseudo-Diogenes *Epistle* 45.

[76]*Nigrinus* 24; cf. *Dialogues of the Dead* 1.1; *The Runaways* 4, 14, 20, 27; Seneca *Epistle* 5.1-3.

[77]Epictetus *Discourses* 3.22.10,50; 4.8.5; Maximus of Tyre *Discourse* 1.9-10 (15,4-18,3 Hobein). Cf. Geffcken, *Kynika und Verwandtes,* 139–40.

[78]Pseudo-Diogenes *Epistle* 15.

[79]Dio Chrysostom *Discourse* 13.10. For an unconvincing debunking of Dio's account, see J. L. Moles, "The Career and Conversion of Dio Chrysostom," *JHS* 98 (1978): 79–100, here 88.

[80]On *syntomos hodos* as a description of Cynicism, see Lucian *Philosophies for Sale* 11; pseudo-Crates *Epistles* 6; 13; 16; 21; pseudo-Diogenes *Epistles* 12; 30; 44, and see V. Emeljanow, "A Note on the Cynic Short Cut to Virtue," *Menemosyne* n. s. 18/2 (1965): 182–84.

[81]Lucian *Philosophies for Sale* 8.

[82]Pseudo-Crates *Epistles* 16; 23; pseudo-Diogenes *Epistle* 34.

[83]Pseudo-Crates *Epistle* 13; pseudo-Diogenes *Epistle* 30 on security; pseudo-Crates *Epistles* 6; 16; 23; pseudo-Diogenes *Epistle* 12 on separating from persons with different standards.

[84]Pseudo-Diogenes *Epistles* 7; 34. Cf. pseudo-Crates *Epistle* 33.2, the Cynic's garb guards him.

[85]Pseudo-Crates *Epistle* 23; pseudo-Diogenes *Epistles* 15; 34.

to sneak up on someone's blind side, nor do they associate it with versatility in speech. On the contrary, it draws attention to them and sets them apart, sometimes becoming the very cause of the ill treatment they receive. Far from being a symbol of adaptability, their garb asserts their independence from the conventions and values of society.[86] These Cynics are also unlike the Stoics who chose to develop Antisthenes' other image. They do not use the image of the fortified city to describe the intellectual exercises by which the sage attains security, as the Stoics did, but in conscious rejection of the need or desirability of intellectual sophistication, they stress the practical life which is lived by willing it.[87] Hans Dieter Betz has shown—but without examining the military metaphor in detail—that discussions of the philosopher's *schema* lie behind part of the debate in 2 Corinthians 10–13.[88] Before turning to Paul, it remains to examine the fate of Odysseus at the hands of his admirers and detractors after Antisthenes.

Odysseus: Hero and Villain

Odysseus continued to meet with a mixed reception. He was sometimes used by the same author as both a positive and negative example.[89] "His traditional qualities, especially the ambiguous ones, are now manipulated and reorientated to suit prevailing policies and doctrines."[90] He is still remembered as crafty, duplicitous, and too much given to expediency,[91] but although he is acknowledged to have done things in secret and without any witnesses, Ovid could also claim that Ulysses was superior in intellect to his allies.[92] According to Stanford, Ovid's account of the contest between Ajax and Odysseus is an exhibition of Roman rhetoric in a mythological setting. The contest had become a subject for declamations, and Ovid intended to illustrate the

---

[86]The Cynic's dress is therefore part of his "falsifying of the currency," on which see Diogenes Laertius *Lives of Eminent Philosophers* 6.21-22, 71; Donald R. Dudley, *A History of Cynicism from Diogenes to the Fifth Century* A.D. (London: Methuen, 1937), 20–22; H. Niehues-Pröbsting, *Der Kynismus des Diogenes und der Begriff des Zynismus* (Munich: W. Fink, 1979), 43–56. However, not all Cynics made that connection. According to Lucian *Demonax* 5, Demonax wore the Cynic garb but lived the same life as everyone else.

[87]The image does appear, e.g., in pseudo-Diogenes *Epistle* 29.1, but not in the Stoic manner. On the Cynic self-understanding, see A. J. Malherbe, "Self-Definition among Epicureans and Cynics," in *Jewish and Christian Self-Definition. Vol. 3: Self-Definition in the Greco-Roman World,* B. F. Meyer and E. P. Sanders (Philadelphia: Fortress Press, 1982): 46–59 (= 11–24 in this volume).

[88]*Der Apostel Paulus,* 47–57.

[89]On the use of examples in Greek and Latin Literature, see B. Fiore, S. J., *The Function of Personal Example in the Socratic and Pastoral Epistles,* AnBib 105 (Rome: Biblical Institute Press, 1986).

[90]Stanford, *The Ulysses Theme,* 118-19.

[91]Statius *Achilleid* 1.784; Horace *Ode* 1.6.7; *Satire* 2.5; Cicero *De officiis* 3.97. Stanford (*The Ulysses Theme,* 266 n. 12) tries too hard to remove any unfavorable assessment of Ulysses from Horace.

[92]Ovid *Metamorphoses* 13.15, 101–4, 360–69. See Stanford, *The Ulysses Theme,* 138–43.

conflict between the man of action and the man of counsel. His own preference is clearly stated: "The event made clear the power of eloquence: the skilful speaker won the brave man's arms."[93] Other orators praised his eloquence and style, and Plutarch refers to him as a defender of the moderate form of the philosopher's bold speech (parrēsia).[94]

In general, the Stoics praised Odysseus.[95] They did have difficulty with his weeping, but were more inclined to see him as an exemplar of virtue and wisdom.[96] Like Hercules, he was to them an ideal wise man because he was unconquered by struggles, despised pleasures, and was victorious over all terrors.[97] He was a man of sense (ho ton noun echōn),[98] an example of the person who controls his passions with his reason (logismos).[99] Yet he was adaptable, striving in every word to be courteous and affable in all.[100]

The way in which Stoics dealt with his weakness is instructive. Epictetus simply dismisses Homer's description of Odysseus's weeping on the ground that if Odysseus had wept, he could not have been a good man, and it is self-evident to Epictetus that he had been.[101] Far more characteristic for Epictetus is that Odysseus trusted in his own judgments about which things are under our control and which not, while at the same time being an example of the way God governs human affairs and of someone who does nothing without calling on God.[102]

Two passages from Pacuvius's Niptra which Cicero quotes are particularly significant. In one, as she washes Ulysses' feet, his nurse recognizes him and approvingly speaks of "the gentleness of (his) speech, the softness of (his) body" (lenitudo orationibus, mollitudo corporis).[103] Cicero is concerned

---

[93]Metamorphoses 13.382-83, according to Stanford's translation.
[94]Cicero Brutus 40, 177; De oratore 1.142; 2.64; 2.120; Tusculan Disputations 5.46; Quintilian Institutio oratoria 11.3.158; 12.10.64; Aulus Gellius Attic Nights 1.15.3; Plutarch How to Tell a Flatterer from a Friend 66F, cf. 74B. Plutarch's discussion of parrēsia is heavily dependent on Cynic and Stoic sources. For other Stoics, see Epictetus Discourse 2.24.26; Heraclitus Homerica Problemata 67.5 (72 Buffière).
[95]Ganss ("Das Bild des Weisen bei Seneca," 122) is wrong when he says that Odysseus had lost his earlier significance as a paradigm in the later philosophial literature. Cf. Stanford, The Ulysses Theme, 118–27.
[96]Cicero De finibus 5.49; Horace Epistle 1.2.17-18. Cf. Lucian The Parasite 10, where Odysseus is criticized for not being a better Stoic. For the problem of his weeping, see Stanford, The Ulysses Theme, 121.
[97]Seneca De constantia sapientis 2.1. As a philosopher, Seneca admired Ulysses; as a dramatist he denigrated him. Cf. Stanford, The Ulysses Theme, 144.
[98]Plutarch Advice to Bride and Groom 139A. For ho noun echōn as a description of the Stoic sage, see SVF 3.548, 563, 701, 717.
[99]Plutarch How to Study Poetry 31B-D.
[100]Cicero De officiis 1.113.
[101]Epictetus Discourse 3.24.13–21, on which see A. J. Malherbe, "Pseudo-Heraclitus, Epistle 4: The Divinization of the Wise Man," JAC 21 (1978): 49.
[102]Cf. Epictetus Discourse 3.26.33–34.
[103]Tusculan Disputations 5.46. According to Cicero, it is Anticlea, Ulysses' mother, but in the scene he and Pacuvius have in mind (Odyssey 19.390-93), Euryclea, Ulysses' nurse, does the washing. For lenis as a description of speech, see Cicero De oratore 2.183; Quintilian, Institutio oratoria 6.1.50; 9.4.127.

whether to accept these qualities as good in the philosophical sense. His other quotation, in a discussion of the soul, is more illustrative.[104] Cicero holds that the soul has two parts, one with and one without reason *(ratio)*. The one without is soft *(molle)*. Reason by its own effort strives and becomes perfect virtue. It is man's duty to enable reason to rule over the other part. He does this when close associates shame a person when the soft part of his soul acts disgracefully. This happened to Ulysses when he was reproved for his wailing. Cicero says that Ulysses did not wail extravagantly but with restraint, and he then quotes Pacuvius. In this respect, Cicero claims, Pacuvius has greater insight than Sophocles, who made Ulysses lament excessively, for Pacuvius says:

> You too, Ulysses, though we see you sore stricken, are almost too soft in spirit
> *(nimis paene animo es molli)*, you who, accustomed to live life-long under arms
> *(consuetus in aevom agere)*.

On his deathbed Ulysses expressed the attitude that it is appropriate to complain at hostile fortune, but not to bewail it. Ulysses is therefore an example of the person in whose spirit the softer part obeyed reason just as a disciplined soul obeys a strict general.

Odysseus, therefore, despite the difficulty that his "softness" represents, was a paradigm for some Stoics.[105] He represented the sage who subdues the passions through reason. However, the military imagery that was often used by Stoics to describe the wise man's fortified soul does not appear to have been used extensively in discussing Odysseus, and other military images appear only incidentally, as they do here in Cicero. Nor does Antisthenes' characterization of the philosopher's garb as his weapons find application to Odysseus among Stoics. The situation with the Cynics is altogether different.

During his Cynic period, Dio Chrysostom repeatedly compared himself with Odysseus.[106] At his conversion to the Cynic life, when he had been banished by Domitian, he consulted Apollo and called to mind Odysseus, who would become his example during his wanderings: "So after exhorting myself in this way neither to fear or be ashamed of my action, and putting

---

[104]*Tusculan Disputations* 2.47–50.

[105]Note also the Stoic allegorists' interpretation of Odysseus and the moly plant. According to Heraclitus *Homerica Problemata* 73.8–10, Hermes, who is the rational intelligence *(logismos)*, gives Odysseus the *molu*, which signifies prudence *(phronēsis)*, to withstand the onslaught of the passions. According to Apollonius Sophista *Lexicon Homericum*, s.v. *molu*, Cleanthes said that *molu* allegorically signifies the reason by which the *hormai* and *pathē* are softened.

[106]Moles ("The Career and Conversion of Dio Chrysostom"; n. 79 above) has called into question Dio's account of his Cynic period and scholarly acceptance of it. On Odysseus and Dio, see J. F. Kindstrand, *Homer in der zweiten Sophistik*, Studia Graeca Upsaliensia 7 (Uppsala: Almqvist & Wiksell, 1973), 34–35; Desideri, *Dione di Prusa*, 174 n. 2; Moles, "Career," 97.

on humble attire *(stolēn tapeinēn)* and otherwise chastening myself, I proceeded to roam everywhere."[107] At the end of his wanderings, when he had heard Domitian's death, he stripped off his rags, quoting *Odyssey* 22.1, "Then Odysseus of many counsels stripped off his rags."[108] Dressed in this fashion, and grateful to the gods for preventing him from becoming an eyewitness to the injustices of Domitian, he went about "demanding crusts, not cauldrons fine nor swords" (*Odyssey* 17.222).[109] According to Dio, Diogenes too was like Odysseus in every respect as he moved among people in the guise of a beggar.[110] In this, we shall see, he does not agree with certain other Cynics. Dio knew that the philosopher's garb was referred to as his armament, and he is careful to distinguish himself from those Cynics who made much of their garb as their weaponry.[111] The philosopher's weapons, defenses, allies, and bodyguards in his battle against the passions, he says, are wise and prudent words and not the outward garb as the majority think. That most people judge philosophers by their dress, rather than by what they really are, is not surprising since the same mistake was made in the case of Odysseus, who was not distinguished from the beggar Irus because they were dressed alike. The professed philosophers Dio has in mind are those "who do many harsh things," that is, the rigoristic Cynics.[112]

Dio reflects the same concerns in *Discourse* 33. In his self-introduction (1-14), he distinguishes the ill-clad philosopher who censures people in order to improve them from the sleekly dressed sophist who flatters then for his own benefit. Thersites, to whom Apollo paid the highest tribute because he first censured himself, is cited as an example of the former.[113] The philosopher enters a world full of vice and filled with enemy upon enemy (15). Like Odysseus, he

---

[107]*Discourse* 13.10-11.

[108]According to Philostratus *Lives of the Sophists* 1.488.

[109]*Discourse* 1.50.

[110]*Discourse* 9.9. Cf. Hoïstad, *Cynic Hero and Cynic King,* 196, for the similarities to Antisthenes's Odysseus.

[111]*Discourse* 49.10-12.

[112]Cf. *Discourse* 32.11, and for the type, Malherbe, "Gentle as a Nurse," 208–10; idem, "Self-Definition among Epicureans and Cynics" (n. 87 above) (35–48 and 11–24 in this volume).

[113]Thersites is usually represented unfavorably as the dour Cynic, e.g., Lucian *Philosophies for Sale* 7; *The Fisherman* 7; *The Runaways* 30; *The Ignorant Book-Collector* 7. On Lucian, see K. Funk, "Untersuchungen über die Lucianische Vita Demonactis," *Philologus,* Suppl. 10 (1907): 597; R. Helm, *Lucian und Menipp* (Leipzig/Berlin: B. G. Teubner, 1906): 53–54, 196. Lucian *(The Ignorant Book-Collector 7)* pokes fun at Thersites as a Cynic making a popular speech *(dēmēgorōn):* If he should get Achilles' armor he would not change immediately nor would he be able to use it. In *Demonax* 61 Thersites is called a mob-orator *(dēmēgoros)* of the Cynic type. Demonax, however, accepted him as an illustration when it suited him (cf. 50), as does Dio. When Dio does characterize him, it is not as *skythrōpos* or *dēmēgoros,* or from material derived from the *Odyssey,* but with words from *Iliad* 2.246, as *ligus agorētēs,* a "clear-voiced speaker."

subdues his body with injurious blows, casts around his shoulders sorry rags, in guise a slave, steals into the wide-eyed town of those who hold debauch *(Odyssey* 4.244-46)

in order to do his neighbors some good. In response, they either stir him up or, what is of greater moment to Dio, summon a philosopher who will appear to them to be an intractable and savage man as a speaker *(dēmēgoros)*, from whom they are eager to hear what they are in no condition to endure.[114]

The type of Cynic whom Dio represents, who submits to ill treatment and hardships in order to benefit his audience, goes back to Antisthenes, and so does Dio's use of Odysseus to describe himself as such a Cynic who wears the humble garb.[115] With Dio we have now moved from distinctions between Stoics and Cynics to differences among the Cynics themselves. The harsh Cynics were most insistent in describing their form of dress as armament, a description that is also ultimately dependent on Antisthenes. But what is at issue here is not merely the continuing influence of Antisthenes in the Cynics' use of the imagery, rather their self-understanding as it is related to the imagery. The differences become clear in the Cynic epistolary literature which reflects the perception of those Cynics whom Dio opposes, and they cast light on his use of the Antisthenic tradition. The letters in question, certain of the ones attributed to Crates and Diogenes, date from the early Empire and represent issues under debate around the time Paul wrote 2 Corinthians.[116]

The Weapons of the Gods

Two of the letters attributed to Crates are hostile to the Antisthenic tradition. They assert that Diogenes and not Odysseus was the father of Cynicism, and that the Cynic's garb are the weapons of the gods or of Diogenes with which the Cynic drives away those who would corrupt him.[117] In *Epistle* 19, the antagonism to Odysseus becomes vituperative.[118] In an attack on the view that

---

[114]For the curious attraction such people had for the public, see A. J. Malherbe, "Medical Imagery in the Pastoral Epistles," in *Texts and Testaments: Critical Essays on the Bible and Early Church Fathers,* ed. W. E. March (San Antonio, Texas: Trinity Univ. Press, 1980): 27 (= 132–133 in this volume).

[115]On Dio as an Antisthenic Cynic, see Hoïstad, *Cynic Hero and Cynic King,* 164–65, 196–97.

[116]On the dates and authorship of the letters attributed to Crates and Diogenes, see *The Cynic Epistles: A Study Edition,* ed. A. J. Malherbe, SBLSBS 12 (Missoula, Mont.: Scholars Press, 1977), 10–21.

[117]Pseudo-Crates *Epistles* 19; 23.

[118]Cf. W. Capelle, "De cynicorum epistulis" (Diss., Göttingen, 1896), 23, 53. Norden ("Beiträge zur Geschichte der griechischen Philosophie" [n. 45 above], 394–95) states that most of the accusations made against Odysseus in the letter appear in the scholia to Homer as *aporiai* and are solved. According to Stanford *(The Ulysses Theme,* 266 n. 12), M. Martorana *(Ulisse nella letteratura Latina* [Palermo & Rome, 1926], 75–80) discusses the Cynic rejection of Antisthenes' conception of Odysseus as the proto-Cynic, and suggests that Horace *Satire* 2.5 may reflect the same attitude.

Odysseus was the father of Cynicism, a bill of particulars against him is drawn up: he was the softest of all his associates,[119] he put pleasure above all else, he put the cloak on only once, always looked to God for aid, and begged from everyone, even the lowly or base *(tapeinoi).* Diogenes is then claimed to be the father of Cynicism: he wore the Cynic garb throughout his entire life, was superior to toil and pleasure, demanded his financial support, but not from the *tapeinoi,*[120] was self-sufficient, had confidence in himself *(eph'heautō tharrounta),*[121] trusted in reason, and was courageous in his practice of virtue. Odysseus is here made to represent the milder Cynic like Dio, from whom the author wants to be distinguished, Diogenes the paradigm of the superior, consistent, rigorous, and demanding Cynic.

Another Cynic, writing in the name of Diogenes, also represents the interest of the period in the original invention of the Cynic garb.[122] It is clear from *Epistle* 34 that the issue revolved around Antisthenes' interpretation of Odysseus. "Diogenes" denies that he had received the lessons of the *schēma* and begging from Antisthenes; what Antisthenes taught had already been anticipated by Homer and the poets. The statement indicates that Antisthenes is still identified with the garb but is removed as its inventor.[123] While "Diogenes" belongs to the same rigoristic type of Cynicism as "Crates," he does not share the latter's low esteem of Odysseus, nor does he shrink from relating the Cynic to the gods, albeit in a typically Cynic manner. In *Epistle* 7, he calls himself heaven's dog who lives free under Zeus, and attributes what is good to Zeus and not to his neighbors. It is his living according to nature *(kata physin)* and not according to popular opinion *(kata doxan)* that is equivalent

---

[119]Softness frequently appears in vice lists describing the self-indulgent person, e.g. Lucian *Timon* 28; Epictetus *Discourse* 2.16.45; pseudo-Diogenes *Epistles* 12; 29.2; 36.5. The self-sufficient Cynic's *schēma* is contrasted to the self-indulgent person's soft garments by pseudo-Lucian *The Cynic* 17; cf. pseudo-Diogenes *Epistle* 28.1; pseudo-Crates *Epistle* 19; Cicero *De oratore* 1.226.

[120]Paradoxically, Cynic begging was viewed as a sign of independence: By surrendering his private property, the Cynic was freed from evil and showed himself superior to the values of popular opinion (pseudo-Crates *Epistle* 7; pseudo-Diogenes *Epistle* 9); begging is really a demand for what belongs to him (pseudo-Crates *Epistles* 26; 27; pseudo-Diogenes *Epistle* 10.2); he begs only from people who are worthy of him and his teaching (pseudo-Crates *Epistles* 2; 19; 22; 36; pseudo-Diogenes *Epistle* 38.3–4).

[121]Cf. pseudo-Diogenes *Epistle* 29: The harsh Cynic clad in the traditional garb will turn Dionysius away from his softness, take away his fears, and instill *tharsos.*

[122]Various persons are credited with it. In addition to the Cynic epistles, the sources behind Diogenes Laertius *Lives of Eminent Philosophers* 6.21 and Lucian *Dialogues of the Dead* 21 refer to Antisthenes. The epistles of Crates, Diogenes Laertius *Lives of Eminent Philosophers* 6.22–23 and Dio Chrysostom *Discourse* 72.11, 16 attribute it to Diogenes, the latter including Socrates, and Lucian *(Philosophies for Sale)* 8 finds it already in Heracles. On the tradition, see F. Leo, "Diogenes bei Plautus," *Hermes* 41(1906): 441–46; Dudley, *A History of Cynicism,* 6-7. Kindstrand *(Bion of Borysthenes,* 162) thinks that the practice may have begun with Socrates.

[123]Victor Emeljanow, "The Letters of Diogenes" (Diss., Stanford University 1974), 41.

to his being free under God.[124] Quoting *Odyssey* 13.434-38, but not mentioning Odysseus by name, he claims that the garb is an invention of the gods and not of men. He lives under their protection, and therefore he calls for confidence *(tharrein)* in his dress.[125] He dons the garb with conscious determination as a reflection of his simplicity of soul and demonstration that his spoken claims conform to his life.[126] No enemy would dare to campaign against such a person.[127]

These formidable Cynics, then, still use the tradition that begins with Antisthenes, but, offended by the relative moderation in Cynic life which had come to be associated with Antisthenes, they denied their indebtedness to him and distanced themselves from Odysseus. The old charges against Odysseus are now applied to their fellow Cynics, namely, that they are not consistent, that they lack courage, associate with the base, and are soft. The Cynic letters do not comment on Odysseus's versatility of speech, but other sources do,[128] and the rigoristic Cynics' criticism of the adaptation of a philosopher's speech to particular circumstances is well documented.[129] Theirs was not a view of Odysseus that would permit treatment like that of the Stoics of Pacuvius's hero, gentle in speech and soft in body, who through reason subdued his weakness. Such an Odysseus was not a positive example for them, but was to be used in their polemic against their competitors.

In sum, two military images that were popular in the first century were derived from Antisthenes. He applied the image of a city fortified against a siege to the wise man's rational faculties with which he fortifies himself, and he applied the image of a soldier's personal armor to the garb of Odysseus the proto-Cynic, who through his versatility and self-humiliation adapted himself to circumstances in order to gain the good of his associates and save them. The imagery of the fortified city was adopted by Stoics and developed in their description of the sage who is secure in the citadel of his reason. The imagery of the philosopher's garb as his armor became popular among Cynics, who do not appear to have used the imagery of the fortified city to any great extent to describe the philosopher's personal security.

Odysseus received the attention of both schools of philosophy. The Stoics were embarrassed by his softness and weeping? but with the aid of their

---

[124]For an attempt to place this passage in the context of Cynic attitudes toward religion, see Malherbe, "Pseudo-Heraclitus, *Epistle* 4" (n. 101 above) 50–51, and for a modification of the view expressed there, idem, "Self-Definition among the Epicureans and Cynics" (n. 87 above), nn. 73–75.
[125]Cf. pseudo-Diogenes *Epistle* 10.1.
[126]Pseudo-Diogenes *Epistle* 15.
[127]Pseudo-Diogenes *Epistle* 46.
[128]E.g., Horace *Satire* 2.5.27–44; cf. Martorana, *Ulisse* (n. 118 above).
[129]See Malherbe, "Gentle as a Nurse" (n. 73 above).

psychology and their view of cosmic determinism they could redeem him as a person who overcame his passions and hardships through his reason and who lived the life assigned him by the divine. The Cynics, who did not possess such a well-developed doctrine of intellectual and moral development, and who placed the greatest value on the volition of the independent man, were divided over him. In their debates, the philospher's garb was taken as a symbol for his disposition and demeanor. Cynics of more moderate bent identified with him as the wandering preacher of Antisthenes who went about clad in rags and suffered humiliation. The rigoristic Cynics, on the other hand, rejected the Odysseus of Antisthenes as their model and claimed that their garb was armament received from the gods. It functioned not only in relation to the masses they excoriated, but also to distinguish themselves from other Cynics who, like Odysseus, appeared to be inconsistent in their behavior, were soft in body, and were abjectly dependent on others, even the base. Some of them decried Odysseus's dependence on the divine, but others interpreted this relation to the divine to refer to the Cynic's life of opposition to society's values and conventions. Not brought up in relation to Odysseus by these Cynics, but frequently discussed by other writers not well disposed to him, was his adaptability in speech, a feature rigorous Cynics rejected.

Paul and the Corinthians

In 2 Corinthians 10:3-6, Paul uses both images, in conjunction with each other, to introduce this polemical section of the letter. He describes his own weapons in terms approximating the self-description of the rigoristic Cynics and describes his opponents' fortifications in terms strongly reminiscent of the Stoic sage. As in the tradition we have surveyed, the imagery represents two types of self-understanding, but by Paul they are brought into conflict with each other in a detailed image of a successful siege. In his warfare *(strateuometha)* Paul is armed to demolish fortifications, and his attack is described as taking place in three successive stages: demolishing all fortifications, taking captives, and punishing resistance.[130] The precise relationship between these verses, and indeed 10:1-6, to the rest of chapters 10—13 is difficult to determine, and cannot be pursued here. A number of observations, however, are in order.

Paul uses this particular imagery only here.[131] Why? It is not unlikely that the opposition he encountered suggested it to him. To determine whether

---

[130]The three participles, *kathairountes, aichmalōtizontes, echontes,* are grammatically dependent on *strateuometha* and explicate how the campaign takes place.
[131]The closest parallel is 2 Cor. 2:14-16, if one accepts the interpretation of some commentators. Cf. E. B. Allo, *Saint Paul: Second Épitre aux Corinthiens,* 2d ed., ÉB (Paris: J. Gabalda, 1956), 45–47; Hughes, *Paul's Second Epistle to the Corinthians,* 77–78; Lietzmann-Kümmel, *An die Korinther,* 198; Barrett, *A Commentary on the Second Epistle to the Corinthians,* 98.

this was indeed the case, it will be necessary to give closer attention to the charges brought against Paul.

It is important for Betz to decide whether 10:1, "I who am humble *(tapeinos)* when face to face with you, but bold *(tharrō)* to you when I am away," is to be interpreted in light of 10:10, "For they say, 'His letters are weighty *(bareiai)* and strong *(ischyrai)*, but his bodily presence is weak *(asthenēs)*, and his speech of no account *(exouthenēmemos)*,' " and to be understood as part of the accusation against Paul, as most commentators do, or whether to read 10:1 as already a reply to 10:10, as Betz does.[132]

What is decisive for Betz is what is understood under the terms *tapeinos-tharrein* which describe the inconsistency and incongruity of Paul's actions. To illuminate the matter, Betz traces a tradition in which the philosopher, particularly Socrates, is described as *tapeinos*. The Cynics appropriated this tradition when they discussed the absurdity of the garb, which rested for them on their principle of "counterfeiting the coinage." The pair *tapeinos-tharrein* could therefore assume the positive value that it also has here in Paul. In 10:1, Betz holds, Paul responds to the charge of 10:10, but does not use the same terms, which suggests that it is Paul himself who introduced the pair *tapeinos-tharrein*. The criticism in 10:10 of Paul's inconsistency in communication between his speech, when present, and his letters, when absent, is formulated in terms derived from the field of rhetoric. In response, Paul also uses such terms. Thus *tolmān* ("to be bold") and *tharrein* both came from contemporary rhetoric, and were used in the conflict between philosophers and sophists.[133] Paul's apology is thus part of this tradition, and Betz interprets 10:1-6 in light of that conflict.[134]

Betz is correct in drawing attention to the philosophical discussions of the philosopher's *schēma* and to the Cynic character of the self-deprecating irony with which Paul begins the section.[135] He does not, however, do justice to the military imagery that dominates 10:1-6, nor does he satisfactorily discuss its relation to the charge against Paul mentioned in v. 2, by "certain persons who reason *(logizomenous)* that we are conducting ourselves according to the flesh *(kata sarka peripatountas;* RSV: 'acting in worldly fashion')." These issues must be explored before interpreting 10:1-6 in light of the reconstructed philosophic-sophistic controversy, especially since the terms explicitly used by Paul to describe criticism of his speech and letters do not appear here.

---

[132]See Betz, *Der Apostel Paulus,* 44–57.

[133]On *tolmān,* see further, Betz, *Der Apostel Paulus,* 67–68, who is followed by Josef Zmijewski, *Der Stil der paulinischen "Narrenrede",* Bonner Biblische Beiträge 52 (Cologne/Bonn: Hanstein, 1978), 234–35.

[134]Betz, *Der Apostel Paulus,* 68.

[135]For the Cynic irony, see Geffcken, *Kynika und Verwandtes,* 55–56, and Kindstrand, *Bion of Borysthenes,* 183.

Exactly what Paul's opponents meant when they accused him of living *kata sarka* is much debated.[136] They may thereby have meant that he had no visions or ecstatic experiences and that he did not "behave in an authoritarian, self-assertive way that could be ascribed to spiritual authority and superiority."[137] But the use of the same phrase in 2 Corinthians 1:17 does lend some concreteness to its use here. In defending himself against the charge that his failure to carry out his announced visit to them proved his insincerity, Paul in two rhetorical questions reflects the language in which the charge was made:[138] "Was I vacillating when I wanted to do this? Do I make my plans according to the flesh *(kata sarka)*, so as to say at the same time 'Yes, yes' and 'No, no'?" Here the inconsistency between his stated plans and his deeds is ascribed to duplicity. In 1:12-14, where he protests his sincerity, consistency, and clarity, he also denies that his conduct in the world and especially in relation to the Corinthians had been in fleshly wisdom *(sophia sarkikē)*. The same concern with his inconsistency is reflected in 10:1, and it is therefore likely that *kata sarka peripatein* is the Corinthians' interpretation of his conduct. It is sufficient for our purpose to note that the occasion for Paul's use of the military imagery is criticism of what is perceived to have been the inconsistency and adaptability of his behavior.

The same criticisms, we have seen, were made of Odysseus, viewed by some as a proto-Cynic. Other elements of 10:1-2, which Betz interprets in terms of contemporary rhetoric, also are part of the tradition we have traced, and when seen from that perspective clarify the connection between vv. 1-2 and 3-6.[139]

Paul's inconsistency of behavior is described in 10:1 in terms of the contrast between the baseness or humiliation *(tapeinos)* he exhibited when present and the confidence *(tharrō)* with which he acted when away. It is not immediately obvious whether Paul's opponents formulated their complaint in these words or whether it is Paul himself who does so. What he is referring to is clarified by 11:7, where he describes his decision to support himself by manual labor as his voluntary self-humiliation *(emauton tapeinōn)*. In referring to his plying his trade as something humiliating, he reflects the upper

---

[136]See the catalogue of interpretations in G. Theissen, *The Social Setting of Pauline Christianity: Essays on Corinth,* trans. and ed. J. H. Schütz (Philadelphia: Fortress Press, 1982), 64 n. 44. Windisch *(Der zweite Korintherbrief,* 295 n. 2) compares the construction to Diogenes Laertius *Lives of Eminent Philosophers* 6.11, which refers to a statement by Antisthenes on the wise man's conduct.

[137]Thus Barrett, *A Commentary on the Second Epistle to the Corinthians,* 250, on the basis of the content of chaps. 10–13.

[138]Cf. Windisch, *Der zweite Korintherbrief,* 64.

[139]Betz concentrates on the former, where he espies traces of the philosophic-sophistic controversy, hence the latter is a difficult passage for him *(Der Apostel Paulus,* 68).

class attitude toward manual labor.[140] However, Paul viewed his employment as belonging to the hardships that characterized his apostleship,[141] and the practice of his trade was therefore part of his apostolic self-understanding. His refusal to accept financial support from the Corinthians when he was with them, but to maintain himself by tentmaking, could thus appear as humiliating, but it also involved Paul's and the Corinthians' understanding of apostleship.

When Paul was away, it was charged, he acted with guile by enriching himself by means of the collection for Jerusalem (12:16). However, in 10:2 Paul does not contrast his humiliation with his purported guile, but with confidence *(tharrō)*. The connection between *tapeinos* and *tharrein* becomes intelligible when viewed in light of the Cynic descriptions of the philosopher's dress as the armament of the gods. The rigorous Crates affirms that, although it is appropriate for the Cynic to receive financial aid from others, he was not to accept anything from the base *(tapeinoi)* but was to show his independence by selective begging[142] and be confident in himself *(eph' heautō tharrounta)*. Stated differently, his confidence was to be in his dress which is an invention of the gods and not men, a symbol of the conscious determination with which he undertakes his campaign and a means by which he distinguishes himself from others. Such a person is different from the two-faced Odysseus who begged from everyone.

Paul appropriates the language of the Cynics, but he applies it to himself in a completely different manner. Paul differs from the rigorous Cynics in not being concerned with the *tapeinotēs* of others but his own, namely, the self-humiliation of which his manual labor is part. In the voluntariness of his self-humiliation, he is like Antisthenes's Odysseus whom these rigorists reject. He further differs from them in that he does not beg and indeed refuses financial aid from his converts. His practice of supporting himself by manual labor was not, however, contrary to the practice or ideals of all Cynics. To some, the independence thus gained was to be strived for, and Ronald Hock has demonstrated that Paul's statements about his work should be seen in that context.[143] Nevertheless, viewed socially, and in the Corinthian debate theologically, his practice was humiliating. Where Paul does agree with Crates, ironically, is that his practice also distinguished himself from others (cf. 11:12).

---

[140]See R. F. Hock, "Paul's Tentmaking and the Problem of His Social Class," *JBL* 97 (1978): 555–64; idem, *The Social Context of Paul's Ministry: Tentmaking and Apostleship* (Philadelphia: Fortress Press, 1980), esp. 36, 60, 64.
[141]Cf. the reference to his manual labor in the list of apostolic hardships in 1 Cor. 4:9-13 (v. 12), and see Windisch, *Der zweite Korintherbrief*, 334.
[142]Cf. n. 120.
[143]*The Social Context of Paul's Ministry,* esp. 39–40, 56–59.

That Paul can describe himself as *tapeinos* does not, however, mean that he accepts abjectness as its corollary. To make that clear, he stresses his confidence *(tharrēsai te pepoithēsei)* and boldness *(tolmēsai)* in 10:2. In this respect he is like the rigoristic Cynics who have confidence in the armor of the gods although, as we shall see, he understands it differently. The boldness in this context refers to boldness in battle, and not to speech. Agesilaus, for example, is reported to have said that a general should have boldness *(tolmān)* toward the enemy and kindness toward the men under him.[144] For our purposes it is noteworthy that Odysseus's boldness or lack of it was a point at issue in Greek literature,[145] and we have encountered it in Antisthenes' account of the contest between Ajax and Odysseus. There Ajax accuses Odysseus of not having the boldness to take up Achilles' arms: he would rather be underhanded and submit to humiliation. Odysseus, who has only his humble garb as armor, sarcastically replies that he would not be so bold as to strive for reputation, but would be content with the maltreatment he receives if he might thereby save others. Implicit in his reply is that his boldness resides in his total behavior as symbolized by his rags. It becomes explicit in the later Cynics who debate his appropriateness as a model for them, although they use *tharrein* instead of *tolmān*. The words, however, are equivalent in meaning,[146] and Paul links them with *pepoithēsis* ("confidence") in 10:2 to stress the confidence with which he threatens to act against those who accuse him of conduct according to the flesh, that is, of acting underhandedly and inconsistently.

The imagery that lies behind 10:1-2 becomes explicit in verses 3-6. Paul rejects the charge that he lived *kata sarka* in such a way as to introduce the military imagery. Instead of saying "For though we live in the flesh we are not living according to the flesh," he says, "For though we live in the flesh *(en sarki)* we are not carrying on a war according to the flesh *(ou kata sarka strateuometha)*." The criticisms leveled against him had to do with his conduct, and he responds to them by describing his conduct in explicitly martial terms. "In the flesh" is to be understood simply as "in the world,"[147] and "according to the flesh" in the sense in which it was used by his opponents, that is, as describing his mean, inconsistent, underhanded, conniving conduct. Paul's warfare, then, consists in his manner of life. Far from being abject, the Paul

---

[144]Plutarch *Sayings of Spartans* 213C; *Gnomologium Vaticanum* 70 (32 Sternbach). Cf. also Epictetus *Discourse* 4.1.19.
[145]See G. Fitzer, "tolmaō," *TDNT* 8 (1972): 181–87.
[146]Cf. Windisch, *Der zweite Korintherbrief*, 294–95; Fitzer, "tolmān," 184 n. 17.
[147]Barrett, *A Commentary on the Second Epistle to the Corinthians*, 250; E. Schweizer, "sarx," *TDNT* 7 (1971): 126: "the earthly life in its totality"; R. Bultmann, *Theology of the New Testament*, trans. K. Grobel (New York: Charles Scribner's Sons, 1951), 1.235: "in the sphere of the obvious, or earthly-human, or the natural."

who is *tapeinos* is combative. In this respect he is like the Cynic who appears in humiliating circumstances and garb but is actually at war.

In an explanatory parenthesis (v. 4), Paul qualifies the nature of his equipment in the war: his weapons are not fleshly *(sarkika)* but powerful in God's service *(dynata tō theō)*. This qualification distinguishes Paul's use of the imagery from that of the Cynics and, while it expresses his confidence, refers it to God. "Fleshly" is used in the Pauline sense of what is opposed to God,[148] thus he does not contrast "fleshly weapons" to "spiritual weapons," which one might expect, but to weapons which are *dynata tō theō,* thereby laying the stress on the effectualness and divine origin of his weaponry.[149] What he means by *dynata tō theō* is not immediately clear. The construction can be intensive and be rendered "very powerful,"[150] or it can be a *dativus commodi,* "powerful for God" in whose service the weapons are wielded.[151] In view of Paul's treatment of weakness and power in this letter, the latter is the correct meaning. It is God's power that enables him to endure the hardships that characterize his apostleship;[152] he will boast in his weakness, for in it God's power is perfected.[153] The hardships may be viewed as demonstrations of weakness[154] and as belonging to his mean life, but Paul reevaluates them by making them the opportunity for the demonstration of God's power.[155]

Paul is like the Cynics in describing his manner of life, which for them was symbolized by their garb, as weapons, and by relating them to God. He differs radically from them, however, in that his confidence is not in himself but in God's power.

When Paul describes his own armament, he makes use of that part of the tradition which originated with Antisthenes and found its way into Cynics' discussions of their self-understanding. However, when he describes the objects of his attack, it is the Stoic appropriation of the other image that he finds useful. The self-sufficient, self-confident Stoic, secure in the fortification of his reason, represents a type antithetical to Paul's own self-understanding and provides him with the description of his opponents. Like Seneca, they feel secure in their elevated citadel. Paul had already made use of such Stoic self-descriptions elsewhere in his Corinthian correspondence to describe certain

---

[148]Cf. Schweizer, "sarx," 128.

[149]Windisch, *Der zweite Korintherbrief,* 297; Plummer, *Second Corinthians,* 276.

[150]Thus C. F. D. Moule, *An Idiom Book of New Testament Greek* (Cambridge: Cambridge Univ. Press, 1953), 184. The construction would then be a Hebraism.

[151]Thus Windisch, *Der zweite Korintherbrief,* 297; Barrett, *A Commentary on the Second Epistle to the Corinthians,* 251, and most commentators.

[152]Note the association of God's power with the so-called *peristasis* catalogues in 4:7-11 and 6:4-7.

[153]See 11:30–12:10 and cf. 13:3-4.

[154]Cf. the ironic references to his weakness which enclose the list of hardships in 11:21-29.

[155]Cf. R. Leivestad, "'The Meekness and Gentleness of Christ' 2 Cor. 10:1," *NTS* 12 (1966): 162.

Corinthians, so it comes as no surprise that he does so here, but now he uses military imagery.[156] The reasonings *(logismoi)* of his opponents are the fortifications that protect their every thought *(pan noēma)* against the knowledge of God *(gnōsis tou theou)*. On the surface, this appears to be an intellectual confrontation: Paul proclaims the knowledge of God which overpowers the corrupt thoughts of his opponents.[157] Paul does speak in 4:4-6 of the *noēmata* of unbelievers and the knowledge of God which is preached, and in 11:6 he does claim knowledge for himself. But the discussion in 10:1-6 has to do with his conduct. His humble life, in which God's power is manifested, is the armament with which he attacks his opponents. Thus he calls on his readers, not to listen to him, but to look at what is right in front of their eyes (10:7).[158]

Conclusion

We return to the question why Paul uses the Antisthenic tradition. His opponents may have described him in terms reminiscent of the unflattering depiction of Odysseus, to which Paul responded by applying the tradition in his own way. The similarities between the criticisms made of Odysseus and Paul are obvious. Only those directly relevant to the argument presented here have been taken up. It is not impossible that a conscious comparison was made by Paul's opponents. However, what was important about Odysseus was that he represented a certain type of preacher who to an observer might appear similar to Paul. There can be no doubt that Paul was familiar with the different types of philosophers, and that he took great care, on the one hand, to distinguish himself from some of them and, on the other hand, to describe himself in terms commonly used to depict certain ideal philosophers.[159] If

---

[156]For the use of Stoic (and Cynic) terminology, see R. M. Grant, "Hellenistic Elements in 1 Corinthians," in *Early Christian Origins: Studies in Honor of Harold R. Willoughby,* ed. A. Wikgren (Chicago: Quadrangle Books, 1961): 60–66. For the terminology in Paul's response to the Corinthian slogans, see S. K. Stowers, "A 'Debate' over Freedom: 1 Corinthians 6:12-20," in *Christian Teaching: Studies in Honor of LeMoine G. Lewis,* ed. Everett Ferguson (Abilene, Texas: Abilene Christian University, 1981): 59–71. Note the parallel between the attitude expressed in Lucian *Hermotimus* 81, that the Stoic, if he learns Stoic cosmology properly, will be "the only rich man, the only king, and the rest slaves and scum *(katharmata)* compared to (him)," and 1 Cor. 4:8, "Already you have become rich! Without us you have become kings!" followed by a *peristasis* catalogue which concludes, "we have become, and are now, as the refuse *(katharmata)* of the world, the offscouring *(peripsēma)* of all things." Windisch *(Der zweite Korintherbrief,* 25) lists a number of the ways Paul describes his opponents in 1 and 2 Corinthians, a major difference being that in 2 Corinthians the opposition is more vehement and personal and the details of the opposition are different in some respects.

[157]*Noēma* always has a negative connotation in 2 Corinthians; cf. 2:11; 3:14; 4:4; 11:3.

[158]Cf. 12:6, where, although he speaks of his speech and boasting, he again draws attention to what people can see in him.

[159]See Malherbe, "The Beasts of Ephesus," *JBL* 87 (1968): 71–80, and idem, "Gentle as a Nurse" (n. 73 above).

Hermann Funke is correct, Paul had already in 1 Corinthians 9:24-27 made use of Antisthenic tradition to describe his ministry.[160] And we have seen that in the immediately preceding verses he describes himself in a manner that echoes Antisthenes' Odysseus. It is therefore likely that it is Paul who in some respect thought of himself along the lines of the Antisthenic ideal. Having once introduced the tradition in the discussion with Corinth, he now also uses it to defend himself.

Paul obviously assumed that his method of argumentation would be intelligible to his Corinthian readers. His use of military imagery in writing to Corinth was particularly apt. The location of the city on the isthmus lent it great strategic importance.[161] It was known for its extensive fortifications, particularly those of Acrocorinth, from which, according to Strabo, one could look down on the isthmus.[162] Formidable in appearance and in fact, it could withstand a direct onslaught but was not immune to stealth.[163] The Spartans, however, appear to have viewed it with contempt, and Corinth came to represent in the apophthegmata the city whose walls offered ineffectual protection to its unworthy citizens.[164] Paul is equally disdainful of his Corinthians' defenses.

[160]"Antisthenes bei Paulus," *Hermes* 98 (1970): 459–71.

[161]Polybius *The Histories* 18.11.5-6. Cf. W. Elliger, *Paulus in Griechenland: Philippi, Thessaloniki, Athen, Korinth* (Stuttgart: Katholisches Bibelwerk, 1978), 202.

[162]Strabo *Geography* 8.6.21. Cf. R. Carpenter and A. Bon, *Corinth. 3.2: The Defenses of Acrocorinth and the Lower Town* (Cambridge, Mass.: Harvard Univ. Press, 1936).

[163]Cf. Plutarch *Aratus* 18.3–4.

[164]See Plutarch *Sayings of Kings and Commanders* 190EF (cf. 190A); *Sayings of Spartans* 215D. Cf. 212E, 221F, 230C; Valerius Maximus *Noteworthy Doings and Sayings* 37; see n. 29 above.

8

Medical Imagery in
the Pastoral Epistles

The author of the Pastoral Epistles makes frequent use of the language of health and disease in polemic leveled at false teachers and their followers. The expressions "sound (healthy) teaching" (1 Tim. 1:10; 2. Tim. 4:3; Tit. 1:9; 2:1), "sound words" (1 Tim. 6:3; 2 Tim. 1:13; Tit. 2:8), and being "sound in the faith" (Tit. 1:13; 2:2) appear in the New Testament only in the Pastorals and represent a major theme of the letters, namely, that orthodox teaching alone issues in a moral life. The entire complex of medical terminology in the letters, however, has not received extensive treatment. Commentators have occasionally discussed "sound teaching" and similar descriptions in brief excursuses, but they have not placed the use of these terms firmly in either their suspected philosophical context or in the argument of the letters them-selves.

Earlier Interpretations

The use of "sound teaching" and related terminology in the Pastorals pre-sented further evidence to Martin Dibelius that Paul was not the author of these letters.[1] The singular use of these terms in the Pastorals, he insisted, could not be explained either as a new designation for the gospel by Paul in his old age or as new terms coined to fight the heresy at hand. The use of the term was as old as Homer and common in the philosophical literature of the author's time. But this terminology should be understood in the con-temporary philosophical sense in which it designated rational speech and not in the original poetic sense in which it described the power of the gospel to bring healing and life. While rationality was not a basic part of the structure of Paul's thinking, Dibelius detected "some shifts toward rationalism" in the

---

[1]M Dibelius and H. Conzelmann, *A Commentary on the Pastoral Epistles,* trans. P. Buttolph and A. Yarbro, Hermeneia (Philadelphia: Fortress Press, 1972), 29–30.

Pastoral Epistles. The gospel, an established part of the church's teaching, is a rational criterion which can be applied.

Subsequent discussion has generally addressed the issues as identified by Dibelius. Some support has emerged for his claim that the terms were derived from the philosophers referring to the teaching of a rational moral life, but not to teaching whose goal is the health of the soul.[2]

Wilhelm Michaelis, however, rejected Dibelius's position and insisted that the terms should not be understood in a philosophical sense but in a context of a polemic against heresy. On this reading, the teaching is described as sound, not because it is rational or makes the readers or hearers spiritually healthy, but because it is free from the disease of heresy.[3] Such usage was not intended in a philosophical sense.

A mediating position was represented by Ulrich Luck, who with Dibelius insisted that the terminology could be understood only against the Greek hellenistic background, but for him that background was not specifically philosophical but represented the "average understanding." We thus have to do, not with a philosophical rationalism, but with "the logical relating of faith and teaching to rational existence in the world." Traditional teaching, in contrast to perverted doctrine, is concerned with "rational and proper life in the world, which as creation is characterised by order and reason."[4] It does not refer to teaching which seeks to make its readers whole.

The way non-Christian material has been utilized to illuminate the use of the terminology in the Pastorals is unsatisfactory. Dibelius did little more than list some parallels, and Luck did not clearly relate his discussion of the Pastorals to what he considered their background. Michaelis and Jeremias did not treat the pagan material at all. Ceslaus Spicq, while citing many parallels indicating that the terminology was not unusual in antiquity, did not present a unified picture that helps in understanding the language.[5] Robert J. Karris, although he assiduously gathered parallels from ancient philosophers to support his thesis that the anti-heretical polemic of the Pastorals was indebted to the philosophers' attacks on sophists, studiously avoided dealing with the terms describing health and disease.[6]

---

[2]E.g., B. S. Easton, *The Pastoral Epistles* (New York: Charles Scribner's Sons, 1947), 234; J. N. D. Kelly, *A Commentary on the Pastoral Epistles,* HNTC (New York: Harper & Row, 1963), 50.

[3]W. Michaelis, *Pastoralbriefe und Gefangenschaftsbriefe: Zur Echtheitsfrage der Pastoralbriefe,* NF, Erste Reihe 6 (Gütersloh: C. Bertelsmann, 1930), 79–85; N. Brox, *Die Pastoralbriefe,* 4th ed., RNT (Regensburg: F. Pustet, 1969), 39–40, 107–8, mentions neither Dibelius nor Michaelis in this context, but represents the latter's view, as does J. Jeremias, *Die Briefe an Timotheus und Titus. Der Brief an die Hebräer* 11th ed., NTD 9 (Göttingen: Vandenhoeck & Ruprecht, 1975), 14–15.

[4]U. Luck, "hygiēs," *TDNT* 8 (1972): 312.

[5]C. Spicq, *Saint Paul: Les Épitres pastorales,* 4th ed., ÉB (Paris: J. Gabalda, 1969), 115–17.

[6]R. J. Karris, "The Function and Sitz im Leben of the Paraenetic Elements in the Pastoral Epistles" (Diss., Harvard Divinity School, 1971) and a summary of the first part of the dissertation published as "The Background and Significance of the Polemic of the Pastoral Epistles, *JBL* 92 (1973): 549–64.

In order to make any advance in understanding the function of these terms in the Pastorals, all the terms describing health and disease must be considered. Inquiry will be made in this essay into the conceptual framework of the Pastorals in which the terminology may fit, and then, in light of these findings, non-Christian material will be investigated for any contribution it may make to understanding the Pastorals' imagery. It is methodologically proper to begin with the assumption that the Pastorals were addressing either an actual situation or sketching one that would be readily recognizable to their readers. Since the language of health and disease was used in the polemic against false teachers, it is reasonable to assume that a particular type of opponent was in view and that it may be possible to outline a picture of the author's perception of this type.

The Polemic of the Pastorals

In using the terminology of health and disease, the author of the Pastorals reveals an understanding of the nature of the church's teaching and also characterizes those who oppose it or do not hold to it. On the positive side, the sound words are thought to form a pattern and to have been received from Paul (2 Tim. 1:13). Such sound teaching cannot be censured (Tit. 2:7). Instruction is given in it, and those who oppose it are reproved so that they might be sound in the faith (Tit. 1:9, 13; cf. 2:2). It is not said that sound teaching makes its recipient sound; at most that is an inference that may be drawn from these latter statements.

The Heretics

The author is more explicit in using the terminology polemically to describe the heretics. In using the language of health and disease, his intention is not so much to describe the content of the heretics' teaching as their demeanor and its causes and results. The details about the heretics given in passages containing medical terminology are echoed and sometimes amplified in other polemical passages in the letters which do not employ such terminology. These details are, therefore, not isolated bits of polemic, but form, in the author's perception, major features of the character as well as preaching method of those opposed. In its salient points, the exhortation of the author, frequently in explicitly antithetic form, urges the readers to the exact opposite mien and method, thus making it clear that the author is operating with a distinct person in mind who is to be shunned. The characterization of that type is vivid and polemical.

To begin with, the person who does not adhere to the sound teachings knows nothing (1 Tim. 6:4). This theme of obtuseness runs throughout the letters. The heretics' mind and conscience are defiled (Tit. 1:15), their conscience is seared or cauterized (1 Tim. 2:4), they fall into many senseless lusts (1 Tim. 6:9), their controversies are stupid and uninstructed (2 Tim. 2:23; Tit. 3:9). Those who listen to them and whom they capture are silly little women who are forever trying to learn but never come to a knowledge of the truth (2 Tim. 3:7). In contrast to the heretics, the orthodox do have knowledge and understanding (1 Tim. 1:7f; 4:3). By applying their minds to what is written by the Apostle, they will receive understanding from the Lord (2 Tim. 2:7; cf. 1 Tim. 3:15). In other words, their knowledge is derived from tradition and Scripture (2 Tim. 3:14-17; cf. 2:2; Tit. 1:9), and as the grace of God had appeared to instruct them (Tit. 2:11-12), so the servant of God instructs his opponents with gentleness (2 Tim. 2:25).

The intellectual condition of the heretics is so wretched that, in contrast to the soundness of orthodox teachings, it can be said that they are diseased (1 Tim. 6:4).[7] Their minds are corrupt *(diephtharmenōn . . . ton noun)* (1 Tim. 6:5; cf. 2 Tim. 3:8) and defiled (Tit. 1:15), and the teaching they produce will eat its way in their hearers like gangrene (2 Tim. 2:17). Their diseased condition is exhibited in their demeanor, in their preoccupation with controversies, verbal battles, and wranglings (1 Tim. 6:4-5) which are unprofitable and useless (2 Tim. 2:14; Tit. 3:9). Their harsh, bellicose, and misanthropic bearing is reflected in other descriptions of them in the letters, especially by the antisocial vices listed in 2 Tim. 3:2-4; they are proud, arrogant, abusive (cf. 1 Tim. 6:4), disobedient to their parents (cf. Tit. 1:16), ungrateful, inhuman, slanderers, fierce, haters of good, treacherous, reckless, swollen with conceit. Furthermore, they are insubordinate (Tit. 1:10), given to strife (1 Tim. 6:4; Tit. 3:9), and factious (Tit. 3:10).

The Orthodox

The contrasting qualities and actions that should characterize the readers, given in the form of exhortations and in lists of qualifications of various

---

[7]*Tetyphōtai, mēden epistamenos, alla nosōn* ("he is puffed up with conceit, he knows nothing; he has a morbid craving"). The combination of *typhoō* with words describing the cognitive element in man is common in the literature. Cf. Lucian *Nigrinus* 1, *anoētos te kai tetyphōmenos* ("senseless and conceited"); Polybius *The Histories* 3.81.1, *agnoei kai tetyphōtai* ("he is ignorant and conceited"). Epictetus was aware that one's great power of argumentation and persuasive reasoning may be an excuse for *typhos* ("vanity"; *Discourse* 1.8.6-7) and it is understandable why, as Julian (*Oration* 6.197D) says, that true philosophers were called *tetyphōmenoi* ("conceited"). The word could also mean to be mentally ill, demented. See Demosthenes *Oration* 9.20, where it is contrasted with being in one's right sense *(hygiainein)*. Plutarch *(Progress in Virtue* 81F) cautions the young man that as he lays firmer hold on reason he will lay aside *typhos,* and he then goes on to expand a medical metaphor. In this light it is quite likely that *tetyphōtai* in 1 Tim. 6:4 is intended to describe mental illness, and that *meden epistamenos, alla nosōn peri zētēseis* is a further specification of the condition. Cf. Theophylact *In epistolam primam ad Timotheum expositio* (PG 125.77), who, in commenting on the passage, thought that ignorance causes delusion, which he interpreted as a tumor of a diseased soul.

functionaries, frequently in antithetic form, serve to further delineate the heretical type who is to be avoided. The readers should avoid useless verbal battles (2 Tim. 2:14; Tit. 3:2, 9; cf. 1 Tim. 3:3, 23-24) and stupid and uninstructed controversies,[8] and should not be swollen with conceit (1 Tim. 3:6), or be arrogant (1 Tim. 6:17), quick-tempered, or violent (1 Tim. 2:8; 3:3; Tit. 1:7). They are to abuse and slander no one (1 Tim. 3:11; Tit. 2:3; 3:2), but are to be gentle to all (2 Tim. 2:24; cf. 1 Tim. 3:3; 6:11; Tit. 3:2), especially in their instruction (2 Tim. 2:25; Tit. 3:2), and show all patience (2 Tim. 4:2).

The terms describing the preaching and pastoral care of the orthodox distinguish them from their opponents: they are to preach (2 Tim. 4:2) and speak what befits sound doctrine (Tit. 2:1; cf. 15) and are to charge (1 Tim. 1:3; 4:11; 5:7; 6:17), instruct (1 Tim. 4:6, 11, 16; Tit. 3:14; cf. 1 Tim. 3:3; Tit. 1:9), correct (Tit. 1:5), and remind (2 Tim. 2:14) others. They should be careful in chastising those within the community (1 Tim. 5:1; cf. 19, 22), and should rather exhort (1 Tim. 5:1; 6:2; 2 Tim. 4:2; Tit. 1:9; 2:6) and honor (1 Tim. 5:3, 17) them. Only seldom are they commanded to engage in censure (2 Tim. 4:20) and severe rebuke, harsh treatments reserved primarily for those who persist in sin (1 Tim. 5:20; cf. 2 Tim. 4:2; Tit. 2:15) and for the heretics (Tit. 1:9, 13) who must be silenced (Tit. 1:11). The evangelists are to present themselves as examples in their speech and conduct, in love, faith, and purity (1 Tim. 4:12), which requires that they constantly give attention to their own progress in the Christian virtues (e.g., 1 Tim. 4:12-16; 5:22; 6:11-14; 2 Tim. 2:1-8, 22; 3:10, 14; 4:5, 15).

All Christians should strive to live quiet and peaceable lives, godly and respectful in every way (1 Tim. 2:2). This demeanor is the exact opposite to that which characterized them once, when they themselves were foolish, disobedient, passing their days in malice and envy, hated by men and hating one another. All that was changed when the goodness and loving kindness of God the Savior appeared (Tit. 3:3-4).

Antisocial Behavior

In addition to the diseased condition that they create in their hearers, the heretics through their harsh verbal battles produce the antisocial vices of envy, strife, slander, and base suspicions, which are summarized as the frictional wranglings of people corrupt in mind (1 Tim. 6:4f).[9] They subvert entire

---

[8]For the theme of avoiding the heretics, see further 1 Tim. 4:7; 6:11; 2 Tim. 2:16.

[9]*Diaparatribai* ("frictional wranglings") clearly describes friction. See Polybius *The Histories* 2.36.5, *en hypopsiais en pros allēlous kai paratribais* ("their relationship was characterized by mutual suspicion and friction"), and cf. Athenaeus *The Deipnosophists* 14.626E and other references in LSJ, *s.v.* "paratribē." John Chrysostom *(In epistolam primam ad Timotheum commentarius,* Hom. 17 [PG 62.392]) proposes an alternative explanation: The heretics are like scab-

households (Tit. 1:11; cf. 2 Tim. 3:6). But all vice is contrary to sound doctrine (1 Tim. 1:10).[10] They have in mind not the good of the people they preach to, but their own gain (1 Tim. 6:5-10; cf. Tit. 1:11). In contrast, the sound teaching has the life of the orthodox as an ordered community in view. The social responsibilities in which that community is instructed are tantamount to the sound teaching (1 Tim. 6:1-3; Tit. 2:1-10), and the behavior inculcated further has in view the approval of the Christian community by the larger society (Tit. 2:5, 8, 10; cf. 1 Tim. 3:7). High value is placed on the home and the instruction that goes on in it (e.g., 1 Tim. 2:15; 3:4f, 12; 4:3; 5:1-4, 14-16; 2 Tim. 1:5; Tit. 1:6), and when the church's leaders are to confront the heretics, it is to stop them from upsetting households (Tit. 1:9ff). The teaching of the orthodox always has in mind the benefit of their hearers, never their own profit (e.g., 2 Tim. 2:24-26; 1 Tim. 1:20-21).

The heretics are received by people who do not endure sound teaching,[11] but who in keeping with their own irrational lusts accumulate teachers for themselves who will merely tickle their ears *(knēthomenoi tēn akoēn,* 2 Tim. 4:3).[12] Among them are the silly little women who are incapable of grasping the knowledge of the truth (2 Tim. 3:7). It is among such people that their teaching will eat its way like gangrene (2 Tim. 2:17).

In sum, the author's use of the medical images is part of his overall perception of the heretics. The author describes them as intellectually inferior, having diseased minds that produce violent preaching and contaminate those

---

covered sheep that infect the healthy sheep when they rub against them. He thus seems to think that *paratribe* is in some way related to *paratrimma,* which is used by medical writers of (infected?) abrasions. Cf. LSJ, *s.v.* "paratrimma" for references. In view of the other terminology in the passage, the fact that *diaphtheirō* ("corrupt") is also used in a medical sense (see LSJ, *s.v.* "diaphtheirō, phtheirō," and see below the use by Dio Chrysostom and pseudo-Diogenes), and the analogous view in 2 Tim. 2:17, the interpretation is not improbable, despite the caution of Dibelius and Conzelmann, *The Pastoral Epistles,* 82 n. 3.

[10]The unique formulation of 1 Tim. 1:10, *kai ei ti heteron te hygiainousē didaskalia antikeitai* ("and whatever else is contrary to sound doctrine"), should not be overstressed. In function it is not different from such endings to vice lists as *kai ta homoia* ("and the like"; Gal. 5:21) and *ta toiauta* ("such things"; Rom. 1:32; 2:3), used to indicate that the list is not all-inclusive. Cf. Gal. 5:23, *kata tōn toioutōn ouk estin nomos* ("against such there is no law"). Karris's statement ("The Function and Sitz im Leben" [n. 6 above], 64), that "no other catalogue of vices employed in Christian writers contains a reference to the "sound teaching," must not include the Pastorals (see 1 Tim. 6:4-5; Tit. 1:9-10, and cf. 2 Tim. 4:3-4).

[11]The conjecture by Price (recorded in the Nestle-Aland apparatus), that *anthexontai* should be read for *anexontai* is attractive in light of Tit. 1:9, but the latter reading is perfectly intelligible in the context. Cf. Dio Chrysostom *Discourse* 33.15-16: Man's ears are dainty when reared on flattery and lies; people cannot endure *(anexesthe)* demanding preaching.

[12]"Irrational lusts": The RSV rendering of *epithymias* by "likings" is too mild. The term in Greek philosophy described "the waywardness of man in conflict with his rationality." Cf. F. Buechsel, "epithymia," *TDNT* 3 (1965): 169, and see below. The element of irrationality is not absent from the Pastorals. Cf. 1 Tim. 6:9, *epithymias pollas anoētous* ("many senseless desires"); 2 Tim. 3:6, of the women who learn without coming to knowledge of the truth; Tit. 2:12, the divine *paideia* ("training") has as its goal the renunciation of worldly *epithymiai* ("passions"); Tit. 3:3, the *anoētoi* ("foolish") were enslaved to their *epithymiai.*

who accept their teaching. They are antisocial and upset the social order by their preaching. They are motivated to preach by their hope of financial gain. Those who welcome them are likewise intellectually and morally inferior and are infected by them. Contrasted to the heretics are the orthodox who have knowledge and hold to sound teaching, who are generally mild in their own teaching, yet know to be severe when the occasion demands severity, who are socially responsible, give constant attention to their own moral progress, and always have the benefit of others at heart.

The Moral Philosophers

When the historical and social setting of the Pastorals is considered, a certain group of teachers, well known in the early Empire, fits well the description noted above. Among the many kinds of philosophers who wandered about was a group, Cynics of a particular type, who were distinguished for the severity with which they delivered their message. They held a strange fascination for those who heard them, and met with both acceptance and repulsion. Contemporary writers used the medical metaphors and images of the Pastorals in discussing the teaching of philosophers in general; however, the language was particularly used in connection with rigoristic Cynics and the questions they raised about the nature of the true philosopher's *parrēsia,* that frankness of speech used in attempting to cure people of their moral illness.

Moral Disease

The description of human vices and passions as diseases was widespread, but was especially used by Stoics and Cynics. Stoics, as was their wont, engaged in minute subdivision and definition of passions as diseases and identified the degrees to which the soul might be subjected to them.[13] The soul, they held, might be in a state of war, with its passions and diseases prevailing over its healthy (rational) principles *(tous hygiainontas logous).*[14] When passion in the soul rages savagely and produces itchings and ticklings which arise from lust and indulgence *(knēsmous kai gargalismous ex hēdonēs kai epithumias),*[15] it is cured by drugs, and if some vice spreads *(epinemomenē)* like festering shingles, it is incised with professional skill with the instrument of

---

[13]See Cicero *Tusculan Disputations* 4.10–13, especially 10, 23, 27, 33. Cf. Galen *De locis affectis* 1.3 (8.32 Kuhn; *SVF* 3.429); Diogenes Laertius *Lives of Eminent Philosophers* 7.115 (*SVF* 3.422); Stobaeus *Anthology* 2.7.10 (2.93,1–13 Wachsmuth-Hense; *SVF* 3.421). See I. Hadot, *Seneca und die griechisch-römische Tradition der Seelenleitung,* Quellen und Studien zur Geschichte der Philosophie 13 (Berlin: Walter de Gruyter, 1969), 142–46.
[14]Philo *On Abraham* 223.
[15]Philo *The Worse Attacks the Better* 110. Cf. 2 Tim. 4:3.

sharp reason *(logō tomei to kat' epistēmēn temnetai)*.[16] After reason has rid the soul of its disease, reason remains in the soul.[17] Such therapy cannot be brought about by eloquence or a specious *parrēsia* which is not genuine or beneficial *(ōphelimon)*, but merely tickles.[18] The person who is aware of moral illness should seek and welcome effective treatment. "Why do you tickle my ears?" asks Seneca, "Why do you entertain me? There is other business at hand; I am to be cauterized, operated upon, or put on a diet. That is why you were summoned to treat me!" *(Epistle* 75.6–7).

The Physician of the Soul

Since philosophy was viewed as intended to cure vices and lead to virtue, it is natural that the philosopher was described as a physician of the soul whose teaching was the means by which the cure was effected.[19] The widespread use of such medical terminology and imagery is not surprising since philosophers (and sophists) were in fact closely related to physicians.[20] The description of the philosopher as a physician became common among the Stoics and Cynics, although it was by no means confined to them.[21] The Stoics Seneca,[22] Musonius,[23] and Epictetus[24] frequently made use of the comparison.

---

[16]Philo *The Worse Attacks the Better* 110. The medical metaphor of the (rational) word as a scalpel is behind Heb. 2:12. It is tempting to force 2 Tim. 2:15, *ergatēn anepaischynton orthotomounta ton logon tēs alētheias* ("a workman who has no need to be ashamed, rightly handling the word of truth"), into a medical sense, for example, "a workman unashamed of the word of truth as it cuts straight (correctly?)," especially since the medical metaphor is continued, *kai ho logos autōn hōs gangraina nomēn hexei* ("and their talk will eat its way like gangrene").

[17]Musonius Rufus *Fragment* 36; cf. *Epistle to Pancratides* 3-4 (137-38 Hense).

[18]Plutarch *How to Tell a Flatterer from a Friend* 51CD. The medical metaphor is not used in this immediate context, but is applied extensively elsewhere in the tractate where *parrēsia* is discussed. It is the basic conviction of all moral philosophers that the philosopher and his speech should be beneficial. See, for example, Dio Chrysostom *Discourses* 1.3–4; 32.2, 5, 12–13, 33; 33.56; Plutarch *How to Tell a Flatterer from a Friend* 55CD, 68C; Lucian *Demonax* 63, 66.

[19]For references, see S. Dill, *Roman Society from Nero to Marcus Aurelius,* 2d ed. (London: Macmillan, 1905), 292; K. Holl, "Die schriftstellerische Form des griechischen Heiligenlebens," *Neue Jahrbucher für das klassische Altertum* 19 (1912): 418; G. Bardy, *La conversion au christianisme durant les premiers siècles* (Paris: Aubier, 1949), 75–76.

[20]Cf. the title of one of the works of the physician Galen: *That the Best Physician is also a Philosopher,* and see G. W. Bowersock, *Greek Sophists in the Roman Empire* (Oxford: Clarendon, 1969), 19, 59–75, esp. 67–68.

[21]Once they found their way into the diatribe, medical images were assured of wide usage. See A. Oltramare, *Les Origins de la diatribe romaine* (Lausanne: Librairie Payot, 1926), 304 (index), *s.v.* "Médicin (compairasons avec le =)," B. P. Wallach, "A History of the Diatribe from Its Origins Up to the First Century B. C. and a Study of the Influence of the Genre Upon Lucretius, III, 830–1094" (Diss., University of Illinois, 1975), 134–36, passim. For extensive non-Stoic and non-Cynic use of the image of the physician, see, for example, Philo of Larissa, the Skeptic teacher of Cicero, in Stobaeus *Anthology* 2.7.2 (2.39,19–42,6; Wachsmuth-Hense), and Plutarch, who does, however, reflect Stoic ideas on the subject, in *How to Tell a Flatterer from a Friend* 61A-F, 73A-D, 74D, and see below.

[22]E.g., *Epistles* 22.1; 27.1; 40.5; 50.4; 64.8; 72.5–6; 94.24; 95.29.

[23]E.g., *Fragment* 1 (1,5-11; Hense).

[24]E.g. *Discourses* 2.15.4–5; 3.21.20; 3.23.27–28, 30; 3.25.7–8; *Fragment* 19 (468; Schenkl).

As the quotation from Seneca reveals, Stoics expected that the philosopher-physician's treatment might need to be severe: not only drugs and diet, but the knife and cautery might need to be used. Epictetus held the same view.[25]

Dio Chrysostom permits the clearest insight into how a Stoic philosopher regarded his own exhortation as analogous to the work of a physician.[26] In *Discourse* 77/78 Dio justifies the philosopher's "fullest frankness" *(pleistē parrēsia)*. A soul is corrupt *(diephtharmenē)* because of the ignorance, depravity, insolence, jealousy, grief, and the countless other lusts *(epithymiai)* that beset it.[27] Such a condition requires surgery, and especially cautery (43). But the philosopher must first begin, and be as unsparing, on himself as on others (45). The philosopher is not to be indiscriminate in severity but as one who is sound *(hygiēs)* in words and deeds, is to adapt his treatment to the condition of the hearers. By sometimes being severe and sometimes gentle, the philosopher hopes thus to rescue others from foolishness, lusts, intemperance, and soft living.[28] The aim is not to cause dissent, greed, strife, jealousies, and desire for base gain, but to remind others of sobriety and righteousness and to promote concord (38–39). The Stoic philosopher-physician is thus concerned with the virtue of individuals, yet takes special care to contrast antisocial vices with social virtues.

The social dimension of instruction in virtue was elaborated by Dio in *Discourse* 32, where the medical metaphor was extended to apply to political officials. For the vices, Dio said, the gods have prepared one remedy and cure, namely, education and reason, and a person who employs this remedy throughout life arrives at last at a healthy and happy end (16).[29] The most depraved flee furthest from reason as the most inflamed sore shrinks from touch. Their treatment will need be the most drastic. The one treatment may be likened to dieting and drugs and is applied by philosophers who, through persuasion and reason, calm and make the soul gentle. They are the saviors of people who can be saved by confining and controlling vice before it reaches its final stage. The severity of their speech saves.

The other treatment may be likened to surgery and cautery and is practiced by rulers, laws, and magistrates, who remove what is abnormal and

---

[25]*Discourse* 3.22.72-73.
[26]Although *Discourse* 77/78 may be from his Cynic period, it nevertheless shows a milder attitude than that of the types of Cynics with which we shall be concerned. The dating of *Discourse* 32 to the middle years of Trajan's reign, thus after his Cynic period, proposed by H. von Arnim, *Leben und Werke des Dio von Prusas* (Berlin: Weidmann, 1898), 435–38, is generally accepted. See C. P. Jones, "The Date of Dio of Prusa's Alexandrian Oration," *Historia* 22 (1973): 302–9, for an attempt to place it in the reign of Vespasian, thus before Dio's Cynic period. In either case, the oration does not belong to his Cynic period, and it in fact shows a definite anti-Cynic bias.
[27]Cf. 1 Tim. 6:4 and n. 9 above.
[28]Cf. 2 Tim. 2:23-26.
[29]Cf. *Discourse* 17.6.

incurable. They are to be milder than the philosophers, for one should be sparing in meting out punishment, but not in imparting instruction (17-18). Dio appears to have difficulty with his metaphors since cautery and surgery, the more severe treatments, ought to belong to the philosophers, if they are the more severe, while dieting and drugs would be the method of milder officials.[30] In any case, what is to be noted is that the metaphors are used of instruction in virtue within the social order and that there is a stress on the need for different degrees of severity corresponding to the differences in the moral condition of those instructed.[31]

The Human Condition

While Dio asserts the need for painful frankness, he has a relatively optimistic view of the human condition which permitted him to adapt his preaching to the condition of his audience.[32] His comparatively rare pessimistic statements on the condition of the masses occur in speeches that show Cynic influence.[33] Stoics in general shared this relatively charitable view of human nature. Musonius, for example, held that people have a natural disposition toward virtue,[34] and that the majority of wrongs are due to ignorance and misunderstanding which can be overcome by instruction.[35] Epictetus insisted that the philosopher should not be angry at those who err, but should pity them.[36] Such a humane view not only permitted but required that the philosopher temper biting frankness with gentleness.

Some Cynics also viewed human nature in this way. Perhaps in reaction to Cynicism's reputation for harshness, there were those who emphasized that some of its heroes had been gentle in demeanor. Indeed, a milder strain of Cynics can be identified at least as early as Crates.[37] The major representative of this type under the Empire known to us was Demonax who, according to

---

[30]For the ruler who practices surgery and cautery like a physician, see Plutarch *Cato Major* 16.5; Epictetus *Fragment* 22 (469; Schenkl).

[31]Dio frequently uses the images of surgery and cautery in connection with his own exhortation toward social harmony, and constantly seeks to justify his own severity. Cf. *Discourses* 33.44; 38.7; cf. 57.5. for his persistent use of the image, see J. Oesch, "Die Vergleiche by Dio" (Diss., Zurich, 1916), 15.

[32]Cf. *Discourse* 32.24-28. See *Discourse* 13.13; 17.2-3 for his view that the crowd does not do what it knows to be best, and for its ignorance, *Discourses* 13.27; 14.2.

[33]Cf. R. Hoïstad, *Cynic Hero and Cynic King* (Uppsala: C. W. K. Gleerup, 1948), 169. Dill (*Roman Society from Nero to Marcus Aurelius* [n. 19 above], 369) generalizes on the basis of orations that are influenced by Cynicism.

[34]See *Fragment* 2, and cf. A. C. van Geytenbeek, *Musonius Rufus and Greek Diatribe* (Assen: Van Gorcum, 1963), 18, 28–33.

[35]*Fragment* 10.

[36]*Discourse* 1.18.3, 7–14. But some are impossible to persuade, cf. *Discourse* 2.15.13–20.

[37]See A. J. Malherbe, " 'Gentle as a Nurse': The Cynic Background to 1 Thess. 2," *NovT* 12 (1970): 210–11 (= 42–43 in this volume).

Lucian, was kind, gentle, and cheerful, was everybody's friend, and avoided only those whose error placed them beyond the hope of cure.[38]

The Severe Cynics

More important, however, is the larger company of Cynics, considered more typical of Cynicism in the popular mind, who were neither sociable nor gentle. Cynics of this type scoffed at the masses[39] and insisted that, since the masses were ignorant, they could not be friends of the philosopher.[40] The true Cynic was an avowed hater of mankind and withdrew from society.[41] While medical metaphors were used by all types of Cynics,[42] our particular interest lies in that group of stern Cynics.

These Cynics held that it was by virtue alone that the soul could be purified of its diseases and that the Cynic was the physician who could bring about the cure.[43] The human condition was so corrupt that only the most painful treatment, the severest *parrēsia,* could avail. The letters ascribed to Diogenes illustrate the attitude and manner of preaching. *Epistle* 28 is a severe condemnation of Greek civilization directed at Sinope.[44] Diogenes calls their laws the greatest delusion, and excoriates them for doing nothing by sound reason *(hygiē logō).* By their ignorance and senselessness they had become a mockery, and Diogenes and nature both hated them. Diogenes punishes them in word, nature does so in deed. They legislate and educate, but to no avail. They are tickled by pleasure *(egargalisthēte hyp' hedonēs).* If they continue to indulge themselves, Diogenes warns, the judges elected by the people, whom they call physicians(!), will treat them. They will cut and cauterize and prescribe drugs for the people, but will not be thanked for their ministrations. As for himself, Diogenes will associate only with those who know his Cynic worth. He will be like Antisthenes, who spoke only with those who knew him, and avoided those who knew neither nature, reason, nor truth.

---

[38]Lucian *Demonax* 10.

[39]E.g., pseudo-Hippocrates *Epistles* 17; 26; 47 (301, 304 Hercher).

[40]E.g., pseudo-Socrates *Epistle* 8.

[41]E.g., pseudo-Socrates *Epistle* 24. On the misanthropy represented by these letters, see G. A. Gerhard, *Phoinix von Kolophon* (Leipzig/Berlin: B. G. Teubner, 1909), 67–68, 166–67, 170–76.

[42]Antisthenes, already, is said by Diogenes Laertius (*Lives of Eminent Philosophers* 6.4, 6) to have compared a philosopher to a physician. To Diogenes is attributed the statement that he, like a physician, does not spend his time among those who are healthy, but among those who need therapy. See Stobaeus *Anthology* 3.13.43 (3.462,11–15; Wachsmuth-Hense), and cf. Dio Chrysostom *Discourse* 8.5. For further references, see J. J. Wettstein, *Novum Testamentum Graecum* (Amsterdam: Dommer, 1752), 1.358–59, on Matt. 9:12. Demonax, according to Lucian (*Demonax* 7), thought that one should pattern oneself after physicians who heal diseases but are not angry at the patients.

[43]Cf. pseudo-Diogenes *Epistles* 27; 49; pseudo-Hippocrates *Epistle* 11.7 (293 Hercher).

[44]See V. E. Emeljanow, "The Letters of Diogenes" (Diss., Stanford University, 1974), 49, 71–72, 136–39; cf. Malherbe, "Gentle as a Nurse" (n. 37 above), 212 n. 3 (= 43–44).

Epistle 29, addressed to Dionysius, tyrant of Sicily, likewise finds justi-fication in the putrid condition of society for the Cynic's harshness and an-tisocial attitude.[45] Diogenes threatens to send Dionysius a hard taskmaster (a Cynic) who will purge him. The tyrant needs someone with a whip, not someone who will flatter him. His disease *(diaphthora)* is far gone, and requires surgery, cautery, and medication for healing. Instead, Dionysius had brought in grandparents and wetnurses! The author seems to be polemicizing against those philosophers who saw the need for occasional gentleness in preaching.

Reaction to the Cynics

The antisocial Cynics did not, of course, withdraw from society, but lambasted it with unrelenting intensity. That they found audiences at all who would listen to them may be surprising, for the harsh treatment the mobs accorded philosophers in general is frequently recorded.[46] The fact, however, that the descriptions of mob-reaction frequently came from philosophers or profes-sional teachers, persons never quite satisfied with the adulation they deserved, should warn of the hazard of overstressing the animosity with which they were regarded.[47] The moral philosophers obviously did meet certain needs or there would not have been as many of them as in fact there were.[48] And, it was not only those of high moral purpose who were accorded a hearing. Lucian provides ample evidence that, although the wandering preachers did not always have motives or demeanor of the purest kind, they nevertheless had little difficulty in securing an audience. This was also, perhaps especially, true of both those Cynics who had a genuinely pessimistic view of mankind and adopted a correspondingly harsh style of preaching, and of those char-latans who affected such a Cynic style as a cover for their true designs.

Lucian is the best source for the sharp reaction with which such preachers met. His polemic is explicit and attaches itself to the medical images that were in vogue. He was familiar with the metaphors of surgery and cautery

---

[45]Cf. pseudo-Heraclitus *Epistles* 2; 9. For the Cynic debate as to whether the true Cynic can associate with rulers, see R. F. Hock, "Simon the Shoemaker as an Ideal Cynic," *GRBS* 17 (1976): 41–53.

[46]For the reception of the philosophers see L. Friedlaender, *Darstellungen aus der Sittengeschichte Roms in der Zeit von August bis Ausgang der Antonine,* 8th ed. (Leipzig: Hirzel, 1910), 4.301–10.

[47]See, for example, the endless discussions by such teachers and philosophers on the proper hearing they should receive, e.g., Plutarch *On Listening to Lectures;* Dio Chrysostom *Discourses* 1.8, 10; 32.2; 72; Seneca *Epistle* 52.11–15.

[48]Dill, *Roman Society from Nero to Marcus Aurelius,* 340-41; Dio Chrysostom *Discourses* 13.12; 72.11.

as applied to the philosopher's speech and with the description of the philosopher as a healer of the passions.[49] In his polemic against the vagabond preachers he repeatedly mentions the attraction they had for the masses. In *Philosophies for Sale,* Lucian describes the work of the Cynic through the mouth of one such physician of men's ills (8). The man claimed that the Cynic should be impudent, bold, and abuse everyone, for then the people will admire him and consider him manly. Education is altogether unnecessary (10-11). Elsewhere Lucian likewise observes that people tolerated the outspokenness of such preachers, delighted in their therapy, and cowered under their censure.[50] Particularly the common, simple people, especially those who had nothing more pressing to do, admired such preachers for their abusiveness.[51] While flailing others, these preachers themselves were immoral and greedy. The masses, however, were reticent to speak against them, both out of fear and because they thought such preachers were superior by virtue of their belligerence.[52] In his inimitable way, Lucian sketches what would be the disastrous effect on society of such preachers: industry would grind to a halt.[53] While Lucian thus satirically polemicized against these severe charlatans, he recognized that they did have a considerable following—his reason, in fact, for taking both them and their followers to task.

Lucian did, however, see much in true Cynicism that he admired.[54] That is most clearly evident in his tractate *Demonax,* but it also emerges from the picture he sketches of the Cynic in *The Downward Journey.* In the latter tractate a Cynic, appointed an observer and physician of men's ills (7), is being judged. Although the Cynic has been free-spoken, critical, and censorious (13), Lucian does not find fault with him. In the final judgment scene, the Cynic is told that wickedness leaves marks on the soul which only the judge can see, but there are no such marks on the Cynic. Then Lucian uses the image of "searing" in a new way. Though no marks of vice are found on the Cynic, there are many traces of searing *(egkaumatōn)* which somehow or other had been removed. The Cynic explains that he had earned them when in his ignorance he had still been wicked, but that when he began to live the philosophic life, after a while he had washed the scars from his soul (24). For Lucian, then, the searing that comes from vice must be removed before a person presumes to correct others.

---

[49]Cf. *The Fisherman* 46, 52; *Apology* 2.
[50]*The Runaways* 12.
[51]*Peregrinus* 18; *The Double Indictment* 11, of Stoics who act in the same manner.
[52]*The Runaways* 12; *The Carousal* 12-19; cf. *The Dream* 10–11.
[53]*The Runaways* 17; cf. *Peregrinus* 18: The wise prefect runs Proteus out of town.
[54]See R. Helm, "Lucian und die Philosophenschule," *Neue Jahrbuch für das klassische Altertum* 9 (1902): 351–69 for what Lucian found attractive in Cynicism.

Another reaction to the upbraiding of the Cynics can be identified. In a context in which every street preacher asserted his right to *parrēsia,* often conceived as the misanthropic railing of the Cynic, it was natural that serious philosophers would, on the one hand, distance themselves from such preachers, and on the other, give renewed attention to the nature of the true philosopher's *parrēsia.* It became customary for philosophers to describe either themselves or their heroes in an antithetic manner that would make the differences between themselves and the interlopers clear. This can be seen clearly in Dio Chrysostom as well as in other philosophers.[55] We have also seen that philosophers of higher culture and milder mien, when reflecting on the proper method of teaching, carefully specified how verbal cautery and surgery were to be used.[56] Yet they were equally careful to avoid specious frankness.

Plutarch's tractate *How to Tell a Flatterer from a Friend,* which utilizes material from discussions of the philosopher's frankness, illustrates the concern of a serious philosopher.[57] True frankness is like a potent medicine, when it is used with moderation (74D),[58] but flattery, at its most insidious, can take the form of a specious *parrēsia* (61D-62C). The flatterer, Plutarch charges, is himself diseased and in need of prudent remedies (62C) but is not thereby deterred from letting his flattery become a pestilence in society (49C). His "frankness" merely titillates *(knā)* and tickles *(gargalizei)* (cf. 51CD, 61B). It adds nothing to the powers of thinking and reasoning, but caters to pleasure, intensifies irrational temper, and engenders a tumor of conceit (cf. 59E). The flatterer's presence is like a growth in that he always assaults the festering and inflamed conditions of the soul (cf. 59C-60B). In criticism of those who open themselves to this specious frankness, Plutarch warns that its vicious, secret attacks will produce in them an itching sore whose scar will remain even after it heals. Such scars or gangrenes lead to destruction

---

[55]See above and cf. Dio Chrysostom *Discourse* 32.11; 34.30; 42.1-2; 77/78.37-38; Lucian *Demonax* 4, 8; Julian *Oration* 6.200BCD. See further, Malherbe, "Gentle as a Nurse" (n. 37 above).

[56]See above and cf. Cicero *De officiis* 1.136.

[57]The type of criticism Plutarch applies to the flatterer's supposed frankness is also leveled by the popular sophist Aristides at the Cynics in *Oration 3: To Plato, in Defense of the Four* 663–81 (511,6–519,19; Behr. English translation in *P. Aelius Aristides: The Complete Works,* trans. by C. A. Behr [Leiden: E. J. Brill, 1986], 1.273-77). On this passage, see further A. Harnack, *The Mission and Expansion of Christianity in the First Three Centuries,* trans. and ed. J. Moffatt, 2d ed., enlarged (New York: G. P. Putnam's Sons, 1908), 500, and A. Boulanger, *Aelius Aristide et la sophistique dans la province d'Asie au IIe siècle de notre ère* (reprint, Paris: É. de Boccard, 1968), 249–56, and 41 n. 39 in this volume. The parallels between the criticism of the harsh Cynics and the heretics in the Pastorals are striking: They preach virtue to others but are themselves corrupt, they are avaricious, their outspokenness is in fact maliciousness, they are antisocial and undermine households, etc.

[58]Cf. Themistius *Oration* 22 (67,4–6 Downey Norman): The *parrēsia* of a true friend is like a physician who uses the proper treatment (drugs instead of cautery and surgery).

(65CD).[59] These scars caused by vice are evidently what Lucian refers to as searings. Like Lucian, Plutarch does not object to frankness when it is properly applied, but demands that the person who presumes to speak with boldness be without disease lest the listeners become infected.

Genuine philosophic frankness, according to Plutarch, should be employed for the philosopher's as well as the listeners' improvement and should not be used out of a desire for reputation or out of ambition. Using a different metaphor, he elaborates on the subject in his tractate *Progress in Virtue,* in which he warns against the bellicosity that might be mistaken for frankness.

> But most of all must we consider whether the spirit of contention and quarreling over debatable questions *(zēteseis)* has been put down, and whether we have ceased to equip ourselves with arguments, as with boxing gloves or brass knuckles, with which to contend against each other, and to take more delight in scoring a hit or knockout than in learning and imparting something. For reasonableness and mildness in such matters, and the ability to join in discussions without wrangling, and to close them without anger, and to avoid a sort of arrogance over success in argument and exasperation in defeat, are the marks of a man who is making adequate progress (80BC).

Those who are insolent and filled with haughtiness and disdain are uninstructed in philosophy and will change when they train their minds, apply their stinging criticism to themselves, and in consequence be milder in their intercourse with others (81BC).

Conclusion

This historical and social context, in which the claims of certain harsh Cynics to be the healers of diseased humanity brought forth various responses, demonstrates how the language of health and disease function in the Pastoral Epistles. Like Lucian, the author accuses harsh opponents of being ignorant, abusive, immoral, antisocial, and charges that they are received only by the ignorant of whom they take advantage. Into this fairly standard picture of charlatans is woven the description of specious *parrēsia* represented by Plutarch. Contemporary harsh preachers intoned their own superiority as physicians and found justification for their pugnaciousness in the diseased condition of their hearers' minds and souls. The author of the Pastorals, in rebuttal, accuses the heretics, as Plutarch did the flatterer, with being diseased of mind and morals. Their verbal battles do not eradicate disease in others, but are the products of their own disease, and will further infect those who, with

---

[59]The comparison with gangrene had already been used by Lucilius (*Fragment* 7 Krenkel). Cf. Wallach, "A History of the Diatribe" (n. 21 above), 276–77.

irrational lusts, will listen to them with itching ears that wait only to be tickled. When the author describes the heretics' consciences as seared, he probably means that they were still seared with sin, as had been Lucian's Cynic before his conversion to philosophy. Therefore, he implies, they are in no condition to heal others. In light of the popularity of the metaphor of cautery, however, his use of the image might perhaps have an added barb: not only are they themselves still seared by sin, their sinful condition is so extreme that their own consciences have been cauterized.

The use of the medical imagery in the Pastorals is thoroughly polemical. There is no picture, as in the moral philosophers, of the intellectually and morally ill person who will be cured by reason through the application of the drugs, surgery, and cautery of *parrēsia*. While it is affirmed that the orthodox do have understanding, it was not the rationality of the sound teaching that made them so, but rather the apostolic tradition. That the "sound words" may bring about health of soul is an inference the reader may be tempted to draw, but it is not part of the function to which the images are put. That function is polemical.

The contrasting picture of the orthodox teacher as gentle and mild, knowing when to be severe, concerned with personal moral progress, who preaches to benefit others, and who promotes social stability, is similar to that sketched by Dio Chrysostom of himself and the ideal philosopher in antithesis to misanthropic, antisocial Cynics. This presentation of the Christian teacher is in harmony with the overall tendency of the Pastoral Epistles to present Christianity as a responsible part of society.

That the author of the Pastoral Epistles makes use of such typical descriptions does not compel us to conclude that they were not applicable to actual situations confronted. Dibelius was correct in his insistence that the language with which we have been concerned be understood as it would have been by the original readers. Those readers would not only have recognized the language, but the types as well. They could see and hear them in the streets. The literary and polemical traditions we have traced developed in and found application to actual situations. In the absence of compelling reasons to believe the contrary, we would hold the same to be true for the Pastoral Epistles.

9

"In Season and Out of Season": 2 Timothy 4:2

Insufficient attention has been paid to what turns out to be a remarkable admonition to Timothy: "preach the word, be urgent in season and out of season *(epistēthi eukairōs akairōs)*, convince, rebuke and exhort, be unfailing in patience and in teaching." Because *epistēthi* ("be urgent") has no object, the relation of the admonition to the rest of the sentence is unclear,[1] but it seems natural to take it as pointing to the preceding *kēryxon* ("preach").[2] Understood thus, Timothy is commanded to have "an attitude of prompt attention that may at any moment pass into action."[3]

Eukairōs akairōs ("in season and out of season") is an oxymoron and is "made still more emphatic by the omission of the copula."[4] It has sounded proverbial to some commentators,[5] and Ceslaus Spicq has pointed out that *eukairia* ("appropriateness") is a rhetorical term.[6] Exegetes have primarily been interested in the person or persons to whom the preaching should be opportune or inopportune. Some have held that the reference is to Timothy,[7]

---

[1]Some commentators do not discuss the relationship to the rest of the sentence or are themselves unclear on how they understand it, e.g., W. Lock, *A Critical and Exegetical Commentary on the Pastoral Epistles,* ICC (Edinburgh: T. & T. Clark, 1924), 112–13; E. K. Simpson, *The Pastoral Epistles* (Grand Rapids: Wm. B. Eerdmans, 1954), 152; J. Jeremias, *Die Briefe an Timotheus und Titus. Der Brief an die Hebräer,* NTD 9 (Göttingen: Vandenhoeck & Ruprecht, 1963), 56; M. Dibelius and H. Conzelmann, *A Commentary on the Pastoral Epistles,* trans. P. Buttolph and A. Yarbro, Hermeneia (Philadelphia: Fortress Press, 1972), 120; C.Spicq, *Saint Paul: Les Épitres pastorales* ÉB, 4th ed. (Paris: J. Gabalda, 1969), 2.799.
[2]As do C. J. Ellicott (*A Critical and Grammatical Commentary on the Pastoral Epistles* [Andover: Draper, 1882], 167), C. K. Barrett (*The Pastoral Epistles in the New English Bible,* New Clarendon Bible [Oxford: Clarendon Press, 1963], 116), J. N. D. Kelly (*A Commentary on the Pastoral Epistles,* HNTC [New York: Harper & Row, 1963], 205) and, apparently, B. S. Easton, (*The Pastoral Epistles* [New York: Charles Scribner's Sons, 1947], 68).
[3]Ellicott, *Pastoral Epistles,* 167.
[4]Ibid.; cf. Spicq, *Épitres pastorales,* 799; Simpson, *Pastoral Epistles,* 152.
[5]Lock, *Pastoral Epistles,* 112–13; Kelly, *Pastoral Epistles,* 205.
[6]Spicq, *Épitres pastorales,* 799.
[7]Thus, the Greek Fathers: John Chrysostom *In epistolam secundam ad Timotheum commentarius,* Hom. 9.2 (PG 62.651); Theodore of Mopsuestia (*Theodori episcopi Mopsuesteni in epistolas b. Pauli commentarii,* ed. H. B. Swete [Cambridge: University Press, 1882] 2.223); Theodoret *In-*

others to Timothy's hearers,[8] while some consider that probably both were in view.[9] The concern with the appropriate or inappropriate occasion on which to speak stretches back to the fourth century B.C., and an awareness of discussions of the subject may help us place 2 Timothy 4:2 in a new light. Spicq is on the right track when he refers to *Phaedrus* 272A, in which Plato requires that a speaker discern whether certain forms of speech are opportune or inopportune; but Spicq does not follow it up, and the other references that he provides are not quite to the point.[10]

Timely Exhortation

According to Dionysius of Halicarnassus *(On the Arrangement of Words* 12), the Sophist Gorgias was the first person to write about the necessity for a speaker to adapt his words to the actual circumstances, the *kairoi,* in which he delivers them.[11] His earlier contemporary, Protagoras of Abdera, had been the first, according to Diogenes Laertius *(Lives of Eminent Philosophers* 9.52), to emphasize the importance of seizing the right moment *(kairos)* for delivering a speech, but Protagoras did not develop the idea and it has been denied that it was part of the so-called *kairos*-Lehre or that Gorgias had derived it from Protagoras.[12] It has been argued that the doctrine was influenced by the field of medicine: as a physician adapts his treatment to the condition and needs of his patient, so should the orator.[13] Whatever the original influences may have been, it will be seen that a speaker's consideration of the proper *kairos* for his speech—especially that brand of speaking described as *parrēsia*

---

terpretatio epistolae II ad Timotheum (PG 82.852); cf. Theophylact *Epistolae secundae divi Pauli ad Timotheum expositio* (PG 125.128). Among modern commentators the interpretation is held by Ellicott, *Pastoral Epistles* (167), Simpson, *Pastoral Epistles* (152), and Spicq, *Épitres pastorales* (799). G. H. Whitaker ("In Season, Out of Season," *ExpTim* 34 [1923]: 332–33) attempts to support Chrysostom's interpretation by adducing references that, however, either do not refer to an opportune time for speech (Polybius *The Histories* 5.26.10; Plutarch *Against the Stoics on Common Conceptions* 1071D) or use *eukaireō* (Plutarch *Sayings of Spartans* 223D), which is not precisely the same as speaking *eukairōs.*

[8]Easton, *Pastoral Epistles,* 69; Jeremias, *Briefe an Timotheus und Titus,* 56; Dibelius and Conzelmann, *Pastoral Epistles,* 120.

[9]Lock, *Pastoral Epistles,* 111–12; Barrett, *Pastoral Epistles,* 116.

[10]Isocrates *Antidosis* 311 and J. C. T. Ernesti (*Lexicon technologiae graecorum rhetoricae,* [reprint, Hildesheim: G. Olms, 1962], 140), whose references are either wrong or beside the point.

[11]See G. A. Kennedy, *The Art of Persuasion in Greece* (Princeton: Princeton Univ. Press, 1963), 66–68. With respect to his statement that *kairos* as a rhetorical term is largely restricted to the classical period, one should note E. Norden (*Die Antike Kunstprosa,* 5th ed. [reprint, Darmstadt: Wissenschaftliche Buchgesellschaft, 1958], 69 n. 1), who refers, among others, to Hermogenes, *Peri ideōn* 2.396.12 Spengel and Quintilian *Institutio oratoria,* 9.3.102. Cf. also W. Schmid, *Geschichte der griechischen Literatur* (Munich: C. H. Beck, 1940), 1.3/1, 65.

[12]See Schmid, *Geschichte,* 1.3/1, 24 n.3.

[13]See the bibliography in Schmid, *Geschichte,* 1.3/1, 24 n.3; 58 n.5; 65 n.3.

("frankness, boldness")—was later frequently compared to a good physician's discernment of his patient's condition.[14]

The use of *kairos* and its cognates became a commonplace.[15] A sampling from a wide range of material will serve to illustrate the point. According to Aeschylus, "words are physicians of ailing wrath if salve is applied at the proper time *(en kairō)*."[16] Philo of Alexandria, in a discussion of the correct *kairos,* claims that untimely bold speech *(parrēsia akairōs)* is not really bold speech, but the products of diseased minds and emotions.[17] *Sentences of Sextus* 163a is somewhat similar: "An untimely word *(logos para kairon)* is proof of an evil mind." Athenaeus (*The Deipnosophists* 14.620f) accuses Sotades of *akairōs parrēsia,* and Dio Cassius (*Roman History* 65.12.1) says that Helvidius Priscus imitated Thrasea's *parrēsia,* but sometimes did so *ouk en kairō* ("unseasonably"). The anthologist Stobaeus, in his collection of *dicta* on *parrēsia,* also records that it should be *en kairō.*[18] Cicero's compliment to his friend Atticus (*Epistle to Atticus* 4.7.1), *Nihil eukairoteron epistula tua,* "nothing could be more apropos than your letter," in which he uses the Greek word *eukairoteron,* reveals the currency that the term had attained by the first century B.C.

The philosophical moralists from the first and second centuries of the Empire provide information that is particularly pertinent to our interest. They reflect the general concern for opportune speech as it relates to their own efforts. Thus Musonius Rufus advises that a philosopher, rather than rehearsing a multitude of arguments, should speak *kairiōs* ("at the proper time") about each.[19] Maximus of Tyre, on the other hand, says that there is no *kairos* appropriate to the philosopher's discourse, but he appears to have in mind the social context peculiarly adapted to receiving philosophical instruction.[20]

In addition to sharing the interest generally, these philosophers were particularly concerned with the appropriate times for their efforts at moral reformation. Their psychagogy required serious consideration of the emotional and moral conditions of those persons they sought to benefit. In deliberating on the proper *kairos* for their instruction, they were careful, as

---

[14]The following fragment from Democritus, Protagoras's contemporary and fellow-citizen, is of interest: *oikeion eleutherias parrēsia, kindynos de hē tou kairou diagnōsis (Fragment* 226 Diels-Kranz). It is not clear, however, whether *diagnōsis* should be understood in its medical sense or simply as "discern." We know nothing about Democritus's possible relationship to Protagoras.
[15]The Stoics' use of *eukairia* in their doctrine of *eutaxia* is here left out of consideration. See Cicero, *De finibus* 3.45; *De officiis* 1.142.
[16]*Prometheus Bound* 380-82, used by Plutarch (*Condolence to Apolloyius* 102B).
[17]*On Dreams* 2.78–92.
[18]*Anthology* 3.13.61 (3.466,17–476,2; Wachsmuth-Hense); cf. 3.13.59 (3.466,6–13; Wachsmuth-Hense), *en hō chrē.*
[19]*Fragment* 1 (6,6; Hense).
[20]1.3 (4,22–5,8; 6,3–9; Hobein).

they were in other matters, to distinguish themselves from persons who did not show similar discrimination. This meant, frequently, that they distanced themselves from the Cynics. Thus, in his depiction of the ideal Cynic, Epictetus contrasts him to what was popularly conceived to be a Cynic trait, namely, to revile at an inappropriate time *(loidoreisthai akairōs)* the people he meets.[21] And Lucian, who gives a Cynic cast to the satirical comments of Momus, has him accused of inopportune censure *(ouk en kairō nyn epitimōn)*.[22] The serious philosopher, on the other hand, is not indiscriminate in his frankness, but only reproves a person when the situation is timely *(eukairōs)*.[23] Dio Chrysostom *(Discourse* 38.4-5) shows that expressing one's fear that one's address might be *akairōs* had become a convention among such philosophers by the end of the century.

Determining the Proper Occasion

In determining the proper *kairos* for their speech, philosophers took into consideration a number of things. To begin with, they had to decide where and to whom they would speak, for example, whether in a school, a salon, upon invitation elsewhere, or in the open air where all could hear them.[24] Except for those of their number who despaired of the human condition and withdrew from society[25] and the few who approved residence at court[26] or taught in their own homes,[27] in this period the majority of Cynics preferred to preach to the public at large.[28] While these differences in practice clearly existed among the Cynics, their critics took no interest in differentiating

[21]*Discourse* 3.22.50. M. Billerbeck (*Epiktet: Vom Kynismus,* Philosophia Antiqua 34 [Leiden: E. J. Brill, 1978], 113–14) thinks that the meaning of *akairōs* here is "importunate" or "tasteless," that is, that it is modal rather than temporal. The distinction, however, does not hold in this kind of context.

[22]*Zeus Rants* 43. Earlier in the dialogue, Momus's *parrēsia* had been permitted because it was thought to be aimed at the common good (19), but his rebuke *(epitimēsis)* was soon rejected (23). On Lucian's use of Momus, see R. Helm, *Lucian und Menipp* (Leipzig/Berlin: B. G. Teubner, 1906), 147–48.

[23]Cf. Epictetus *The Encheiridion* 33.16; and on the different attitudes toward *parrēsia,* see A. J. Malherbe, " 'Gentle as a Nurse'; The Cynic Background to 1 Thess. 2," *NovT* 12 (1970) 203–17 (=35–48 in this volume).

[24]See "Gentle as a Nurse," esp. 204–7 (=37–40).

[25]See, e.g., pseudo-Heraclitus *Epistles* 2; 4; 7; 9; see A. J. Malherbe, *Paul and the Thessalonians: The Philosophic Tradition of Pastoral Care* (Philadelphia: Fortress Press, 1987), 21 n. 59; pseudo-Socrates *Epistle* 24; pseudo-Diogenes *Epistle* 28.

[26]See R. F. Hock, "Simon the Shoemaker as an Ideal Cynic," *GRBS* 17 (1976): 41–53.

[27]As, e.g., Lucian's *Demonax.*

[28]See, e.g., pseudo-Socrates *Epistles* 1; 6; Dio Chrysostom *Discourse* 32.7–11.

between them, but generally described all Cynics as street preachers, gross in their behavior and importunate in their speech.[29]

It was disconcerting to Stoics that little difference was seen to exist between themselves and the Cynics. Juvenal, for instance, said that Stoics differed from Cynics only in the shirt that they wore (*Satire* 13.122), thus reducing the issue to a matter of class and style, as some modern scholars also have done.[30] Some Stoics may indeed themselves have drawn the distinctions in this way.[31] It should be noted also that as early as the first century B.C. there were Stoics abroad in the streets[32] who used the Cynics' means of propaganda.[33] Seneca himself much admired his contemporary, the Cynic Demetrius, who is the first Cynic in the Empire about whom we have information, supplied largely by Seneca.[34] Yet Seneca wanted it to be clearly understood that proper instruction differed from that of the Cynics. Unlike the Cynics, who were indiscriminate in their use of freedom of speech and "scattered advice by the handful" to all within hearing distance, Seneca would speak only to those who were in a condition to receive a benefit and would not threaten to drag the philosopher down to their level.[35]

In order to attain the most good, the philosopher might find it desirable or necessary to deal with people individually rather than in groups.[36] This

---

[29]For the diversity among the Cynics, see A. J. Malherbe "Self-Definition among the Epicureans and Cynics," in *Jewish and Christian Self-Definition. Vol. 3: Self-Definition in the Greco-Roman World,* ed. B. F. Meyer and E. P. Sanders (Philadelphia: Fortress Press, 1983), 46–59 (= 11–24 in this volume).

[30]See W. Nestle, *Griechische Geistesgeschichte von Homer bis Lukian in ihrer Entfaltung vom mythischen zum rationalen Denken dargestellt* (Stuttgart: A. Kroner, 1944), 390–91; R. MacMullen, *Enemies of the Roman Order: Treason, Unrest, and Alienation in the Empire* (Cambridge, Mass.: Harvard Univ. Press, 1966), 60, 308 n. 17. For other ancient evidence, see Dio Cassius *Roman History* 65.13 and the comments by D. R. Dudley (*A History of Cynicism from Diogenes to the Fifth Century* ᴬ·ᴰ· [London: Methuen, 1937], 137) and W. Liefeld "The Wandering Preacher as a Social Figure in the Roman Empire" [Diss., Columbia University, 1967], 40–41).

[31]Lucian (*Hermotimus* 18) has the Stoic Hermotimus say, "I used to see the Stoics walking with dignity, decently dressed, always thoughtful, manly in looks, most of them close-cropped; there was nothing effeminate, none of that exaggerated indifference which stamps the genuine crazy Cynic. They seemed in a state of moderation and everyone says that is best."

[32]See Horace *Satire* 2.3; see also E. V. Arnold, *Roman Stoicism* (Cambridge, Mass.: Cambridge Univ. Press, 1911), 111; Jose F. Mora, "Cyniques et Stoiciens," *Rev. de metaph. et de morale* 62 (1957): 22.

[33]For their propaganda, see P. Wendland, *Die hellenistisch-römische Kultur in ihren Beziehungen zu Judentum und Christentum. Die urchristlichen Literaturformen,* 3d ed. HNT 1 (Tübingen: J. C. B. Mohr [Paul Siebeck], 1912), 75–96; A. Oltramare, *Les Origines de la diatribe romaine* (Geneva: Librairie Payot, 1926), 10; M. Spanneut, *Le Stoicisme des pères de l'Église, de Clément de Rome à Clément d'Alexandrie* (Paris: Éditions du Seuil, 1957), 49-50. For modification of the view that the diatribe was used by Cynics in their public preaching, see S. K. Stowers, *The Diatribe and Paul's Letter to the Romans,* SBLDS 57 (Chico, Calif.: Scholars Press, 1981).

[34]See M. Billerbeck, *Der Kyniker Demetrius,* Philosophia Antiqua 26 (Leiden: E. J. Brill, 1979).

[35]*Epistle* 29.1–5; cf. 108.4. See I. Hadot, *Seneca und die griechisch-römische Tradition der Seelenleitung,* Quellen und Studien zur Geschichte der Philosophie 13 (Berlin: Walter de Gruyter, 1969), 171–72.

[36]For the desirability of personalized instruction, see A. J. Malherbe, "Exhortation in First Thessalonians," *NovT* 25 (1983): 244–45 (= 55 n.32 in this volume); idem, *Paul and the Thessalonians,* 56–57, 75, 81, 82, 86, 88. See further, below, 153 n. 38.

required that the correct *kairos* for the instruction be determined. The Epicurean communities provide examples of the procedure,[37] as do other philosophers.[38] Dio Chrysostom (*Discourse* 77/78.38-39) reflects the attitude as well as the medical language that was commonly used in this kind of context. The philosopher, he says, should admonish people privately and individually as well as in groups as frequently as he finds any *kairos,* spending his life sound *(hygiēs)* in words and deeds.

Plutarch shows deep concern for attaining the greatest good in instruction,[39] and in *How to Tell a Flatterer From a Friend* he provides the handiest discussion for our immediate interest. The latter half of the treatise (65E-74E) is a detailed treatment of *parrēsia* ("frankness, boldness"). The conviction that people are injured if they are either praised or blamed *akairōs* (66B) leads Plutarch to a careful consideration of the proper and improper times for frank speech. Drinking parties clearly do not constitute the right *kairos* for frankness (68CD), nor do times of misfortune (68E-69E). The person who applies frankness and stinging rebuke during the latter is like someone who applies a vision-sharpening stimulant to a disordered and inflamed eye and thereby increases the pain (69AB). In such circumstances it is preferable to exhibit the gentleness of a nurse or to follow the example of Crates (69CD).

The proper *kairos* is when the philosopher sees himself called to check the headlong course of vice (69E-70B). Plutarch gives advice on the specific ways in which this is to be done. In particular, it should be recognized that a *kairos* for admonition is found after people have been reviled by others and are downcast. Then frankness is to be applied, but privately (70DE). Error should be treated as a foul disease, and all admonition and disclosure should therefore be made secretly, "with nothing of show or display in it to attract a crowd of witnesses and spectators" (70F-71A).

> And least of all is it decent to expose a husband in the hearing of his wife, and a father in the sight of his children, and a lover in the presence of his beloved, or a teacher in the presence of his students; for such persons are driven almost insane with grief and anger at being taken to task before those with whom they feel it necessary to stand well (71C).

Frankness should be therapeutic *(therapeutikē parrēsia),* and that it can be when, like a physician, the philosopher acts at the correct *kairos* (73D-74A). As physicians continue their treatment after surgery, so those who use

---

[37]See M. Gigante, "Philodème: Sur la liberté de parole," *Actes du VIIIe Congrès, Assoc. Guillaume Budé* (Paris: Les Belles Lettres, 1969): 206–7.

[38]See Hadot, *Seneca und die griechisch-römische Tradition der Seelenleitung,* 65–66.

[39]See, e.g., *On Listening to Lectures* 43E-44A: Someone who listens to a lecture should approach the lecturer privately after the lecture, for what a philosopher says to an individual privately may bear profitable fruit.

admonition should not abandon people after stinging them with their words (74DE).

Timothy's Preaching

In light of this sustained concern with the opportune time for speech, the command to Timothy to preach *eukairōs akairōs* is remarkable. That the author knew it to be so is suggested by the omission of the copula for the sake of emphasis. He wanted to draw special attention to this part of his admonition. The medical language frequently found in discussions of opportune and inopportune speech is also found in verse 3 and is part of the use the author makes of such language throughout the Pastorals.[40] Some of the Church Fathers discerned something similar to medical treatment already reflected in the sequence *elegxon, epitimēson, parakaleson* ("convince, rebuke, exhort," in v. 2). Attributing to Paul the kind of concern one sees in Plutarch, they understood Paul to be advising Timothy to move from the harshest to the mildest admonition in the way a physician progressively administers surgery, strong drugs, and mild medicines.[41]

There is the strongest likelihood, therefore, that *eukairōs akairōs* should be understood in light of the material that has been presented here. Since in this material *kairos* invariably refers to the time or circumstances with respect to the listeners and their condition or mood, it is reasonable to think that it also does so in 2 Timothy 4:2. If it does, however, one is left with the task of explaining this deliberate flying in the face of the convention to determine and choose the right *kairos* and avoid being *akairōs*. The problem becomes more acute when it is observed that at this point the author appears to be at cross-purposes with the way in which he has used the larger complex of philosophical traditions of which this one is part. Throughout the Pastorals the heretics are depicted as harsh, bellicose, and undiscriminating in their relations and speech, while the readers are advised to be gentle, understanding, and discriminating in their treatment of those within the community.[42]

---

[40]See A. J. Malherbe, "Medical Imagery in the Pastoral Epistles," in *Texts and Testaments: Critical Essays on the Bible and Early Church Fathers*, ed. W. E. March (San Antonio, Texas: Trinity Univ. Press, 1980), 19-35 (= 121–36 in this volume). Jerome D. Quinn thinks that the polemical use of the medical imagery could be viewed in the wider perspective of the *sō(s)*-cluster of terms in the Pastorals, which is used for a rescue or healing of persons ("Jesus as Savior and Only Mediator [1 Tim. 2:3-6]," in *Fede e cultura alla luce della Bibblia*, Atti della Sessione Plenaria 1979 della Pontificia Commissione Biblica [Turin: Elle Di Ci, 1981]: 251-53). I wish to thank him for this reference and for other comments he has made on this chapter.

[41]See n. 7. John Chrysostom speaks more generally of the physician's surgery and drugs. Theophylact likens rebuke *(epitimēsis)* to surgery, and exhortation *(paraklēsis)* to milder drugs, while Theodoret likens reproof *(elegchos)* to surgery, and exhortation to milder measures. J. D. Quinn reminds me that Theodore of Mopsuestia (n. 7 above) and Oecumenius *In epistolam primam ad Timotheum commentarius* (PG119.229) continue this exegetical tradition.

[42]For the remainder of this paragraph, see my "Medical Imagery in the Pastoral Epistles."

The description of the heretics matches that of the misanthropic, antisocial Cynics, that of the orthodox, the ideal philosopher who has in mind the nurture and progress of his hearers. Yet in 2 Timothy 4:2, Timothy is commanded to speak *akairōs*, precisely what Cynics who were regarded as irresponsible were accused of doing. And, notwithstanding the addition of the dangling "in patience and teaching," the characterization of the preaching provided by the middle three of the five imperatives is precisely that of the harsh and demanding Cynic speech.

Furthermore, although medical language is used so frequently elsewhere in the letters, despite the Fathers' efforts to see in the verse an example of "Seelenleitung" (spiritual care) analogous to medical treatment, the fact remains that it is not utilized here in the way one might expect it to have been used. Finally, neither in this passage nor anywhere else in the Pastorals is there an interest in private or individual instruction as there is, for example, in 1 Thessalonians 2:12 and Acts 20:20, 31. On the contrary, Timothy's duties are consistently portrayed as out in the public, for all to see.[43]

We shall take these problems up in reverse order. The lack of interest in private instruction may be explained by the circumstances envisaged in the letters. The heretics are the ones who sneak into households to upset the faith.[44] Yet their folly will be plain to all. They will not progress *(prokopsousin)* far, or, ironically, will only "progress" to a worse condition (2 Tim. 3:11, 13). Timothy, in contrast, is to preach and teach in public so that his progress *(prokopē)* may be visible to all (1 Tim. 4:15). The situation the author has in mind therefore does not permit the adoption of a standard "pastoral" method. Timothy must distinguish himself from his opponents in his method of teaching as much as in its content.

That *eukairōs akairōs* is brought into conjunction with medical imagery in 2 Timothy 4:2-3 is quite understandable in light of the tradition that has been traced, and the Fathers' attempt to extract a pastoral therapy in the way they did is not unexpected. But it is not surprising that the author himself does not develop such a therapy. That he does not is in keeping with the way in which he uses medical imagery throughout the letters. His use of the imagery is thoroughly polemical. It describes the diseased condition of the heretics, but is never utilized to describe a therapy for those sick souls. It is never explicitly said that the morally or religiously ill person will actually be

---

[43]E.g., 1 Tim. 4:12-15; 5:19-21, 24-25; 2 Tim. 2:2; cf. Tit. 2:7-8.
[44]2 Tim. 3:6; Tit. 1:11. Cf. Spicq (*Épitres pastorales,* 799), who adduces (*Épitres pastorales,* 777) Jude 4 and *Letter to Flora* 7.1 in commenting on *endynō* in 2 Tim. 3:6. On the danger of women being led astray, see D. L. Balch, *Let Wives Be Submissive: The Domestic Code in 1 Peter,* SBLMS 26 (Chico, Calif.: Scholars Press, 1981), 84–85; and for women upsetting entire households, see Athenaeus *The Deipnosophists* 13.560c.

cured by sound or healthy words. That the speaker will in fact bring about health of soul in his opponents by applying sound words is at most an inference that the reader may wish to draw on the basis of such passages as Titus 1:13. But that is by no means certain and is not the case in 2 Timothy 4:3, where it is said that they would not endure healthy teaching. In light of this consistently polemical use of the imagery, developing a therapy of the word which uses the same imagery would have been incongruous.

The admonition to preach *akairōs* is more problematical, but it too should be understood in light of the Pastorals' perspective. The persons the author has in mind are not well-meaning individuals who have gone astray and are open to reason and persuasion which would effect their return to the truth. They are obstinate and their unwillingness to endure sound teaching would appear to place them beyond the pale. There seems to be no prospect of amelioration in their condition that could justify that adaptation of speech which is at the heart of the admonition to speak *eukairōs* only. Given the extremity of their condition, Timothy is directed to preach without giving consideration to whether it is opportune or inopportune to do so. That is the thrust of the oxymoron. In this respect the attitude is that of the pessimistic Cynic who flays his deluded audience.

Conclusion

There is another aspect of the matter, however, that distinguishes this admonition from the Cynic attitude. The reason (*gar,* "for") given for the command is that there will be a *kairos* when people will not heed sound words and will refuse to listen to the truth (v. 3). That *kairos* is in fact already present. These are the last days when people apostatize from the faith.[45] But the seasons are divinely determined; they are *kairoi idioi,* the proper time, in which things are made known. The testimony to the ransom of Christ was or is made at the proper time (1 Tim. 2:6), and God will make manifest the appearing of Christ at the proper time (1 Tim. 6:15). Ages ago God promised eternal life and at the proper time manifested his word in the apostolic preaching (Tit. 1:3). The *idioi kairoi* are thus part of a history of salvation in which preaching of the word belongs to the process of revelation. Timothy, as recipient of the apostolic message, continues in this process, but it is God who enacts the work of salvation.[46] The process is determined by God, not by the inclination of people to accept the word or not. The preaching should therefore take place irrespective of the condition of the listeners, which, in the case of the heretics, is beyond the hope of cure anyway.

---

[45]1 Tim. 4:1; 2 Tim. 3:1; cf. Spicq, *Épitres pastorales,* 800; Dibelius and Conzelmann, *Pastoral Epistles,* 64, 115.
[46]Dibelius and Conzelmann, *Pastoral Epistles,* 43, 131.

10

"Not in a Corner":
Early Christian Apologetic
in Acts 26:26

In 1960 W. C. van Unnik could with justification state that insufficient attention had been given to the purpose of the Book of Acts.[1] During the past twenty-five years, however, since Acts has become a storm center of scholarly discussion,[2] there has been no lack of attempts to fill the need; and its purpose has been defined more variously, frequently in theological terms.[3] A particular purpose that had earlier been discerned, an apologetic one, has also again received attention and been perceived in different ways.

The Apologetic of Acts

It is frequently stated that Acts is an *apologia pro ecclesia,* written, with Rome in mind, for two purposes: to convince the civil authorities of the falsity of charges brought against Christians and to argue that Christianity should be extended the privileges of a *religio licita.*[4] This argument has recently been

---

[1]W. C. van Unnik, "The 'Book of Acts' the Confirmation of the Gospel," *NovT* 4 (1960): 26–59 (= *Sparsa Collecta: The Collected Essays of W. C. van Unnik,* 3 vols., NovTSup 29 [Leiden: E. J. Brill, 1973] 1.340–73).

[2]W. C. van Unnik, "Luke-Acts, a Storm Center in Contemporary Scholarship," in *Studies in Luke-Acts,* ed. L. E. Keck and J. L. Martyn (reprint, Philadelphia: Fortress Press, 1980), 15–32.

[3]For the theological context of much of the recent discussion, see U. Wilckens, "Interpreting Luke-Acts in a Period of Existentialist Theology," in *Studies in Luke-Acts,* 60–83; for the purpose of the work, see R. Maddox, *The Purpose of Luke-Acts* (Göttingen: Vandenhoeck & Ruprecht, 1982). An account of the investigation of Acts up to 1969 is provided by W. W. Gasque, *A History of the Criticism of the Acts of the Apostles* (Grand Rapids: Wm. B. Eerdmans, 1975).

[4]For example, J. Weiss, *Ueber die Absicht und den literarischen Character der Apostelgeschichte* (Marburg/Göttingen: Vandenhoeck & Ruprecht, 1897); B. S. Easton, *The Purpose of Acts* (London: SPCK, 1936), reprinted in his *Early Christianity* (Greenwich, Conn.: Seabury Press, 1954); and, with greater reservation, H. J. Cadbury, *The Making of Luke-Acts* (London: SPCK, 1927), 299–316. This view seems to be that of H. Conzelmann, *The Theology of St. Luke,* trans. G. Buswell (Philadelphia: Fortress Press, 1980 [1960]), although he is unclear on the matter (see Paul W. Walaskay, *'And So We Came to Rome': The Political Perspective of St. Luke,* SNTSMS 49 [Cambridge:

stood on its head by Paul Walaskay, who claims that the author is pro-Roman, and that what he writes for his church is in fact an *apologia pro imperio*.[5] Also regarding Acts as apologetic, but not in political terms, are those writers who think that it was directed to the wider Jewish community to settle internal disputes between Jewish sects, of which Christianity was one,[6] and those who regard Acts as presenting an intramural Christian defense of Paul.[7] The term apology as applied to Acts has also been extended to describe its author's perceived intention of converting the educated readers for whom he ostensibly wrote.[8]

I am here interested in the way Luke's presentation of Christianity, particularly in the person of Paul, may reflect an awareness of pagan criticisms of Christianity, and shall focus on Acts 26:26, where Paul makes claims for the public character of Christianity and his own preaching. Usually, when the purpose of Acts is seen to be the offering of a defense to non-Jews or non-Christians, the apology is defined in terms of political rights,[9] and attempts are then made to describe the historical, and in particular, political conditions which were likely to have been the occasion of the writing. I am not prepared to offer a hypothesis on the latter, but, before turning to Acts 26:26, do wish to broaden the understanding of external apologetic with which the nature of Acts might be examined. Extensive comparisons between Luke-Acts and the apologists, particularly Justin, have been made,[10] but they have concentrated on questions of theological affinity, literary dependence, or style of argumentation, while I wish to pursue social factors. The Christian apologists

---

Cambridge Univ. Press, 1983], 9–10), and E. Haenchen, *The Acts of the Apostles,* trans. B. Noble and G. Shinn (Philadelphia: Westminster Press, 1971), 630, 693–94. For problems with this understanding, see R. Karris, "Missionary Communities: A New Paradigm for the Study of Luke-Acts," *CBQ* 41 (1979): 80-97.

[5]*'And So We Came to Rome'* (n. 4 above).

[6]For example, Conzelmann, *The Theology of St. Luke,* 148, who thus thinks of both internal and external apologetic interests (see n. 4 above).

[7]Already represented by F. C. Baur, this view has recently been advanced most vigorously by J. Jervell, *Luke and the People of God: A New Look at Luke-Acts* (Minneapolis: Augsburg, 1972); idem, *The Unknown Paul: Essays on Luke-Acts and Early Christian History* (Minneapolis: Augsburg, 1984). See also N. A. Dahl, "The Purpose of Luke-Acts," *Jesus in the Memory of the Early Church* (Minneapolis: Augsburg, 1976), 87–98.

[8]J. C. O'Neill, *The Theology of Acts in Its Historical Setting,* 2d ed. (London: SPCK, 1970), 176.

[9]This is not always the case. See, for example, Gerd Luedemann, *Paul, Apostle to the Gentiles: Studies in Chronology,* trans. F. S. Jones (Philadelphia: Fortress Press, 1984), 18–19, who does, however, refer to nonpolitical features that are properly apologetic as "closely related to the apologetic aspect of Luke-Acts."

[10]See, for example, F. Overbeck, "Ueber das Verhältnis Justins des Martyrers zur Apostelgeschichte," *ZwTh* 15 (1872): 305–49; E. Zeller, *The Contents and Origin of the Acts of the Apostles Critically Investigated* (London: Williams & Norgate, 1875), 1.114–39; O'Neill, *The Theology of Acts;* N. Hyldahl, *Philosophie und Christentum. Eine Interpretation der Einleitung zum Dialog Justins* ATD 9 (Copenhagen: Munksgard, 1966), 260–72; W. S. Kurz, "The Function of Christological Proof from Prophecy for Luke and Justin" (Diss., Yale University, 1977).

of the second and third centuries enable us to gain such a broader understanding of the charges made against Christians and the nature of the Christian apologetic response. Their apologies reveal that, while one of their purposes was to secure political rights, they were occupied at great length with what might broadly be described as social criticism of Christians, only part of which might have had political implications.[11]

I suggest that a number of characteristic features in Acts take on special, and in some cases new, significance when viewed in the light of such criticisms. For our immediate purpose, it will suffice to draw attention, by way of illustration, to two kinds of charges leveled at Christians before turning to Acts 26:26.

It is well known that Christianity was regarded as a lower class movement and that Christians were viewed as uneducated and socially insignificant, if not downright irresponsible or dangerous. According to one critic, they were "untrained in education, outcasts from humane studies, ignorant of even the meanest skills,"[12] and they collected as converts "from the lowest possible dregs of society the more ignorant fools together with gullible women."[13] Until recently, that view of the social status of early Christians was widely held, if not so pejoratively stated, but it has come to be seen as an oversimplification.[14] The description, as abuse of a rival group or sect, was standard

---

[11]The subject of pagan views of Christians, discussed extensively by W. Nestle ("Die Haupteinwände des antiken Denkens gegen das Christentum," *ARW* 73 [1941–42]: 51-100) and P. de Labriolle (*La réaction paienne: Étude sur la polémique antichrétienne du Ier au VIe siècle,* 2d ed. [Paris: L'Artisan du livre, 1948]), has recently enjoyed renewed interest. See, for example, W. Speyer, "Zu den Vorwürfen der Heiden gegen die Christen," *JAC* 6 (1963): 129–35; M. V. Anastos, "Porphyry's Attack on the Bible," in *The Classical Tradition: Literary and Historical Studies in Honor of Harry Caplan,* ed. L. Wallach (Ithaca, N. Y.: Cornell Univ. Press, 1966): 421-50, with bibliography in notes 1 and 2; S. Benko, "Pagan Criticism of Christianity during the First Two Centuries A.D.," *ANRW* 2.23.2 (1980): 1054–1118; idem, *Pagan Rome and the Early Christians* (Bloomington, Ind.: Indiana Univ. Press, 1984); R. L. Wilken, "Roman Criticism of Christianity: Greek Religion and Christian Faith," in *Early Christian Literature and the Classical Intellectual Tradition: In Honorem Robert M. Grant,* ed. W. R. Schoedel & R. L. Wilken (Paris: Editions Beauchesne, 1979): 117–34; idem, "The Christians as the Romans (and Greeks) Saw Them," in *Jewish and Christian Self-Definition, Vol. 1: The Shaping of Christianity in the Second and Third Centuries,* ed. E. P. Sanders (Philadelphia: Fortress Press, 1980), 1:100–25; idem, *The Christians as the Romans Saw Them* (New Haven, Conn.: Yale Univ. Press, 1984); D. Rokeah, *Jews, Pagans and Christians in Context* (Leiden: E. J. Brill, 1982).

[12]Minucius Felix *Octavius* 5.4; Origen *Against Celsus* 6.13. For a collection and discussion of the charges, see *The Octavius of Marcus Minucius Felix,* trans. and annotated G. W. Clarke, ACW 39 (New York: Newman Press, 1974), 183-84, n. 38.

[13]Minucius Felix *Octavius* 8.4; cf. Clarke, *The Octavius,* 206–7 n. 105; A. J. Malherbe, "Apologetic and Philosophy in the Second Century," *Restoration Quarterly* 7 (1963): 19-32.

[14]For the social stratification that already marked the Pauline churches, see G. Theissen, *The Social Setting of Pauline Christianity: Essays on Corinth,* trans. and ed. J. H. Schütz (Philadelphia: Fortress Press, 1982); W. A. Meeks, *The First Urban Christians: The Social World of the Apostle Paul* (New Haven, Conn.: Yale Univ. Press, 1983), 51–75; A. J. Malherbe, *Social Aspects of Early Christianity,* 2d ed., enlarged (Philadelphia: Fortress Press, 1983), 29–59, 118–21.

polemic.[15] Luke, in contrast, stresses the relatively high social standing of converts to Christianity, mentioning, among others, priests (Acts 6:7), a royal treasurer (Acts 8:26-39), a centurion (Acts 10:1-48), a proconsul (Acts 13:6-12), and a ruler of the synagogue (Acts 18:8).[16] The women who populate his story are not of the sort easily led astray,[17] but are examples of good works (Acts 9:36-41; cf. Luke 8:2-4), and they teach (Acts 18:26), provide meeting places for the church (Acts 12:12), and are generally from a professional class (Acts 16:14-15) or of high official standing (Acts 17:3, 12).[18]

Related to this view of Christians as uneducated was their critics' denial that they were in any sense philosophical.[19] Such denials may have been occasioned by Christians' representation of the faith as philosophical and their demands that they receive the same treatment as philosophical sects.[20] Luke does describe the leaders of the church in Jerusalem as simple and uneducated (Acts 4:17), but, as the later apologists would find philosophical qualities exemplified in the most simple Christians,[21] so he, too, sketches a picture of the Jerusalem church in which it realizes the philosophical ideal of a communal sharing of resources, and does so in language that would have made his intention clear to a cultivated reader (Acts 2:44-45; 4:32).[22]

The Philosophical Paul

It is particularly in the person of Paul that Luke provides a paradigm of the educated Christian preacher. According to him, Paul is well-educated in the

---

[15]Cf. the descriptions of Epicureans in Cicero *De natura deorum* 1.72,89; 2.74, as ignorant, and see M. *Tulli Ciceronis De natura deorum,* ed. A. S. Pease, 2 vols. (reprint, Darmstadt: Wissenschaftliche Buchgesellschaft, 1968), 1.381–83.

[16]See H. J. Cadbury, *The Book of Acts in History* (New York: Harper & Row, 1955); E. Plümacher, *Lukas als hellenistischer Schriftsteller,* SUNT 9 (Göttingen: Vandenhoeck & Ruprecht, 1972), 22ff., 26, 30; Luedemann, *Paul,* 19. Cf. Eusebius *Ecclesiastical History* 7.32.2–4; 8.1.2–6.

[17]Cf. 2 Tim. 3:6-7, applied to women led astray by heretics, and see Tatian *Oration* 33; Origen *Against Celsus* 6.24.

[18]For Luke's interest in women from the upper classes, see M. Hengel, "Maria Magdalena und die Frauen als Zeugen," in *Abraham unser Vater,* ed. O. Betz, M. Hengel, & P. Schmid, AGJU 5 (Leiden: E. J. Brill, 1963): 243–56. J. Jervell ("The Daughters of Abraham: Women in Acts," *The Unknown Paul,* 146-57) unconvincingly argues that Luke's women are subordinate, and are simply devout Jews.

[19]See, for example, Origen *Against Celsus* 1.9; 3.44, 75; 6.1.

[20]For Christianity as philosophical, see Justin *Dialogue with Trypho* 8; Tatian *Oration* 35; Melito, according to Eusebius *Ecclesiastical History* 4.26.7; Miltiades, according to Eusebius *Ecclesiastical History* 5.17.5, and for equivalent treatment to the philosophers, Athenagoras *Embassy* 2; Tertullian *Apology* 39, on which see R. L. Wilken, "Collegia, Philosophical Schools and Theology," in *The Catacombs and the Colosseum: The Roman Empire as the Setting of Primitive Christianity,* ed. S. Benko & J. J. O'Rourke (Valley Forge, Penn.: Judson Press, 1971), 271–78.

[21]See Justin *Apology* 1.60; *Apology* 2.10; Theophilus *To Autolycus* 2.35; Minucius Felix *Octavius* 16.5-6, and Athenagoras *Embassy* 11, on which see A. J. Malherbe, "Athenagoras on Christian Ethics," *JEH* 20 (1969): 1–5.

[22]See Iamblichus *The Life of Pythagoras* 30.168, and cf. Plümacher, *Lukas,* 16–18, for the philosophical background of "one soul" and "all things in common."

Jewish tradition (Acts 22:3), but it is his description of Paul in the conventions used of moral philosophers that is of interest here. The scene of Paul in Athens is the most explicit.[23] In the marketplace Paul is confronted by Epicureans and Stoics who raise a question about him: "What does this babbler *(spermologos)* want to talk about?" (Act 17:18). He is then taken from the marketplace to the Areopagus, where he is asked, "May we know what this new teaching is which you present?" (Acts 17:19). The first question, using the pejorative *spermologos,* effectively ranks him with the no-good street preachers of the day as described by Dio Chrysostom: they post

> themselves at street-corners, in alleyways, and at temple-gates, pass around the hat, and play upon the credulity of lads and sailors and crowds of that sort, stringing together rough jokes and much babbling *(spermologian)* and that rubbish of the marketplace.[24]

Celsus gives a similar picture of Christians:

> Moreover, we see that those who display their secret lore in the marketplaces and go about begging would never enter a gathering of intelligent men, nor would they dare to reveal their noble beliefs in their presence; but whenever they see adolescent boys and a crowd of slaves and a company of fools they push themselves in and show off.[25]

Having had Paul receive such abuse, Luke then removes him from the marketplace to precisely such a "gathering of intelligent men." As has often been noted, to underscore the philosophical setting in which Paul here operates, Luke describes the scene with allusions to Socrates.[26]

The second question, on the newness of Paul's teaching, contains one such allusion, and represents what was a matter of major concern in antiquity.[27] Despite the fascination preachers of novelties had for the crowds,[28] innovation

---

[23]See M. Dibelius, "Paul on the Areopagus," *Studies in the Acts of the Apostles,* ed. H. Greeven (New York: SCM Press, 1956), 26–77; H. Conzelmann, "The Address of Paul on the Areopagus," in *Studies in Luke-Acts* (n. 2 above), 217–30; E. Haenchen, *The Acts of the Apostles* (n. 4 above), 514–31. For the philosophical material, see B. Gaertner, *The Areopagus Speech and Natural Revelation* ASNU 21 (Uppsala: C. W. K. Gleerup, 1955). C. K. Barrett, "Paul's Speech on the Areopagus," in *New Testament Christianity for Africa and the World: Essays in Honor of Harry Sawyer,* ed. M. E. Glasswell & E. W. Fasholé-Luke (London: SPCK, 1974), 69–77, is especially suggestive on the function of the reference to the Epicureans. Cf. also the description of Apollos as *anēr logios* ("a cultured man," Acts 18:24).
[24]*Discourse* 32.9.
[25]According to Origen *Against Celsus* 3.50; see 5.65 for Christian misunderstanding of philosophy. Lucian's picture of Peregrinus, who became a Christian, is similar, cf. Lucian *Peregrinus* 11–13.
[26]See Plümacher, *Lukas* (n. 16 above), 19, 97–98, for the literature, to which should be added K. Döring, *Exemplum Socratis: Studien zur Sokratesnachwirkung in der kynisch-stoischen Popularphilosophie der frühen Kaiserzeit und im frühen Christentum,* Hermes Einzelschriften 42 (Wiesbaden: F. Steiner, 1979), and cf. O'Neill, *The Theology of Acts* (n. 8 above), 160–71.
[27]For Socrates's introduction of new gods, see Xenophon *Memorabilia* 1.1.1; cf. Plato *Apology* 24B; *Euthyphro* 3B.
[28]Dio Chrysostom *Discourses* 8.9–10; 9.5.

was suspect, for it could be a menace to the established order.[29] The newness of Christianity was therefore a damaging criticism, and the Christian apologists constantly strove to meet it by stressing Christianity's continuity with Judaism[30] or the pagan philosophical tradition.[31] Luke elsewhere has Paul do the former,[32] here he does the latter. By having Paul explicitly quote from popular Stoicism (Acts 17:28), Luke aligns him with a venerable philosophical tradition in a manner reminiscent of the apologists. It is noteworthy that Luke describes the Athenians and resident aliens as those delighting in novelties: "they spent their time in nothing except telling or hearing something new" (17:21). There is therefore a subtle turning of the tables: the pagan philosophers who question the apostle do not themselves hold to the legitimating tradition; it is Paul who does.[33] Luke does not here argue the way the apologists later would, that biblical religion was older than pagan philosophy, which, they claimed, was derived from it. He in fact does not even quote from the Old Testament at all. Nevertheless, by juxtaposing Paul's appeal to the philosophical tradition to the philosophers' preoccupation with novelties, he does adopt a strategy that would accommodate the apologists' claim of the priority of biblical religion.[34]

Another speech in which Paul speaks as a philosopher is his farewell address at Miletus (Acts 20:17-35). Coming at the end of his missionary labor in the eastern Mediterranean, the speech offers a summary of his work as a founder of churches. In recent years the speech has been compared to the departure speeches of scriptural characters, with which it clearly has affinities, but the Greco-Roman elements used to describe Paul's psychagogy have been

---

[29]See A. D. Nock, *Conversion: The Old and New in Religion from Alexander the Great to Augustine of Hippo* (Oxford: Clarendon Press, 1933), 161; T. D. Barnes, "An Apostle on Trial," *JTS* N. S. 20 (1969): 415 n. 3, 417–18; Minucius Felix *Octavius* 6.1, and Clarke, *The Octavius*, 189 n. 64.

[30]Note Celsus's contrasting of Jews and Christians in Origen *Against Celsus* 5.25–26, 33, 61: Christians rebelled against the Jews, hence they could claim no continuity with them. In 2.4, Celsus sides with the Jew who similarly rejects the Christian attempt. Cf. Overbeck, "Ueber das Verhältnis Justins des Martyrers zur Apostelgeschichte" (n. 10 above), 322–23; R. MacMullen, *Paganism in the Roman Empire* (New Haven, Conn.: Yale Univ. Press, 1981), 2–3.

[31]Cf. Nock, *Conversion*, 249–52; Clarke, *The Octavius*, 15-16.

[32]For example, in Acts 13:16-41, Luke's stress on the church's continuity with Israel has been clarified by Jervell, *Luke and the People of God* (n. 3 above), 41–74. Dahl, "The Purpose of Luke-Acts" (n. 7 above), 94, notes that "Luke-Acts is unique in its insistence that it was the God of the fathers who raised Jesus and in whose service Paul mediated salvation to the Gentiles." For Paul's adherence to the ancestral laws and customs, see Acts 22:3; 24:14; 28:17. For the rejection of pagan ancestral customs, cf. 1 Pet. 1:18 and D. L. Balch, *Let Wives Be Submissive: The Domestic Code in 1 Peter,* SBLMS 26 (Chico, Calif.: Scholars Press, 1981), 82–84, who argues that the intention of the code was apologetic.

[33]Cf. K. Loening, "Das Evangelium und die Kulturen. Heilsgeschichtliche und kulturelle Aspekte kirchliche Realität in der Apostelgeschichte," *ANRW* 2.25/2 (1984): 2632–36.

[34]See K. Thraede, *s.v.* "Erfinder," *RAC* 5(1962): 1247–68.

neglected.[35] I shall identify only enough of those elements to illustrate the point I am making. When Paul claims that he did not shrink from teaching his hearers what was profitable to them (Acts 20:20, 27),[36] that he taught publicly and privately (Acts 20:20; cf. 18:28; 16:37),[37] and that he gave them individual attention (Acts 20:31),[38] he is detailing procedures that were followed by responsible moral philosophers and were widely discussed. His description of rival teachers as fierce wolves (Acts 20:29-30) is standard fare,[39] as is the procedure of using them as a foil for sketching his practice as an example to be followed.[40] The example itself is sketched in normal paraenetic style:[41] it is introduced with an imperative (20:31) and concluded with what is functionally an imperative (*dei,* 20:35), it calls his hearers to remembrance (20:31), and draws their attention to what they already know (20:34). The conduct he outlines is similarly standard: a disavowal of greed (20:33) and working in order to help those in need (20:34-35). This last point may seem surprising in a moral-philosophical self-commendation, but Ronald Hock has

---

[35]For the so-called *Abschiedsrede,* see, for example, J. Munck, "Discours d'adieu dans le Nouveau Testament et dans la littérature biblique," *Aux sources de la tradition chrétienne. Mélanges offerts à Maurice Goguel a l'occasion de son 70e Anniversaire* (Neuchâtel and Paris: Delachaux & Niestlé, 1950), 155–70; H. Schürmann, "Das Testament des Paulus fur die Kirche—Apg. 20, 18-35." *Traditionsgeschichtliche Untersuchungen zu den synoptischen Evangelien* (Dusseldorf: Patmos, 1968), 310–40; H.-J. Michel, *Die Abschiedsrede des Paulus an die Kirche—Apg. 20, 17-38* (Munich: Kösel-Verlag, 1973); J. Lambrecht, "Paul's Farewell Address at Miletus," *Les Actes des Apôtres: Traditions, rédaction, théologie,* ed. J. Kremer (Gembloux: J. Duculot, 1979), 306-37. J. Dupont, *Le discours de Milet: Testament pastoral de saint Paul* (Paris: Éditions du Cerf, 1962), does not place Paul's pastoral practice in the context of contemporary Greco-Roman discussion. For the speech as a personal apology of Paul, see Dibelius, *Studies in the Acts of the Apostles* (n. 23 above), 155–57; Barnes, "An Apostle on Trial" (n. 29 above).

[36]For speaking *anypostolōs,* see pseudo-Plato *Clitophon* 407A; Dio Chrysostom *Discourse* 11.27; 13.16; Plutarch, *How to Tell a Flatterer from a Friend* 60C. This is tantamount to speaking with *parrēsia,* on which see the discussion below. For the orators, see Demosthenes 1.16; 4.51; Isocrates 8.41.

[37]On speaking privately as well as publicly, see Epictetus 3.23.33–34; Dio Chrysostom *Discourse* 13.31; 77/78.37–38; Synesius *Dio* 1.11, and cf. P. Desideri *Dione di Prusa: Un intellettuale greco nell'impero romano* (Messina/Florence: D'Anna, 1978), 24 n. 44. For criticism of speaking in only well selected places, see Dio Chrysostom, *Discourse* 32.8-11, on which cf. A. J. Malherbe, " 'Gentle as a Nurse': The Cynic Background to 1 Thess. 2," *NovT* 12 (1970): 203-17 (=35–48 in this volume).

[38]For individual, personalized instruction, see Dio Chrysostom *Discourse* 77/78.37-38; Plutarch *On Listening to Lectures* 43-44A; *How to Tell a Flatterer from a Friend* 70D-71D, and cf. P. Rabbow, *Seelenführung: Methodik der Exerzitien in der Antike* (Munich: Kösel-Verlag, 1954), 272–78, 317 n. 99; and I. Hadot, *Seneca und die griechisch-römische Tradition der Seelenleitung* (Berlin: Walter de Gruyter, 1969), 64–66. See further above, 141 n. 36.

[39]For the harshness and greed of false philosophers, see Lucian *The Fisherman* 35-36, and cf. A. J. Malherbe, "The Beasts at Ephesus," *JBL* 87 (1968): 71–80 (=78–79 in this volume).

[40]For the contrast between such brutal, demanding preachers and the genuine philosopher, see Lucian *Demonax* 6-8. For the use of personal example, see B. Fiore, S. J., *The Function of Personal Example in the Socratic and Pastoral Epistles,* AnBib 105 (Rome: Biblical Institute Press, 1986).

[41]For these characteristics of paraenesis, see A. J. Malherbe, "Exhortation in First Thessalonians," *NovT* 25 (1983): 240–41 (=49–66 in this volume).

convincingly shown that the moral philosopher who so demonstrated his self-sufficiency and took care of others was a well-known ideal.[42]

Paul's speeches are most frequently examined for evidence of Luke's theology, but their apologetic value in the sense we have used the term should be obvious.

Paul's Defense to Agrippa

We turn now to Acts 26, which contains Paul's last defense, delivered to Agrippa II in the presence of Festus, the Roman procurator, and a gathering of military tribunes and prominent men of the city.[43] In the style of a forensic defense speech,[44] Paul undertakes a defense against "all the accusations of the Jews" (26:2) and rehearses his autobiography: his exemplary religious life as a youth, his persecution of the church, his call on the Damascus road, and his fulfilling of his commission in Damascus, Jerusalem, Judea, and to the Gentiles, for which he was seized by the Jews. When he declares that Christ's death, resurrection and proclamation to the people and the Gentiles were all in fulfillment of the prophets (26:22-23), Festus interrupts him by shouting that Paul's great learning had driven him mad (26:24). The interruption and the dialogue that ensues (26:26-49) are of interest to us, particularly Paul's *captatio benevolentiae* that Agrippa knew what he had been talking about, "for this was not done in a corner" (26:26).

Not in a Corner

Commentators have paid insufficient attention to *ou gar estin en gōnia pepragmenon touto* ("this was not done in a corner"). The majority refer to it simply as a classical tag, well-known idiom, or proverb,[45] although it has also

---

[42]R. F. Hock, *The Social Context of Paul's Ministry: Tentmaking and Apostleship* (Philadelphia: Fortress Press, 1980). The true philosopher does not take money from others: Dio Chrysostom *Discourse* 3.14–15; Lucian *Nigrinus* 25-26.

[43]Acts 26:2-23; cf. 22:1-21; 24:10-21. See R. F. O'Toole, *Acts 26. The Christological Climax of Paul's Defense (Ac 22:1—26:32)*, AnBib 78 (Rome: Biblical Institute Press, 1978), for an extensive treatment of this section of Acts.

[44]See A. A. Trites, "The Importance of Legal Scenes and Language in the Book of Acts," *NovT* 15 (1974): 278–84; F. Veltman, "The Defense Speeches in Acts" (Diss., Graduate Theological Union, 1975); idem, "The Defense Speeches of Paul in Acts," in *Perspectives on Luke-Acts*, ed. C. H. Talbert (Danville, Va.: Association of Baptist Professors of Religion, 1978), 243–56; J. Neyrey, "The Forensic Defense Speech and Paul's Trial Speeches in Acts 22–26: Form and Function," *Luke-Acts: New Perspectives from the Society of Biblical Literature Seminar*, ed. C. H. Talbert (New York: Crossroad, 1984), 210–24. In Acts 26 Paul is "an orator of some distinction," according to C. J. A. Hickling, "The Portrait of Paul in Acts 26," in *Les Actes des Apôtres* (n. 4 above), 501.

[45]E.g., F. F. Bruce, *The Acts of the Apostles* (Grand Rapids: Wm. B. Eerdmans, 1952), 448–49; A. Wikenhauser, *Die Apostelgeschichte*, RNT 5 (Regensburg: F. Pustet, 1956), 273; C. S. C. Williams, *A Commentary on the Acts of the Apostles* (London: A. & C. Black, 1957), 265; I. H. Marshall, *The Acts of the Apostles* (Grand Rapids: Wm. B. Eerdmans, 1980), 399.

been identified as a means by which Luke elevates his subject to the plane of world history.[46] Ernst Haenchen is correct when he states that "these words light up Luke's presentation in Acts from beginning to end. . . . The entire history of Christianity—it is no secret society!—is enacted publicly and before high and exalted personages. Christianity is not an inconspicuous event any longer, but a factor of world history."[47] One can go further than Haenchen does: Luke's use of the tag reflects his awareness of an old charge, already encountered in the New Testament, that Christianity was obscure,[48] and he here offers a defense against it. Christians would later respond to the charge by asserting that the faith had been disseminated throughout the world,[49] and Orosius (*Histories* 5.2.10) eventually used the tag when describing how widespread Christianity was. A close investigation, however, will reveal that much more than geographical expansion is in view in Acts 26:26. Some major occurrences of "in a corner" were collected by Wettstein, and have been repeated without examination of their function in polemic.[50] Such an examination, of a larger collection of occurrences, will illuminate Luke's use of the phrase in this context and demonstrate that here, too, he is presenting Paul as speaking in the manner of a philosopher and that this presentation is part of his apologetic program.

We begin with Plato, *Gorgias* 485D, where an old man who still gives himself to philosophical study is criticized. It is charged that he will become unmanly by fleeing from the centers and marketplaces of the city and would cower down and spend the rest of his days whispering in a corner with three or four lads and never utter anything free or high or spirited. Five hundred years later, Aulus Gellius quotes extensively in Greek from this section of the *Gorgias* and applies it to those who pay "futile and childish attention to trifles which contribute nothing to the conduct and guidance of life,"[51] and two hundred years after him Themistius refers and alludes to *Gorgias* 485D when he repeatedly speaks of those who withdraw from society.[52] For at least seven

---

[46]Dibelius, *Studies in the Acts of the Apostles* (n. 23 above), 2.

[47]Haenchen, *The Acts of the Apostles* (n. 4 above), 691–92; cf. Conzelmann, *Acts of the Apostles,* trans. J. Limburg, A. T. Kraabel, and D. H. Juel, Hermeneia (Philadelphia: Fortress Press, 1987), 212; Plümacher, *Lukas* (n. 16 above), 21, 22–25. For the public impact of Jesus's ministry already, according to Luke, see J. Nolland, "Impressed Unbelievers as Witnesses to Christ (Luke 4:22a)," *JBL* 98 (1979): 219–29, esp. 226–28.

[48]See G. Stählin, *Die Apostelgeschichte,* NTD 5 (Göttingen: Vandenhoeck & Ruprecht, 1962), who refers to Matt. 2:6; 4:14ff.; John 1:46; 7:3-4, 41, 52; 18:20; Luke 24:18.

[49]See the collection of texts in A. Harnack, *The Mission and Expansion of Christianity in the First Three Centuries,* trans. and ed. J. Moffatt, 2d ed., enlarged (New York: Putnam, 1908), 2.1–32.

[50]J. J. Wettstein, *Novum Testamentum Graecum* (Amsterdam: Dommer, 1752), 2.635, repeated, for example, by J. Reiling, *Hermas and Christian Prophecy: A Study of the Eleventh Mandate,* NovTSup 37 (Leiden: E. J. Brill, 1973), 54–55 n. 8, and O'Toole, *The Christological Climax,* 139 n. 45.

[51]Aulus Gellius *Attic Nights* 10.22.17–24.

[52]Themistius refers to *Gorgias* 485D in *Oration* 22.265bc, and alludes to it in *Orations* 23.284b; 28.341d; 34.12; 26.322b.

hundred years, therefore, "to speak in a corner" was used pejoratively, especially by orators or philosophers of rhetorical bent, of people, particularly philosophers, who did not engage in public life. In addition, the tag was used in a general, proverbial manner.[53]

It would appear that philosophers were put on the defensive by such criticism. Two Stoics from the latter half of the first century, thus roughly contemporary with Luke, illustrate this concern in their intramural use of the phrase. Their discussions reflect the intense preoccupation among certain philosophers of the period with the propriety or legitimacy of retiring from public life.[54] Seneca, drawn to leave the imperial court for the contemplative life, is aware of the danger of withdrawal and the criticism with which it would meet.[55] He therefore advises his correspondent Lucilius to retire from public affairs but to hide his retirement (*Epistle* 68.2). He justifies himself by asserting that, since the entire universe is the sage's field, when the Stoic withdraws he is not apart from public life, but has abandoned only one little corner of it. Seneca here alludes to the pejorative description of philosophers who seek privacy and defends them, not without Stoic superiority, by drawing out the implications of the Stoic view of world citizenship and applying the tag to the arena of his would-be critics.[56]

Epictetus is especially valuable for our purpose. He conducted a school of philosophy to prepare young men for participation in public life, and constantly had to counter their tendency to take refuge in the school. Aware of the criticism of retiring philosophers, he uses the tag to chide those of his

---

[53]See also Cicero *De oratore* 1.56; *De re publica* 1.2.2; Seneca *Consolation to Polybius* 13.3; Plutarch *On Being a Busybody* 516B; Lucian *The Parliament of the Gods* 1.1. I am indebted to Rabbi Saul Leeman of Providence, R. I., for drawing to my attention Midrash Gen. Rabbah 39:2, on Gen. 12:1,

> To what can we compare Father Abraham? To a vial of perfume lying in a corner and its fragrance was not spread about. However, when it was moved around its fragrance was spread about. Thus the Holy One, blessed be He, said to Father Abraham, "Move yourself about from place to place and your name will become great in the world" (Leeman's translation).

Leeman also points out that *yoshuai keranot* ("those who sit in corners") means "idlers," and that the phrase is used in the *Hadran* to distinguish idlers from diligent students of Torah.

[54]See the material collected by F. Wilhelm, "Plutarchos *Peri Hēsychias*," *RhM* 73 (1924): 466–82; cf. A. Festugière, *Personal Religion among the Greeks* (Berkeley/Los Angeles: University of California Press, 1954), chap. 4.

[55]For the political dimension of withdrawal, see R. MacMullen, *Enemies of the Roman Order: Treason, Unrest* (Cambridge: Harvard Univ. Press, 1966), chap. 2.

[56]See R. degl' Innocenti Pierini, *"In angulo defixus:* Seneca e l'emarginazione dell' esilio," *Studi Italiani di Filologia Classica* 53 (1981): 225–32, for a discussion of Seneca *Consolation to Polybius* 13.3; *Epistle* 28.4. For the Cynic view of the world citizen's superiority, see A. J. Malherbe, "Pseudo Heraclitus, *Epistle* 4: The Divinization of the Wise Man," *JAC* 21 (1978): 62–63; H. C. Baldry, *The Unity of Mankind in Greek Thought* (Cambridge: Cambridge Univ. Press, 1965), 101–12 (for Stoic cosmopolitanism, 151–66, 177–94); see also G. R. Stanton, "The Cosmopolitan Ideas of Epictetus and Marcus Aurelius," *Phoenix* 13 (1968): 183–95.

students who were hesitant to assume the challenges of public life (*Discourse* 1.29.36). He criticizes them when they are content to confine themselves to a corner and quibble, when they should be examples of the philosophic life (*Discourse* 1.29.55-57), and he draws a sharp contrast between the philosopher who practices his dialectic discourse in a corner and the one who takes on someone of consular rank (*Discourse* 2.12.17). He offers Socrates and Diogenes as examples of men who spoke fearlessly to people in power. If his students set such a premium on their classroom exercises, he thinks it best that they left such matters to the brave and slink to their corners, there to spin syllogisms and propound them to others of similar inclination (*Discourse* 2.13.24–26).

Toward the end of his discourse on the ideal Cynic, Epictetus introduces another element (*Discourse* 3.22.95–98).[57] Speaking of the philosopher who does involve himself in human affairs, he insists that it cannot be said that such a man is a busybody or meddler in others' affairs, for he speaks with the boldness *(parrēsiazesthai)* of a friend and servant of the gods, always with the prayer, "Lead thou me on, O Zeus and Destiny," at hand (95-96). The person whose life cannot stand public scrutiny, however, had best retreat to his own little corner (97). Thus, in contrast to whispering in his corner, Epictetus's ideal philosopher, always guided by the divine, does not cower in a corner, but speaks fearlessly to rulers and presents himself as a public example. We shall see the same elements appearing in Luke's presentation of Paul.

It is informative to examine pagan comments on Christian secretiveness against this background. Arthur Darby Nock has pointed out that while Christians may have been in the public mind, they were not in the public eye,[58] and Stanley Stowers has recently corrected the popular view that Paul's practice corresponded to that of the philosophers who regularly preached in the marketplace.[59] As we have seen, Celsus on occasion described Christians thus, but that was standard polemic. More characteristic is his view of Christians as forming sacred conventicles and his description of them in the language we have examined. Christians, he says, "perform their rites and teach their

---

[57]On this discourse, see M. Billerbeck, *Epiktet: Von Kynismus,* Philosophia Antiqua 34 (Leiden: E. J. Brill, 1978). On the Stoic features in his description of the ideal Cynic, see A. J. Malherbe, "Self-Definition among Epicureans and Cynics," in *Jewish and Christian Self-Definition. Vol. 3: Self-Definition in the Greco-Roman World,* ed. B. F. Meyer & E. P. Sanders (Philadelphia: Fortress Press, 1982): 3.194 n. 27 (= 13 n. 10 in this volume).

[58]A. D. Nock, *Conversion,* 192. Cf. R. M. Grant, *Augustus to Constantine: The Thrust of the Christian Movement into the Roman World* (New York: Harper & Row, 1970), 174–75, on the Christians' "almost Epicurean avoidance of publicity."

[59]S. K. Stowers, "Social Status, Public Speaking and Private Teaching: The Circumstances of Paul's Preaching," *NovT* 26 (1984): 59–82.

doctrines in secret" to escape prosecution, to which Origen replies by referring to the secrecy of the Pythagoreans and "other philosophers" (*Against Celsus* 1.3), thus finding precedence for Christian conduct among philosophers.[60]

The vehemence with which Celsus attacks Christians on this score is more evident in *Against Celsus* 4.23, where he inveighs against Jews and Christians, comparing them all "to a cluster of bats or ants coming out of a nest, or frogs holding council round a marsh, or worms assembling in some filthy corner." One reason for his abusiveness was the domestic unrest Christianity caused, which he associated with Christian gatherings in private homes.[61] Celsus was not alone in viewing with suspicion what Christians gabbled in corners.[62] To such charges, Minucius Felix, as did many other Christians, referred to *Timaeus* 28C, "It is difficult to find the Maker and the Father of this universe, and when one has found him, one cannot speak of him to the multitude," and he argued that Plato, too, recognized the difficulty of speaking of God to the multitude.[63] Origen claimed that the structured Christian catechumenate was superior to the Cynics' practice of preaching to anyone they chanced to meet.[64] For his part, Tatian, adept in anti-philosophical polemic that he was, turned the sophists' charge on the pagan philosophers.[65]

It is in this context of the polemical and apologetic use of the tag that Paul's defense and reply to Festus should be understood. Luke has Paul, like the moral philosophers, claim divine guidance (26:16-17, 22), deny that his activity has been confined to a corner (26:26), speak fearlessly to rulers (26:26), and offer himself as an example to all (26:29). Luke's apologetic aim in this scene, to present Christianity in Paul's person as philosophical, would seem to be clear.

---

[60]Elsewhere, Celsus takes issue with the particularity of the Christian claim that the divine Spirit was present in Jesus. Making use of an Epicurean taunt, he asks why God, at last waking from slumber, sent this spirit into one corner and not all over the world (*Against Celsus* 6.78; cf. 5:50). See J. Geffcken, *Zwei griechische Apologeten* (Leipzig/Berlin: B. G. Teubner, 1907), 256, and cf. *Against Celsus* 4.36 for the Jewish fable of the creation, composed in some dark corner of Palestine.

[61]See *Against Celsus* 3.55, and cf. Harnack, *Mission and Expansion,* 1.393-98; E. R. Dodds, *Pagan and Christian in an Age of Anxiety: Some Aspects of Religious Experience from Marcus Aurelius to Constantine* (Cambridge: Cambridge Univ. Press, 1965), 115–16.

[62]Cf. Minucius Felix *Octavius* 8.14, and Clarke, *The Octavius,* 209 n. 108.

[63]Minucius Felix *Octavius* 19.14; cf. Clarke, *The Octavius,* 272 n. 260. Celsus knew this application of *Timaeus* 28C, but denied Christians the ability to understand it properly. Cf. Origen *Against Celsus* 7.42; A. J. Malherbe, "Athenagoras on the Pagan Poets and Philosophers," in *Kyriakon, Festschrift J. Quasten,* ed. P. Granfield and J. A. Jungman (Münster: Aschendorff, 1970): 1.218–19.

[64]Origen *Against Celsus* 3.51. For Seneca's uneasiness about preaching to the masses, see Hadot, *Seneca und griechisch-römische Tradition der Seelenleitung* (n. 38 above), 171–72.

[65]Tatian *Oration* 26.3; cf. Hermas (*Mandate* 11.13), who applies it to false prophets, and see Reiling, *Hermas and Christian Prophecy* (n. 50 above), 54–55.

Paul's Madness

Other elements in the dialogue initiated by Festus's interruption further support the claim that part of Luke's apologetic intention is to present Paul as a philosopher, and I now turn to them. By having Festus say that Paul's great learning had driven him mad (Acts 26:24), Luke achieves two things: an acknowledgment of Paul's learning by the Roman Festus and an occasion for Paul to claim that he had been conducting his mission in a manner befitting a responsible philosopher. Having secured the former, Luke has Paul disavow a charge often slung at Cynics, namely, that they were mad.

Commentators have been reluctant to take Festus's charge at face value and have attempted to relate it to ancient ideas of the madness of divine inspiration.[66] Whatever justification for his charge Festus might have found in Paul's preaching is beside the point for our purpose. We are not here concerned with what may have been the historical situation, but rather with Luke's account of it. On the literary level, it is important to note that Paul denies the charge and counters by claiming that he spoke words of truth and prudence (26:25). John O'Neill has drawn attention to Justin *Dialogue with Trypho* 39.4, where Trypho similarly accuses Justin of madness and Justin denies it. This seems to O'Neill "to be a stock apologetic situation which no doubt occurred often enough, but which may have been a common ingredient in the accounts of debates between Christians and unbelievers."[67] I agree with him on the apologetic nature of the interchange, but would suggest that Paul's response is illuminated by statements from the moral philosophers of Luke's day.

Cynics were frequently regarded as mad because of their rigorous, ascetic life,[68] or their unconventional or vulgar behavior.[69] More moderate philosophers who spoke in public had to come to terms with this attitude. Dio Chrysostom was such a philosopher and contemporary of Luke, and he illustrates how they did so. Despite being thought mad, he says, the true philosopher would be outspoken and hide nothing, but would persist in speaking the truth.[70] Especially instructive are places in Dio's public speeches where he introduces himself to his audience in such a way as to distinguish himself from the unscrupulous street preachers. In contrast to those who think the philosopher mad, Dio claims that his audience comes to him because he speaks the truth (*Discourse* 12.8-9). In *Discourse* 34 he begins by saying

---

[66]E.g., Bruce, *The Acts of the Apostles* (n. 45 above), 448.
[67]O'Neill, *The Theology of Acts* (n. 8 above), 15.
[68]Pseudo-Socrates *Epistles* 6.1; 9.3; Dio Chrysostom *Discourses* 66.25; 77/78.41; pseudo-Lucian *The Cynic* 5.
[69]Dio Chrysostom *Discourses* 8.36; 9.8.
[70]Dio Chrysostom *Discourse* 77/78.41-42, cf. 33.

that Cynics are thought not to be of sober mind *(sōphronein)* but crazy *(mainomenous)* (2), and then makes a pun on the concept of madness (4). If they do consider him mad, they should listen to him because, and here Dio plays on the Greek association of divine inspiration with madness, he came to them by divine counsel. Elsewhere *(Discourse* 45.1), he introduces himself by referring to his teaching throughout the world and claims that he is not goaded by "madness or desperation to do these things, but (trusts) in a greater power and source of aid, that which proceeds from the gods, though most men deem it useless."

In these self-introductions of Dio we find the same elements that are present in Paul's response to Festus's interruption: the contrast between the public preacher's madness and the genuine philosopher's speaking words of truth and prudence.[71] The similarities between the two extend further. Earlier in Acts 26, in the account of his call, Paul claimed that he had been sent by the divine to witness for him (26:16), that he had done so throughout his mission in the eastern Mediterranean (26:20), constantly depending on help from God as he spoke fearlessly to great and small (26:22), as he now does to Festus and Agrippa (26:26).

Paul's Boldness of Speech

Another element from the philosophical context that Luke includes in this account is found in his characterization of Paul's speech. When Paul describes his speech to Agrippa as boldness *(parrēsiazomenos),* he uses a word that had come to be associated with the philosopher's boldness of speech.[72] The philosopher's outspokenness betokened a fearlessness in pointing out human shortcomings; it also reflected the speaker's confidence in his right to do so. Every philosopher's *parrēsia* should therefore be backed by character, especially when he attempts to bring other people to their senses *(sōphrosynē).* That, Plutarch claims, is what happened when Xenocrates converted Polemo to the rational life.[73] Thus, as we have already seen from Epictetus, the outspoken philosopher was to give himself to freedom and *parrēsia* and to present his life as an example to others.[74] That is the direction Paul's dialogue with Agrippa will take.

---

[71]For the contrasts between *mania* and *sōphrosynē,* see Plümacher, *Lukas* (n. 16 above), 22 n. 86, who refers to Plato, *Phaedrus* 244A; *Protagoras* 323B; Xenophon *Memorabilia* 1.1.16.

[72]See A. J. Malherbe, "Gentle as a Nurse" (n. 37 above), 208–16 (= 35–48), and the literature cited there. For another perspective, see W. C. van Unnik, "The Christian's Freedom of Speech in the New Testament," *Sparsa Collecta: The Collected Essays of W. C. van Unnik,* NovTSup 30 (Leiden: E. J. Brill, 1980): 2.269–89; idem, "The Semitic Background of parrhesia in the New Testament," *Sparsa Collecta,* 2.290–306; S. B. Morrow, "Parrhesia and the New Testament," *CBQ* 44 (1982): 431–46.

[73]Plutarch *How to Tell a Flatterer from a Friend* 71E.

[74]Cf. Lucian *Demonax* 3.

Instantaneous Conversion

The philosophical tradition may also cast some light on yet another element in the dialogue which has puzzled commentators, namely Agrippa's response to Paul: "So rapidly would you persuade me to become a Christian!" (26:28).[75] Of interest here is the contemporary philosophical discussion of instantaneous changes people might undergo. Stoics held the view that the person who made consistent moral progress would experience a change to the stage of the wise man so suddenly that he might be unaware of it.[76] Some Platonists accepted the possibility of such a sudden change,[77] but others, for polemical reasons, resurrected an earlier form of Stoicism more susceptible to attack, and derided the idea of sudden change.[78] More generally, the notion was conveyed in the many accounts of conversion to philosophy,[79] and it finds its Christian counterpart in Augustine's account of his conversion.[80]

Accounts of such conversions, or the claim that one had undergone a sudden change, expectedly met with ironic, if not outright sarcastic, responses.[81] Such responses are the more intelligible when it is recognized that the conversion accounts had a protreptic purpose,[82] especially when they drew attention to the speaker or another convert as an example to follow.[83] This is what Justin does after recounting his conversion: "And, further, I could wish that all should form a desire as strong as mine, not to stand aloof from the Savior's words" *(Dialogue with Trypho 8.2)*. Paul's rejoinder to Agrippa,

---

[75]For discussion of the problems of this statement, see K. Lake and H. J. Cadbury, *The Beginnings of Christianity*, ed. F. J. Jackson & K. Lake, 5 vols. (London: Macmillan, 1933), 5.322–24; Haenchen, *The Acts of the Apostles* (n. 4 above), 689; O'Toole, *The Christological Climax* (n. 43 above), 141–45.

[76]See J. M. Rist, *Stoic Philosophy* (Cambridge: Cambridge Univ. Press, 1969), 90–91.

[77]E.g., Apuleius, *De Platone,* 2.20.

[78]E.g., Albinus *Didaskalikos* 30.2; Plutarch *Progress in Virtue* 75C-E; *The Stoics and the Poets* 1057E-1058C; *Against the Stoics on Common Conceptions* 1062B. See D. Babut, *Plutarque et le Stoïcisme* (Paris: Universitaires de France, 1969), 15–18.

[79]For example, the stock example of Polemo, who responds instantly to Xenocrates' teaching on *aretē* and *sōphrosynē:* Lucian *The Double Indictment* 17; Diogenes Laertius *Lives of Eminent Philosophers* 4.16 (for Christian use of the account, see Ambrose *Hel.* 12.45 [PL 14.712]; Augustine *Contra Julianum, haresis Pelagiana defensorum* 1.4.12 [PL 44.647]). Cf. A. D. Nock, "Conversion and Adolescence," *Essays on Religion and the Ancient World,* ed. Z. Stewart (Cambridge: Harvard Univ. Press, 1972), 1:471–72. For example, see Plutarch *On The Delays of the Divine Vengeance* 563CD; Diogenes Laertius *Lives of Eminent Philosophers* 2.48; 7.2; Philostratus *Life of Apollonius of Tyana* 4.20. In actuality, conversion more likely was a gradual process. Cf. A. D. Nock, *s.v.* "Bekehrung," *RAC* 2 (1954): 107–8.

[80]Augustine, *Confessions* 6.7.11–12.

[81]See, e.g., Lucian *Nigrinus* 1.

[82]See O. Gigon, "Antike Erzählungen über die Berufung zur Philosophie," *MusHelv* 3 (1946): 10–11.

[83]Cf. Lucian *Nigrinus* 38. For a collection of Christian texts, see J. Foster, *After the Apostles: Missionary Preaching of the First Three Centuries* (London: SCM Press, 1951), 86–91. For the motives of conversion accounts, see E. Fink-Dendorfer, *Conversio: Motive und Motivierung zur Bekehrung in der Alten Kirche,* Regensburger Studien zur Theologie 33 (Frankfurt: Peter Lang, 1986).

closing his last account of his sudden conversion, "I could wish that rapidly or gradually, not only you, but all who are listening to me would be as I am—except for these chains" (Acts 26:29), could be seen as functioning in the same manner. That the apologetic dialogue should end on a protreptic note is not surprising, for early Christian apologetic had strong affinities with the protreptic tradition.[84]

There is a difference, however, between Justin and Paul. Justin makes use of the *topos* of going from one philosophy to another,[85] until his search culminated in Christianity, to score the point that Christianity could not only bear philosophical scrutiny, but that it satisfied his inquiring mind as the philosophical school could not. This description has the protreptic function of inviting the reader to follow Justin's example and join him in the true philosophy. It also functions apologetically in that it would put the lie to pagan accusations that Christians demanded that people simply believe, without any rational demonstration, and that they flee scientific inquiry, which required greater intellectual capacity and commitment.[86]

Luke, on the other hand, describes Christian conversion as an instantaneous response to preaching,[87] which might appear to leave him open to the pagan charge that Christian conversion was simple-minded acceptance of outlandish claims made by hucksters. Paul's appeal to the prophets (26:27) might also seem to be a departure from the philosophical mode. His appeal can, however, be compared to the Christian apologists' insistence that the prophets were philosophical and that they could contribute to one's conversion to Christianity.[88] The sermons elsewhere in Acts, moreover, either make use of a proof from prophecy that has affinities with the Aristotelian enthymeme,[89] or, as we have seen, are attached to the philosophical tradition. It

---

[84]Cf. J. Daniélou, *Message évangélique et culture hellénistique aux IIe et IIIe siècles* (Tournai: Desclée, 1961), 86–91. For the relationship between missionary preaching and apologetic, see A. J. Malherbe, "The Apologetic Theology of the *Preaching of Peter,*" *Restoration Quarterly* 13 (1970): 205–23.

[85]*Dialogue with Trypho* 2.3–6. See Hyldahl, *Philosophie und Christentum* (n. 10 above), 148–59.

[86]Cf. Celsus, according to Origen *Against Celsus* 1.9; 3.75; Nock, *Conversion,* 205; and esp. R. Walzer, *Galen on Jews and Christians* (London: Oxford Univ. Press, 1949), 14–15, 48–56, 57–65, 89–91.

See Acts 9:1-22; 13:42-43, 48; 16:14-15, 29-33; 17:2-4, 10-11; 22:6-16, and cf. Luke 15:17; 19:1-8 for other examples of sudden conversions. Apollos, the *anēr logios* ("cultured man") from Alexandria, represents another side (Acts 18:24-26). Already instructed in the faith, he speaks with *parrēsia* in the synagogue, but receives further detailed instructions from Prisca and Aquila. Cf. Eusebius *Ecclesiastical History* 3.37.3 for multitudes converting "at the first hearing."

[88]E.g., Justin *Dialogue with Trypho* 7-8, and Hyldahl, *Philosophie und Christentum* (n. 10 above), 227-31. On the superiority of the prophets and their philosophical character, see Malherbe, "Athenagoras on the Pagan Poets and Philosophers" (n. 63 above), 220–22. For the strength of the Christian argument, see Nock, *Conversion* (n. 29 above), 237–41; and cf. Harnack, *Mission and Expansion* (n. 49 above), 1.279–89.

[89]See W. S. Kurz, "The Function of Christological Proof" (n. 10); idem, "Hellenistic Rhetoric and the Christological Proof of Luke-Acts," *CBQ* 42 (1980): 171–95.

is for Luke, therefore, their inherent persuasiveness, not the credulity of the audience, that results in conversion.[90] It is typical, then, that Paul's *apologia* begins with an allusion to the prophets (26:6) and ends by aligning him with the prophets and Moses (26:22-23), and that the appeal to Agrippa is based on the prophets (26:27). Nevertheless, Agrippa rejects the impetuous response that he understands Paul to call for. And to this, Paul can only intimate that conversion could be either sudden or gradual.

Conclusion

In sum, the dialogue that follows the last account of Paul's conversion in Acts contains themes that Luke had developed earlier. Specifically, he had represented Paul as speaking in language derived from discussions by and about the moral philosophers of his day. An important feature of his depiction of Christianity is the public character of the church. He combines these two themes in the dialogue that follows Paul's last defense. There Paul argues apologetically in a manner analogous to the apologists of the second century, which suggests that Luke was aware of the same issues that would confront them. This is not to say that Acts is to be understood purely as apologetic, even in a broader sense than that in which the term is generally used; it is to maintain that an examination of its apologetic intent deserves a wider focus than it has received.

---

[90]See D. W. Kemmler, *Faith and Human Reason: A Study of Paul's Method of Preaching as Illustrated by 1—2 Thessalonians and Acts 17, 2-4*, NovTSup 40 (Leiden: E. J. Brill, 1975), 11–142. For Luke, it is not so much the content of this speech that is philosophical as Paul's conduct and means of persuasion. The resurrection is still the bone of contention in this defense (26:23-29), as it had been at Athens (17:31-33).

11

A Physical Description
of Paul

When Paul is placed in his Greek context, it is generally his thought, vocabulary, and literary style that receive attention. This is to a degree at least also true when attention is given to the early church's interpretation of his letters. This essay, on the other hand, examines the Greek influence that can be perceived in early Christian reflections on the physical appearance of Paul. The artistic representations of Paul are less well known to most students of early Christianity than the literary evidence,[1] chief of which is the curious literary portrait of Paul in the *Acts of Paul and Thecla,* which in some respects agrees with early Christian paintings. There, Onesiphorus sees Paul as "a man small of stature, with a bald head and crooked legs, in a good state of body, with eyebrows meeting and nose somewhat hooked, full of friendliness; for now he appeared like a man, and now he had the face of an angel."[2]

Paul's Appearance

This description, which in sometimes modified forms proved popular among later writers,[3] does not accord with our view of beauty, and has been regarded as hardly flattering,[4] as "naivunheroisch,"[5] and as representing Paul as quite

---

[1]The artistic material is conveniently gathered by E. von Dobschütz, *Der Apostel Paulus: II. Seine Stellung in der Kunst* (Halle: Buchhandlung des Waisenhauses, 1928); Giuseppe Ricciotti, *Paul the Apostle,* trans. Alba I. Zizzamia, (Milwaukee: Bruce, 1953), 151–59.

[2]*Acts of Paul and Thecla* 3 (= *Acta Apostolorum Apocrypha,* ed. R. A. Lipsius & M. Bonnet, reprint [Darmstadt: Wissenschaftliche Buchgesellschaft, 1959], 1.237,6–9). The translation is that of W. Schneemelcher, *New Testament Apocrypha,* trans. R. McL. Wilson, (Philadelphia: Westminster Press, 1964), 2:354.

[3]See J. Fürst, "Untersuchungen zur Ephemeris des Diktys von Kreta," *Philologus* 61 (1902): 407-12; von Dobschütz, *Der Apostel,* 45–46.

[4]W. M. Ramsay, *The Church in the Roman Empire Before* A.D. *170* (London: Hodder & Stoughton, 1890), 32; L. Vouaux, *Les Acts de Paul et ses lettres apocryphes* (Paris: Letouzey et Ané, 1913), 122.

[5]E. Dassmann, *Der Stachel im Fleisch: Paulus in der frühchristlichen Literatur bis Irenäus* (Münster: Aschendorff, 1979), 279.

plain,[6] ugly, and small,[7] "ein Mann von numinoser Hässlichkeit,"[8] and as being "the typical portrait of a Jew."[9] Luther's view is still that of the majority of commentators: "Ego credo Paulum fuisse personam contemptibilem, ein armes, dirs menlein sicut Philippus" ("I believe Paul was a contemptible, poor little man like Philip").[10]

That this description does not appear to us an idealization may suggest that it was indebted to memory of what Paul actually did look like.[11] If Sir William Ramsay's argument, that the *Acts of Paul and Thecla* goes back ultimately to a first-century document, were accepted,[12] the description of Paul might have some claim to historical accuracy. But Ramsay's argument has proved to be unconvincing.[13] It is more likely that, writing in Asia toward the end of the second century, the author of the *Acts* knew the canonical Acts and other New Testament writings as well as current legendary tradition, and that he used all of them to construct a work intended for edification.[14] In doing so, he was more concerned with current conceptions of Paul than the Paul of the New Testament, although he used the New Testament material freely. Yet there are hints in Paul's letters that he was not an outstandingly robust physical specimen (e.g., 2 Cor. 10:10; 13:7-12[?]; Gal. 4:13-16), which do not make the description in the *Acts* incongruous.[15] Furthermore, early portraits of Paul from the catacombs and elsewhere, showing him with a sparsely covered head, have been taken to represent more or less accurate knowledge.[16]

These efforts to find clues to Paul's physical appearance underscore a peculiarity of the New Testament; it provides no physical descriptions of its

---

[6]T. Zahn, "Paulus der Apostel," *RE* 15 (1904): 70.

[7]J. Geffcken, *Christliche Apokryphen* (Tübingen: J. C. B. Mohr [Paul Siebeck], 1908), 27.

[8]H. D. Betz, *Der Apostel Paulus und die sokratische Tradition: Eine exegetische Untersuchung zu seine "Apologie" 2 Korinther 10–13*, BHT 45 (Tübingen: J. C. B. Mohr [Paul Siebeck], 1972), 54.

[9]W. Michaelis, *Die Apokryphen Schriften zum Neuen Testament*, 2d ed. (Bremen: Carl Schunemann, 1958), 313.

[10]Martin Luther, *Werke: Tischreden* (Weimar: Hermann Bohlaus, 1913), 2 no. 1245.

[11]Von Dobschütz, *Der Apostel Paulus*, 1.

[12]Ramsay, *Church in the Roman Empire*, 381–428.

[13]E.g., A. Harnack, *Geschichte der altchristlichen Literatur bis Eusebius* (Leipzig: J. C. Hinrichs, 1897), 2.1, 505; A. F. Findlay, *Byways in Early Christian Literature: Studies in the Uncanonical Gospels and Acts* (Edinburgh: T. & T. Clark, 1923), 335 n. 226; *New Testament Apocrypha*, 2.332-33.

[14]*New Testament Apocrypha*, 2.348–49; W. Schneemelcher, "Die Apostelgeschichte des Lukas und die Acta Pauli," in W. Eltester & F. H. Kettler, eds., *Apophoreta: Festschrift für Ernst Haenchen zu seinem 70. Geburtstag am 10. Dezember 1964*, BZNW 30 (Berlin: Alfred Töpelmann, 1964), 236–50.

[15]See, e.g., A. Plummer, *A Critical and Exegetical Commentary on the Second Epistle of St. Paul to the Corinthians*, ICC (Edinburgh: T. & T. Clark, 1915), 283; A. Deissmann, *Paul: A Study in Social and Religious History*, 2d ed., enlarged; trans. W. E. Wilson (reprint, New York: Harper & Row, 1957), 55. On the question of Paul's health, see Ricciotti, *Paul the Apostle*, 160–67.

[16]See G. Wilpert, *Roma Sotterranea: Le pitture delle catacombe romane* (Rome: Desclée, Lefebure & Co., 1903), 106; Ricciotti, *Paul the Apostle*, 159.

main characters. Such descriptions were common in ancient biographies and in descriptions of so-called divine men, where they tend to appear toward the beginning, as they do in the *Acts*.[17] It is not impossible that the description in the *Acts* contains some historical truth, but on the basis of our present evidence it is impossible to verify that it does. Rather, recognizing that the *Acts* follows one literary convention in providing a description of Paul early in the work, it is worth inquiring whether other conventions cast light on the description itself. Physiognomy had long been a topic of considerable interest before it attained its greatest popularity in the second century A.D., and Christians shared this interest.[18]

Descriptions of Heroes

Here I wish only to ascertain, with the help of the manuals on physiognomy and descriptions of honored figures, whether the *Acts* description would have appeared as unflattering to Greeks as it does to us. Of the features mentioned, it is Paul's baldness, bowed legs, meeting eyebrows, hooked nose, and perhaps smallness of stature, that lead to our negative assessment of his appearance. For the rest, his aspect is described in terms so favorable that they may appear to the modern reader designed to balance his negative physical features. The physiognomic literature repeatedly discusses these features. It has been denied that the physiognomic manuals provided the basis of the description,[19] yet they do supplement other material, and to that extent are valuable corroborating sources.

Robert Grant has found the basis for the *Acts* description in a passage from Archilochus (*Fragment* 58 Bergk[4]), which was popular in the second century: "I love not a tall general nor a straddling one, nor one proud of his hair nor one part-shaven; for me a man should be short and bowlegged to behold, set firm on his feet, full of heart."[20] On the ground that, according

---

[17]See Elizabeth C. Evans, "Physiognomics in the Ancient World," *TAPA* n. s. 59 (1969): 51–58; Patricia Cox, *Biography in Late Antiquity: A Quest for the Holy Man* (Berkeley: Univ. of California Press, 1983), 14–15; R. Reitzenstein, *Hellenistische Wundererzählungen,* (reprint, Darmstadt: Wissenschaftliche Buchgesellschaft, 1963), 39; L. Bieler, *Theios Aner: Das Bild des "göttlichen Menschen" in Spätantike und Frühchristentum* (reprint, Darmstadt: Wissenschaftliche Buchgesellschaft, 1967), 1.49–50.
[18]See Evans, "Physiognomics in the Ancient World"; J.-C. Fredouille, *Tertullien et la conversion de la culture antique* (Paris: Études augustiniennes, 1972), 60–62.
[19]Bieler, *Theios Aner,* 1.50 n. 1; R. M. Grant, "The Description of Paul in the *Acts of Paul and Thecla,"* *VC* 36 (1982): 1.
[20]Translation by J. M. Edmonds, *Elegy and Iambus* (LCL) 2.127; Grant, "The Description of Paul," 1-4. The major testimonies are Galen *In Hippocratis librum de articulis* 3 (18.1, 537 and 604 Kuhn); Dio Chrysostom *Discourse* 33.17; Schol. Hippocr. ex Erotian 13.32 Klein (*Fragment* 43 [112,13–15 Nachmannson]; Schol. vet. Theocr. 4.49a (148,19–21 Wendel). See Giovanni Tarditi, *Archiloco* (Rome: Ateneo, 1968), 116.

to the Pastoral Epistles, the bishop should have such qualities of a general as are detailed by Onasander, and in view of Paul's liking for military metaphors,[21] Grant thinks it natural for an admirer of Paul to have used the well-known language of Archilochus to depict him as a general. Grant is correct in drawing attention to this somewhat similar description, and thus in recognizing the positive element in the description of Paul in the *Acts*. The two features of interest in the passage from Archilochus are the shortness of the general and his bowleggedness. These and other features are also found in descriptions not indebted to Archilochus, and I suggest that these descriptions point to a different source for the description in the *Acts*.

Three of Paul's features, his small stature, hooked nose, and meeting eyebrows, also appear in Suetonius's description of Augustus (*The Lives of the Caesars* 2.79.2):

> His teeth were wide apart, small, and ill-kept; his hair was slightly curly and inclining to golden; his eyebrows met. His ears were of moderate size, and his nose projected a little at the top and then bent slightly inward. His complexion was between dark and fair. He was short of stature, . . . but this was concealed by the fine proportion and symmetry of his figure.

Suetonius used such physiognomic descriptions, which have parallels in the handbooks, to describe his ideal political leaders.[22] Meeting eyebrows were regarded as a sign of beauty,[23] and a person with a hooked nose was thought likely to be royal[24] or magnanimous.[25] Tallness was preferred; nevertheless, since men of normally small height had a smaller area through which the blood flowed, they were thought to be quick.[26] The main things were that one not be excessive in either direction, and, as in the case of Augustus, that one be well proportioned.[27]

A Description of Heracles

The same features were also attributed to Heracles, who may be of particular relevance. According to Clement of Alexandria (*The Exhortation to the Greeks* 2.26), Dicaearchus, a pupil of Aristotle, and Hieronymus of Rhodes described

[21]See A. J. Malherbe, "Antisthenes and Odysseus, and Paul at War," *HTR* 76 (1983): 143–73 (= 91–119 in this volume).
[22]See Cox, *Biography in Late Antiquity,* 13–15; Evans, "Physiognomics in the Ancient World," 53–54.
[23]Cf. Philostratus *Heroicus* 33.39 (46,16-17 de Lannoy), and on the handbooks see Fürst, "Untersuchungen zur Ephemeris des Diktys von Kreta," 386–88.
[24]Cf. Plato *Republic* 5.474D; Pollux *Onomasticon* 2.73 (2.281, 26-27 Foerster).
[25]Cf. pseudo-Aristotle *Physiognomics* 811a36-38; Anonymous *On Physiognomy.* 51 (91 Jacques Andre).
[26]Cf. pseudo-Aristotle *Physiognomics* 813b.
[27]See Evans, "Physiognomics," 10, 53.

Heracles as follows: "Hieronymus the philosopher sketches his bodily strengths also—small stature, bristling hair, great strength. Dicaearchus adds that he was slim, sinewy, dark, with hooked nose, bright gleaming eyes and long straight hair."[28] Heracles, like other Greek heroes, is also elsewhere described as small,[29] having a hooked nose,[30] and eyebrows that met.[31]

The closest parallel to the *Acts* description is found in Philostratus *Lives of the Sophists* 2.552, where a certain Agathion, who was also called Heracles, is described. Philostratus's description is based on a letter of Herodes Atticus, who had been a pupil of Dio Chrysostom.

> He says that his hair grew evenly on his head, his eyebrows were bushy and they met as though they were one, and his eyes gave out a brilliant gleam which betrayed his impulsive temperament; he was hook-nosed, and had a solidly built neck, which was due rather to work than to diet. His chest, too, was well formed and beautifully slim, and his legs were slightly bowed outwards, which made it easy for him to stand firmly planted.

This Agathion-Heracles is usually identified with the Sostratus of Lucian *Demonax* 1. While Lucian partly described him in Cynic terms, Philostratus adapted his sources and added mystic-religious features, including the heroification of Sostratus.[32] Whether Herodes Atticus had derived the description from Archilochus is unclear. What is important is that we have to do with a description that came to be attributed to Heracles.

Paul the Christian Heracles

It is clear by now that Paul's hooked nose, bowed legs, and meeting eyebrows were not unflattering features in the context in which the *Acts* was written. Furthermore, Heracles and traditions associated with him were used extensively in early Christianity,[33] and I suggest that the author of the *Acts* derived his description of Paul from these sources. Two features distinguish Paul from Agathion-Heracles. Agathion was eight feet tall, while Paul is said to have been small of stature. But tallness was not an absolute requirement for beauty, and

---

[28]Translation by G. W. Butterworth, *Clement of Alexandria* (LCL), 63. See Geneva Misener, "Iconistic Portraits," *CPh* 19 (1924): 108.

[29]E.g., Pindar *The Isthmian Odes* 4.53; cf. Fürst, "Untersuchungen zur Ephemeris des Diktys von Kreta," 409 n. 82; Evans, "Physiognomics," 44–45, 51.

[30]E.g., Plutarch *Antony* 4.1: "A shapely beard, a broad forehead, and an aquiline nose were thought to show the virile qualities peculiar to the portraits and statues of Heracles."

[31]E.g., Philostratus *Imagines* 2.15.5.

[32]See J. F. Kindstrand, "Sostratus-Hercules-Agathion—The Rise of a Legend," *Kungl. Humanistika Vetenskaps-Samfundet i Uppsala. Annales Societatis Litterarum Humaniorum Regiae Upsaliensis* (Arsbok, 1979-80), 50–79.

[33]See A. J. Malherbe, "Herakles," *RAC* 10(1988): 559–83. For Paul and Heracles, see idem. "The Beasts at Ephesus," *JBL* 87 (1968): 71–80 (= 79–89 in this volume).

Heracles himself could be described as small. More puzzling is Paul's baldness, for the physiognomic descriptions drew attention to the hair. Translations of the *Acts* were sensitive to this part of the description.[34] The Armenian gives him curly hair,[35] the Syriac scanty hair,[36] and the Latin a shaven head.[37] Two possible explanations of this odd feature suggest themselves. It is possible that Paul indeed was bald, and that the *Acts* was faithful to memory. The paintings that represent him as thin on top may support such a surmise. On the other hand, baldness may have been suggested by the reference to the shaving of heads in Acts 18:18 and 21:24.

Conclusion

This short excursion into the strange world of ancient physiognomy may cast some light on how Paul was represented as a hero among the Greeks. It calls for further attention to the description in the interpretation of the *Acts*. The basic assumption of physiognomics was that "dispositions follow bodily characteristics and are not themselves unaffected by bodily impulses."[38] It remains to be determined whether there is such a correlation between the description of Paul's physical appearance and his deeds in the *Acts*.

---

[34] See also pseudo-Lucian *The Patriot* 12, which describes Paul as having receding hair; cf. Fürst, "Untersuchungen zur Ephemeris der Diktys von Kreta," 381, 407–12.

[35] Cf. F. C. Conybeare, *The Apology and Acts of Apollonius and Other Monuments of Early Christianity* (New York: Macmillan, 1894), 62.

[36] Cf. W. Wright, *Apocryphal Acts of the Apostles* (London: Williams & Norgate, 1871), 2.117.

[37] See the textual variants in Vouaux, *Les Actes*, 150 n. 6.

[38] Pseudo-Aristotle *Physiognomics* 805a; cf. Cicero *De Fato* 10; Evans, "Physiognomics," 5–6; Cox, *Biography in Late Antiquity*, 13–14.

Indexes

Index of Passages

Index of Authors

184

Index of Subjects